HOW TO BE COMFY

HOW TO BE COMFY

Hundreds of tips to make your house a home

Shannon Lush & Jennifer Fleming

ABC
Books

DISCLAIMER

The material in this book is intended for general information purposes only. It particularly is not intended to be used as a tool to diagnose or treat any physical conditions or to be seen as a substitute for medical advice. The authors and publishers recommend that medical help be sought in the event of any medical emergency by telephoning the emergency 000 number.

Published by ABC Books for the
AUSTRALIAN BROADCASTING CORPORATION
GPO Box 9994 Sydney NSW 2001

First published September 2007

ISBN 978 0 7333 1933 4

Designed by saso content & design pty ltd
Illustrations by Alan Laver
Author photograph on cover and photographs on pages
    23-25 and page 39 by Rick Lush
Typeset by saso content & design pty ltd
Cover design by saso content & design pty ltd

Set in Leawood BT 10/13 pt
Printed and bound in Australia by Griffin Press

10 9 8 7 6 5 4 3 2 1

CONTENTS

KEY TO SYMBOLS

You will find that different types of cleaning information are included in this book. To make finding the correct cleaning tips easier, we've included symbols and boxes.

Information box — practical tips and information are boxed like this.

Hints box — general hints are boxed like this.

Tips box — tips are boxed like this.

Comfy Craft ideas — are boxed like this.

HOW WE USED TO KEEP COMFY ...

Priceless box — hints from yesteryear are boxed like this.

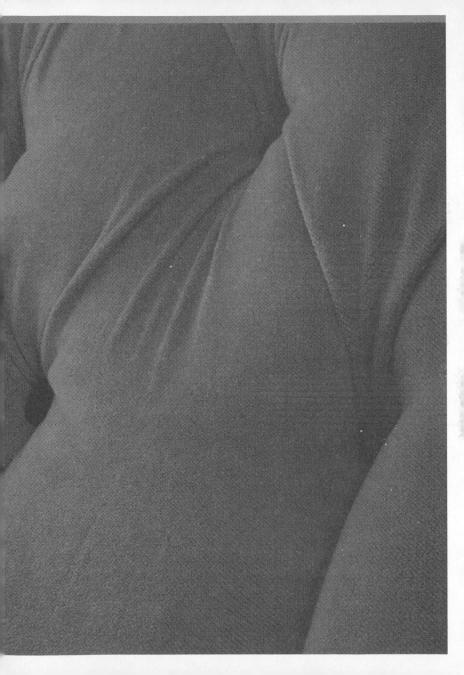

WHO WE ARE

Thank you for making *Spotless* the biggest selling book in Australia in 2006. Its companion, *Speedcleaning*, also enjoyed time in the best-seller lists for several months. It's not because we're a nation of grubs. We think it shows people want old-fashioned, non-toxic cleaning remedies they can use themselves. And it's not just Australians showing an interest. *Spotless* has gone global and can now be found on bookshelves in Norway, Italy, Brazil and the United Kingdom.

Shannon Lush is a fine arts restorer who uses a range of tools, adhesives, solvents and techniques to restore broken artefacts. Add to this a family tradition of sharing handy hints, throw in a passion for organic chemistry and you get a woman who can offer more solutions for stain removal than you can imagine.

Jennifer Fleming is a broadcaster and writer whose interest in stains and cleaning accelerated after meeting Shannon through ABC Radio. She has a first class honours degree in Industrial Relations, is a producer and presenter for ABC Radio and a home renovator.

ACKNOWLEDGEMENTS

Jennifer Even though writing is about spending lots of hours alone at the computer, it takes many people to transfer your efforts into a book. Big thanks to collaborator, Shannon Lush, for her enormous information base and energy. Thanks to our agent, Elizabeth Troyeur for her patience. Editor Megan Johnston had terrific insights and suggestions. Thanks to Stuart Neal, Susan Morris-Yates, Jane Finemore and the team at ABC Books. Thanks to designer Nanette Backhouse and illustrator Alan Laver. Family, friends and colleagues have been very patient and encouraging during the writing process. Special thanks to Pat and John Fleming, Tony Speede, Andy Palmer, Virginia Lloyd and Brett Stone, who cast a forensic eye over early drafts. Thanks to James Valentine. And big thanks to my god-daughter, Charlotte Moss, for being such a bright spark.

Shannon 'Comfy' really came out of the early training that so many members of my family contributed to. All of them need to be thanked: My grandma, who taught me that everyone has a right to feel nice; my mother, who taught me that this was not only a right but an essential and practical way of living; my dad, who taught me to appreciate the excitement of discovery, imagination and invention; and finally my entire family, who showed me that giving one hundred per cent to any task is always appreciated.

So many people involved in the production of this book have given one hundred per cent but I'd like them to know just how much they are appreciated. Jennifer Fleming, who works like a mad woman. Elizabeth Troyeur, who manages to make sense out of madness. The wonderful ABC team: Stuart Neal, Susan Morris-Yates, Jane Finemore (another mad woman), James Valentine, Richard Fidler, Annie Gastin, Carol Whitelock, Bernadette Young, Ingrid Just, Fiona Wyllie, Kathie Bedford and David Kilby, who have all been incredibly supportive.

The biggest thank you of all must go to the love of my life, my husband Rick Lush, and my lovely daughter Erin, who are always there for me.

Introduction

How To Be Comfy is about making your house a home. Your home could be filled to the rafters with loved items, or be completely minimalist. It could have bold feature walls or be subdued and plain. It could be filled with high-tech gadgetry, collectables or items from travels. It could be eclectic or themed. The important point is that you, and others under the same roof, are comfy.

Making a home comfy is about satisfying all the senses: it's about the look, touch, smell, sound, taste and that often-elusive X factor. It's about elements like the colour on your walls, the feel of a mohair blanket, the fragrance of a bunch of flowers, the sound of your favourite music, the taste of a delicious meal or the feeling of warmth from a crackling fire on a cold evening. *How to be Comfy* will help you hone your senses to create a haven.

WHERE TO BEGIN

In *How To Be Comfy* we take you on a room-by-room guide through your home and offer a range of ideas for you to think about. Whether the design of your home is open plan or traditional, being comfy is about how it feels and looks, but also about how it operates. There's no point in having a stunning-looking home that's impractical.

But before you rush out and buy paint or move furniture around, think about what happens in different rooms in your home. What is their function? If your dining room is also where homework is done, factor that in. Think about how the air flows, how much natural light there is and the mood you want to create. If you're not happy with a room, take some graph paper and sketch how the room can be arranged or rearranged to its best advantage.

HOW TO SELECT ITEMS

How To Be Comfy also offers advice on how to select the most comfy items for your home, from towels to tables, fridges to fans, pillows to pots. It looks at how to arrange them, care for them and fix them. There are also lots of economical tips to improve items, from reupholstering a scratchy couch to re-grouting your tiles. There's plenty of do-it-yourself and craft for those who are so inclined.

COLOUR

Colour affects mood, so take time with your colour scheme and pay particular attention to how you feel around certain colours—there are thousands of shades to choose from. A good way to work out what colours you like is to spend time in different houses and see how they make you feel, then use these experiences as a base to construct a colour palette for your home. Decorators use colour wheels to help them.

As a general guide:

Black—is not an energising colour. It can be cold, making a space feel dank and dark like a cave. To make black cosy, add warm shades of colour, such as red, chocolate and orange. Touches of silver and white can make it elegant. To chill black, add blues, purples or blue-greys.

Purple—light purple is artistic, dark purple is moody and rebellious, which is why teenagers often like it. It can also be elegant. A purple dining room with grey, cream, gold or silver can be quite classy.

Red—is energising and exciting and encourages communication. Strong vivid reds are great for dining rooms because they stimulate appetite, excite people and encourage them to eat more quickly. With a more burgundy shade, people want to linger. Red is not good for bedrooms.

Pink—is a warm, loving colour. Soft pinks are calming. Hot pink is exciting and stimulating. When teamed with chartreuse and white, it makes a great colour scheme for a garden room.

Blue—is reflective of nature. It has many shades, each with its own mood and character. It can be clean and fresh, cosy and dim or restful. And because of its versatility, it's one of the most-used colours in homes.

Green—is associated with well-being and nature. It makes a good base colour for walls because many other colours go with it. Ignore the advice that blue and green should never be seen!

Yellow—in the right hue is sunny and happy. If it's strong, it can make you feel unwell. If too vivid, it can be oppressive. Yellow is a thirsty colour and draws moisture from a room, but it can also lift a dank room.

Grey—is the ultimate neutral. A hint of another colour next to it can change it dramatically. It's a great base palette. If you're not sure of the task of a room, opt for grey. Too much can be boring and depressing, but when teamed with any other colour, it can be a great mood enhancer.

White—can be pure, clean, formal or clinical. It can be comforting and warm, chilling and forbidding or anything in between. But it also shows dirt. Touches of white can brighten and clean a room. It provides a good background because people think of it as a blank canvas.

Different colour shadings change the shape of a room. For example, to make the ceiling of a room appear higher, use light colours on the ceiling and a slightly darker shade on the walls. If you want the ceiling to become lower and the walls to extend out, select lighter wall colours and a darker ceiling.

BICKERING OVER HOUSEWORK

In some homes, there's a huge amount of tension about who does the housework. It's not comfy if you spend time bickering about whose turn it is to unload the dishwasher or clean the toilet. One suggestion is to do the housework together. Another is to expand the idea of what housework is so that jobs like paying the bills, fixing the computer and changing a light bulb are also included.

It may also help to know that men and women clean differently. Men tend to clean by line of sight and if they can't see it, they won't clean it. Women tend to clean by program and will often clean something even if it's not dirty. Allow for these different styles of cleaning. Neither way is better, they're just different.

There can also be conflict between hoarders and minimalists. Hoarders have lots of stuff and like to display it, using every bit of space available. Minimalists love surfaces to be clear. The best way to resolve these different decorating styles is to divide the house into areas: each can have their own zone. Storage areas are important for both types. In shared rooms, some patience and tolerance is needed.

One way to deal with household issues it to have house meetings: the busier the people in the home, the more meetings will be needed. Discuss anything that affects the running of the home. Allow people to air their grievances and try to find resolutions with which everyone is happy. House rules need to be developed by everyone: if only one person makes the rules, they won't work.

DITCH THE DRUDGERY

The word drudgery is often used in relation to cleaning and keeping house. And let's face it, some elements can be monotonous. Change that by altering your attitude and intention. Make it a challenge rather than a chore. It's not about being an obsessive perfectionist; see it instead as taking pride in creating a clean and comfy home. Capitalise on your strengths and outsource your weaknesses.

Have fun in your home. It's not just a place to eat, sleep and work, it's an extension of you and a way to express your personality. It should be exciting, peaceful, entertaining or calm when you need it to be. Most of all, it should be comfy!

The Entrance

The entrance to your home should be welcoming, clean and easy to access: no one wants to undertake an obstacle course trying to find your front door. If you've got a cracked path, a broken buzzer or masses of cobwebs, you, your guests and the pizza-delivery guy will feel a bit stressed standing at the front door. The front of your home is its face and says a lot about you. It's a visitor's first point of call, so their initial experience here will influence how they feel about the rest of your home. Read on and we'll show you how to make this part of your home as comfy as possible.

HOW WE USED TO KEEP COMFY FROM *FORTUNES IN FORMULAS FOR HOME, FARM AND WORKSHOP* BY HISCOX AND SLOANE (1944)

To make your own oil stains for hard floors: burnt sienna, slate brown or wine black is ground with strong oil varnish in a paint mill thinned with turpentine and applied with a brush.

GETTING ORGANISED

OUTSIDE THE FRONT DOOR

This part of your home should look clean and inviting, but also reflect the household's personality. Remember: first impressions are lasting. Here are some comfy considerations:

Check the state of your gate, front fence, letterbox and house number. Your fence should be secure and upright, the letterbox should be large enough to fit various sizes of mail and your house number should be easy to see.

Can you easily navigate your way to the front door? If your pathway is a series of humps and bumps, it's going to impact on how comfortable you and your visitors feel. If needed, use white or pale-coloured pebbles, white-painted lines or pale tufts of grass to help guide people along your path. Ensure any steps are delineated with a painted edge or a step tread tile.

Can people easily identify where the front door is? There's nothing worse than wandering around a house looking for the entrance.

How clean is the door? Nobody wants to knock on a door covered with peeling paint and cobwebs. If it's exposed to the weather, check that it doesn't have splinters. If it does, sand the splintery area. If you want your front door to have a weathered look, at least give it a good polish. Carnauba wax is ideal for this. Refresh the door with a coat of paint if it needs it.

Does the doorbell or knocker work?

Do the outdoor lights work?

Make sure your front door has a solid core so it's secure. It's best when hinge pins are heavy and located on the inside of the door.

Doorbells, chimes and knockers

Whether it's a rat-a-tat-tat, a ding-dong or a buzz, the important thing is that you can hear people when they're at the front door. If you don't have a dedicated doorbell or knocker, visitors could get sore knuckles or even resort to thumping your door with a foot or an umbrella handle. It's generally pretty easy to install plug-in, remote-controlled and wireless chimes or even an old-fashioned twist bell.

For more sophisticated buzzers, use an electrician. If your doorbell
sounds wonky, the operating mechanism could be dirty. Clean it with
a dry cotton bud or an old toothbrush. Just make sure your doorbell
doesn't sound like the bells of doom!

Doorknobs

The most important feature of a doorknob is that it's easy to turn.
Choices range from circular, lever, boss, oval or hexagonal. Keep in
mind that circular ones in the centre of a door often require two hands
to open them. Clean your doorknob with some dampened pantyhose. If
it's made of brass, clean with bicarb and vinegar on a lint-free cloth.

Cobwebs

Having a sticky mess of cobwebs all over you isn't comfy. Spiders are
robust creatures, continuing to build their homes even though you
may crash through them frequently. The best way to stop them
making their home at the entrance to your home is to wipe lemon oil

HINT

HOW TO FIX A SAGGING OR SQUEAKY GATE

If your front gate is wedged into the ground and difficult to open,
several elements could be at play. If the support post is at an
angle, it will have to be straightened and secured. The easiest
way is with quick-set cement powder. After realigning the post, put
the cement powder into the hole around the base, add water
according to the instructions and hold the post in position until the
cement sets. Quick-set cement is also handy for patching holes in
your pathway. If your gate lets out a noisy squeak every time you
move it, lubricate the hinges with axle grease. Wipe the axle
grease into the hinge line and swing the gate backwards and
forwards. Don't forget to wipe the excess grease off or you could
get it on your clothes! (If you do, see page 201 for the solution.)

over the area. Wipe the outer part of a lemon over a cloth or use a few drops of essential lemon oil and apply it to the spidery area. For higher areas, wrap the cloth around a broom head, secure it with elastic bands and wipe. Spiders hate lemon oil!

TIP

Make your own lemon oil impregnated cloth by finely zesting a lemon peel, sprinkling it over a piece of clean cloth and rolling it into a sausage shape. Place it in the microwave on high for 30 seconds (for a 600-watt microwave). The oil transfers to the cloth and can be used for polishing and deterring spiders.

Mats and boot scrapers

You'll be surprised at how a welcome mat can warm up the look of an entrance. It's also stops dirt on soiled shoes being tramped into your home. Welcome mats come in many shapes and designs from brown or dyed copra, recycled rubber tyre, multi-coloured *AstroTurf*, timber grid or metal spiral mesh. Metal spiral mesh has an added advantage of being able to be secured to the step so it can't be stolen. To do this, place some eye screws into the step and attach the mesh to it with some wire. You can even have mats made to fit your front door in a style and design you choose.

Boot scrapers are available in traditional or modern designs in cast iron, stainless steel, brass or bronze. Encourage people to use them so they don't track mud, grease and grime through the house.

Resting Area

Keep a chair and table, stool or well-bracketed shelf at seat height at the front door. This is useful if you're not at home and someone has to wait. It's also good to have a spot to put heavy shopping while you're unlocking the door. You'll have somewhere to wait for a taxi and a comfy spot for elderly or infirm visitors to catch their breath.

COMFY CRAFT

HOW TO MAKE YOUR OWN BOOT SCRAPER

If you're feeling crafty, make your own boot scraper with an old broom. Cut the handle so that it's about 30 centimetres in length and hammer the cut spike into the ground so that the bristles face upwards. When people wipe their shoes, any mud will fall onto the garden rather than over the front doorstep.

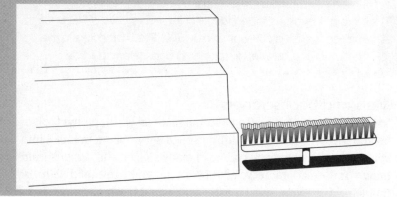

Plants

A dowdy entrance can be transformed instantly with some potted plants. Consider placing some flowering plants here. Add a fragrant touch with plants like lavender, mint and pyrethrum daisy. Not only do they release a lovely scent when you brush past them, they also deter some insects. Don't choose anything spiky because people could catch their clothes on them.

Lighting

No one likes stumbling around in the dark. There are several options to consider with lighting. One is sensor lighting that is activated with movement. You can vary the responsiveness of the light so it doesn't switch on if a dog wanders past or if there's a sudden gust of wind.

You can also vary the length of time the light stays on once it's activated. Another option is a light that can be turned on and off from outside the house. Determine what works for you. When working out where to position a light, have someone shine a torch where the light will be as you walk up and down the path. You don't want it to shine directly into your eyes. Make sure it illuminates the yard and not inside your house. Lighting can be practical as well as decorative. A torch placed in each light position allows you to plan before you spend.

Wet weather

Ideally, the entrance should have some cover so that guests can keep dry once they put their umbrella down. Many entrances may not have the space, but if you do, it's great to have a spot for a brolly. Some people are happy to have them sit just outside the front door against the wall, but an umbrella stand, decorative pot, old spaghetti jar, bin or terracotta pot is just as easy to put there. Consider having a towel available for damp guests.

Security

Feeling secure at home is important. People shouldn't be able to see inside your home except when you want them to. Glass panels should be obscured or coloured. You can apply decorative window film or use frosting cream (see The Bathroom, page 146). A peep hole or door viewer in the front door is a convenient way to see who is outside, which helps you decide whether or not you want to open your front door. Make sure it's at a height that everyone in the house can look through or you'll be like a certain height-challenged grand-mother who had to use a chair to see through her peep hole. Fortunately, Uncle Eddie put in a new peep hole at a more appropriate height.

HOW TO MAKE TEMPORARY COVERS FOR WINDOW OR DOOR PANES

COMFY CRAFT

If you don't want to permanently frost glass in windows or doors, try this temporary cover. **1.** Cut a sheet of waxed paper to the size of the pane. **2.** Place it against the window and hold it firmly with your hand. **3.** Then aim a warm hair dryer at the waxed paper for a few seconds until it softens and melts. **4.** Rub out any bubbles for a good seal. The paper will stick to the glass.

If you want to add a bit of colour, use strips of cellophane and attach your design to transparent contact. Apply to the window for a stained-glass effect.

Many burglaries happen when people are at home but spending time outside. Keep your front door and windows locked when you are outside the house. Don't leave car keys in easy-to-reach areas and don't leave your name and contact details on your keys in case you lose them and they get into the wrong hands.

Be careful about the stipulations with your insurance. If you say you have deadlocks and you don't and you're broken into, you may not be covered by insurance. It's worth making sure you get this right.

If you live in an area with a higher burglary rate, extra security measures, such as security alarms, can be effective and will lower your insurance premiums. Even if you have a box with a blue light you're less likely to be burgled. Back-to-base security is another option. In city areas where glass windows can be broken, window grilles are a good idea, but make sure they can be safely removed from the inside in case of fire. Another consideration with fire is deadlocks. We suggest allocating a secure place for spare keys in case of an emergency. It needs to be out of sight to burglars but known to the household. You might secure a key with masking tape to the back of the stairs or under a windowsill. Just make sure it's easy to get to and release in an emergency.

When you are going away on holiday, it's important to know your home is secure. It is hard to relax if you are worried! You can put some of your internal lights on a timer so the house isn't always in darkness. You can get intermittent timers that go on at different times each night. One security switch even records the weekly pattern of appliance use in a household and can replicate that pattern when you're away. Wireless network timers are also available. You can also hire a security company to look after your home while you are away.

HINT

HOW TO SECURE YOUR HOUSE

You might be surprised to learn that someone is burgled in Australia every minute. It's an experience to avoid. What's more, if you've been burgled, you're more likely to be broken into again. Minimise the risk by making sure all doors and windows are locked when you leave the house. If you're on holiday, organise for someone to collect your mail or get the post office to hold it. An overflowing letterbox screams 'no one at home'. You can also hire a house-sitter: check their references. Store valuables while you're away: Shannon often has to do restoration work for house-sitters when they break things.

TIP

IN CASE YOU LOCK YOURSELF OUT

Have a special spot for a spare key somewhere outside the house in case you lock yourself out. Just make sure it's not in the obvious places like under the mat or in the nearest pot plant. Use your imagination and only tell those who need to know where the key is. Jennifer almost smashed a window to get into her parents' house when she was minding it before she remembered there was a hidden spare key!

As part of your security strategy, it's a great idea to have an inventory of all your possessions. Either photograph or video all your goods and store these records in a safe place. If you don't have a video camera, hire one. A record like this is handy for insurance claims and it's also great to have a history of your valued possessions for your children. Include information such as who in the family owns the item and where it came from. Give detailed descriptions of what's in the house, particularly items of sentimental value. It makes replacement much easier because you can identify goods and offer proof of their condition. Store the inventory somewhere safe, or leave it with the insurance company or your solicitor. If items are not recovered, an artist may be able to provide a copy. Also make a note of serial and model numbers of your goods. You can also get an identification number from police and apply it with a special pen that fluoresces under ultraviolet light.

Security screens

In Australia, many homes have security screen doors to keep insects and burglars out, but let fresh air in. Make sure your screen door has robust locks. It's also important that the grille can't be pulled away from the frame. Ensure that the mesh is strong and that the hinges are secured internally so they can't be knocked out.

TIP

Deter flies by keeping the area clean. Wipe doorways and flyscreens with lavender oil so flies won't travel inside on people's backs. In the past, people used to heat camphor with a flame to deter flies, but this is a very dangerous practice as camphor can explode when it comes into contact with a naked flame—as Shannon found out when camphor tipped over and ignited.

Locks

Should you get new locks when you move into a new house? It's a new house for you, but the previous owners or tenants may still have copies of the keys. For peace of mind, when you move into a new house it's a good idea to change the locks. It's cheaper to replace the barrels rather than the whole lock.

HINT

HOW TO FIX STICKY LOCKS

Changes in the weather can cause locks to expand, contract and corrode. When it's wet or humid, lubricate sticky locks with a graphite puffer or talcum powder. You can use WD-40, but if you have a lot of dust, it can clog up the mechanism; so be careful.

INSIDE THE FRONT DOOR

This area is the threshold between the outside world and your inner sanctum. When you walk in the front door, you want to get the 'I'm home' feeling. Comfy considerations include:

If this is the place you dump the day's paraphernalia, make sure you have a space for it.

If you store coats, hats and shoes here, have appropriate spots for them to go.

Have a spot for keys, umbrellas, tissues, sunglasses, scarves and sun-block. Keys should be stored in a drawer for safety.

If you love clutter, that's fine, but it must be organised; otherwise it's just a mess.

Because there's a lot of traffic in this part of the house, think about flooring. If carpeted, have a mat at the front door and Scotchgard it and the carpet. Plastic runners also protect carpet.

Think of walkways around the home as arteries: if the blood can't flow, it can't get into the muscles of the room. Make sure the entrance hallway is clear because it's a throughway. Doorways leading off the hallway should be easy to get to, open and close.

Many people leave oil burners at the entrance to their home. Be careful with them, particularly near children. The hot oil doesn't extinguish like a candle but remains hot. If you do have one, make sure it's caged.

Hallstand

If you have the space, a hallstand is great for storing all those household bits and bobs: there are hooks for coats and hats and drawers for keys. If you don't have the space, use hooks on the back of the door or install hooks on the wall. You could also use a hatstand. Just be careful with the placement of your hatstand or hallstand: if you have furniture blocking the line of sight, you shorten the view.

If possible, have a mirror near the front door so you can make one last check of yourself before heading out into the world. It's nice to know if your skirt is wedged in your knickers, or your hair is looking like a cockatoo's crest, or you've got that 'panda-eyes' look.

Decorative touches

This is the first part of your home guests will see, so think about some easy decorative touches. Just be aware that there's a lot of dust here because of its proximity to the outside world. During summer, fill a vase with fragrant fruit, such as lemons and limes, or have some frangipani or gardenia flowers in a pretty dish of water. In autumn, fill a vase with autumnal leaves or some colourful berries, such as rosehips. Fragrance is important. Place a scented candle here but never leave a lit candle unattended. Rub lavender oil over doorjambs with a damp cloth or rag. Potpourri in a decorative container with a lid provides a fresh scent when the lid is removed. Avoid cut flowers in this area as they tend to die more quickly because of the draught coming from the door. If you love having flowers here, choose ones that retain their scent after they die, such as lavender, everlasting daisies, salvia, or even cut herbs, such as rosemary.

HOW WE USED TO KEEP COMFY FROM *FORTUNES IN FORMULAS FOR HOME, FARM AND WORKSHOP* BY HISCOX AND SLOANE (1944)

To stiffen hats, use 5 ounces of powdered borax, 1½ ounces of potassium carbonate, 25 ounces of dry shellac and water. Borax and potassium carbonate should be dissolved in enough hot water to immerse the hat and when in the solution, the shellac should be added and the solution boiled until the shellac is dissolved. Then remove from the fire. This can be applied to the hat with either a sponge brush or by immersion of the hat while cold then removing the hat and dipping in a very dilute solution of sulphuric acid or acetic acid (vinegar). This is done to neutralise the alkali and fix the shellac. The hat should then be shaped and allowed to dry.

HOW TO MAKE CITRUS CANDLES

1. Select a mould. It could be the bottom of a milk carton, a plastic container or an old tin (make sure it's not corrugated or the set wax won't be able to slide out). 2. Work out how much wax you will need by placing rough blocks of dried wax into the mould until it reaches the top then double this amount. 3. Set up a double boiler. Have the bottom pan three-quarters filled with water and bring to the boil. 4. Slowly melt the wax in the top pan until it's liquid. Add 2 drops of essential citrus oil (available from herbalists, health food stores, chemists, hardware stores, art suppliers and supermarkets). 5. Have a length of wick and dip it into the wax, remove and allow it to cool. Then run your fingers along the wick pulling it firmly in a straight line. Tie the non-waxed part of the wick to a bamboo skewer and position it on top of the mould with the wick hanging down the centre of the mould. 6. Pour wax from the double boiler into the mould. Leave 10 per cent of the wax in the double boiler because as wax cools, it leaves a well in the centre. Allow the wax in the mould to set and then top it up at the centre.

Another way to make a candle is through continuous dipping. Dip a wick in melted wax, hold it in the air from the top of the wick and allow it to cool, then dip this into the wax again and repeat until the candle is the size you want. Add different candle-colouring dyes and essential oils to each layer. You'll get different colours and aromas as the candle burns.

Never leave hot wax unattended.

How noisy is the entrance?

Imagine yourself coming home in the middle of the night when the house is asleep. Will you clunk your way inside? If you don't have carpet, consider using a runner or mat. You can also put a rubber strip along the door jamb to reduce the noise and draughts.

HOW TO FIX SQUEAKY FLOORBOARDS

Firstly, determine the source of the squeakiness. If the floorboards are rubbing together, sprinkle talcum powder between them. Other problems could be loose boards, loose nails or sunken brick piers. You'll need professional help with these. If there are gaps between your floorboards, close the gap with wood-coloured filler or twine. Place the twine along the gap and tap it in with a rubber hammer. Twine is often used on boats or in boatsheds because timber shrinks when exposed to salt and twine expands with moisture creating a seal. (That's why twine is used to create a nautical decoration effect).

HOW TO REPAIR CRACKS IN THE WALL

What to do will depend on the wall's surface. If it's plasterboard, fill the hole with plaster, allow to dry, then sand and paint. If an entire brick is broken, it will need to be replaced. If the mortar line is cracked, you can refill it. For cement render, proprietary filling products are available. To give it the same finish as the rest of the wall, lay some sandpaper sandy side down as the filler is drying, then remove. You'll get a matching sandy finish.

SPOTTY BRICKS: Tim's question

Q: I've got lots of paint spots on the bricks at the front of my home. I've heard that using hydrochloric acid works. Is that right?

A: Hydrochloric acid will eat away at the brick as well as the paint so it's best not to use it. Use vinegar. If you have lots of paint to clear, use a heat gun and a wire brush.

A place for shoes

Many people heel their shoes off at the front door. If this is the case at your place, create a storage area for shoes. Use an attractive box or a small cupboard. You could also keep a shoe frou—a homemade odour-absorbing mixture inside a muslin cloth (see page 130)—here to dust your shoes. Those with stinky feet can wipe the shoe frou over their feet on entering the house. Guard against dirty shoe marks with a mat or Scotchgard the carpet.

HINT

HOW TO DEAL WITH POWER FAILURES

The first thing to do is work out whether the power outage is affecting just your house or the whole street. Do this by popping outside and looking at the streetlights. If they're all off, it's likely to be an electricity supply issue. Ring the energy supplier: they usually have a recorded message with an estimation of how long the outage will be. If the outage is just at your place, check the meter box. There are two main types: fuses or circuit breakers. For fuses, turn the mains power off, remove the fuse and check the fuse wire. A broken fuse looks burnt. To replace a fuse, unscrew and replace the fuse wire with the appropriate amperage. You can use fuse wire with a lower amperage but never higher and you can't make a twenty out of two tens. Store spare fuse wire in the meter box.

If you have circuit breakers, see which button has flicked off. Then turn off at the power points as many items as possible. Return to the mains box and flick from off to on. If it stays on, gradually restore electrical items until it flicks off again. The last item you put on will be at fault. If it flicks off again, call an electrician. You need to be very careful around electricity—if in doubt, call an electrician.

TIP

As well as spare fuse wire, keep a small torch or a candle and lighter inside the meter box.

Emergency phone numbers

Keep a list of emergency phone numbers that everyone in the house is aware of and can access. Include the hospital, doctor, police, fire, electrician, plumber, security firms, family and friends.

DECORATING FOR SPECIFIC OCCASIONS

The entrance is the perfect spot for decorations. Just make sure your creation doesn't impede access in and out of the front door.

Here are some suggestions for:

Birthday parties—buy or hire a gas cylinder and fill the hallway with helium-filled balloons. Tie the balloons with coloured ribbons that match the party colours. Everyone can take a balloon home.

Twenty-first birthdays—use big gold keys and have photos from birth to twenty-one decorating the party space.

Fortieth birthdays—make a video/DVD. As guests arrive, ask them to tell a story or anecdote about the birthday boy or girl and play the video/DVD during the party.

Baby showers—tie a large baby rattle to the front door. Tie safety pins in blues and pinks along some cord, string the cord along the wall and attach baby shower cards to the safety pins. Arrange lolly dummies in a large bowl at the front door.

Kitchen showers—arrange kitchen utensils in a vase at the front door. Hang a utensil from the front door or even make a rubber glove wreath. To do this, refashion a coat-hanger into a circle and thread rubber gloves one by one onto the coat-hanger through the cuff and up through the middle finger until the entire coat-hanger is covered with rubber gloves!

Halloween—get an old pair of pantyhose, trim the elastic off the top and secure the waistband tightly over the doorframe with thumb tacks. Spread the legs around the frame. Use a hot knife or lit cigarette to burn holes in the pantyhose so that it looks like cobwebs.

Christmas—place tinsel or Christmas lights around the doorframe and secure with *Blu-tak*. Put a wreath on the front door and place a collection of Christmas baubles or decorations in a large bowl near the door.

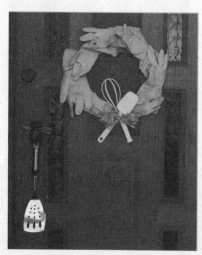

The Lounge, Family and Dining Rooms and the Study

THE LOUNGE/FAMILY ROOM

It can be annoying flicking through furniture catalogues to see their too-perfect lounge and dining room layouts: the cushions on the lounge are always plumped, there's a pristine white rug on the floor and the coffee table has tasteful *objets d'art* on display. While some lounge rooms might look like this, most do not, which is largely because there's always 'stuff'. Even if your lounge, dining and family rooms don't resemble the glossy catalogues, don't despair. The essential point to remember is that *you* feel comfy—and there are plenty of ways to make this a reality.

How we used to keep comfy from *Fortunes in Formulas for Home, Farm and Workshop* by Hiscox and Sloane (1944)

Books may be varnished against the ravages of insects and cockroaches that feed upon books. Mix 2 ounces of dammar resin, 2 ounces of mastic, 2 ounces of Canada balsam, ½ ounce creosote, 20 ounces of spirits of wine. Macerate with occasional shaking for a few days, if wanted at once. For a longer time when possible, a better varnish will result from a maceration of several months.

GETTING ORGANISED

The best way to get organised is to work out the optimal layout for your lounge/family room by creating a floor plan. Create flat cut out models of your furniture using scissors and paper and position them on graph paper. You can arrange and rearrange the cutouts until you have the ideal layout for your room (furniture plans are located at the back of *Speedcleaning*). Keep these considerations in mind:

Place the largest pieces of furniture against the longest wall; don't locate big or tall items near doorways or you'll create a crowded look. Instead, place them near corners.

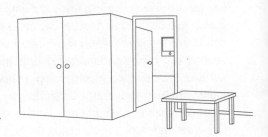

If you have an uninterrupted wall and furniture of different heights, arrange the furniture sloping upwards with the lowest items at one end arcing to the highest items at the other. That way, you avoid a higgledy-piggledy look.

Whenever possible, don't divide a room into two. If doorways are diagonally opposite, create a right-angle pass so people walk around the room rather than through it.

Define the walking area using rugs or create corridors with the backs of lounges or armchairs. It's better to have one big rug rather than several small ones in a small space. If you have lots of small rugs, tie them together by their tassels or fringes to create one big rug.

WALLS

Choosing colours and finishes for walls is subjective—make a selection based on what works for you. When it comes to paint, the higher the sheen, the less likely the wall will mark, but be aware that it also reflects light and will show up imperfections. High-sheen paints are a good choice if you have children and pets. Paint effects, such as rag rolling and marbling, hide marks better than a plain surface. Matt surfaces can develop a sheen when washed so avoid having them in high-traffic areas. Regardless of the paint surface, most commercial cleaning products break down the paint and leave a bleached shiny spot; avoid using them if you can. One of the best ways to clean dirty walls is with brown bread! Just roll it into a ball and rub it against the wall. Some dirty marks, such as grit, grime and metal scratches, will come off with a pencil eraser. Often, white vinegar and old pantyhose will remove dirt, grime and mud splashes. For stubborn marks, try a very diluted solution of sugar soap applied with a soft cloth. Wring the cloth tightly before applying or you'll leave drip marks. Another way to avoid drip marks is to start from the bottom and work your way up the wall, drying as you go.

Wallpaper is great if you need to cover an uneven surface, but the downside is that it tends to date very quickly. When choosing, have a look at designs with a multi-mirror (at wallpaper suppliers). That way you can see how an entire wall will look rather than just one square. Make sure wallpaper in children's rooms has a vinyl finish that is washable.

ART

Art is a matter of personal taste. You can build a room around art, or build art around the room. Don't buy art for fashion: you should have works that you like and want to look at, that way they'll never date.

HINT

HOW TO HANG A PICTURE

The appropriate method for hanging a picture will depend on its weight. For a standard picture (75 x 75cm), attach two self-tapping screw-in eyes to the back of the frame. Make a mark 10 per cent above halfway on the back of the picture, then twist the eyes in along the frame. Fix cord or piano wire through the eyes, using squeeze-on clamps rather than knots. Choose the wall fastening according to the type of wall the picture is to hang from. For plasterboard, use self-drilling *WallMates*. For masonry, drill a hole using a masonry bit, tap a wall plug into it then put in a screw or screw-backed hook. Before drilling into walls, check you're not drilling into any electricals or water pipes!

To work out where to hang pictures, it's important to get balance. Start by drawing the wall or space on some paper and see how the art fits in various spots. Either fit the pictures into a shape, or balance the art with the room's furniture. For walls without furniture, it's better to line up the bottom or the tops of the frames; don't line them up using the middle of the picture. To make a room seem higher, arrange pictures vertically. To make a room seem wider, hang pictures horizontally.

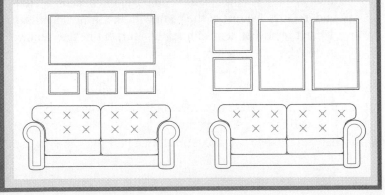

TIP

Jennifer's friend works in an art gallery and offers this hint: cut old corks into discs and glue them to the bottom back corners of a painting to stabilise it and allow air to circulate around the back.

HINT

HOW TO LIGHT A PICTURE

Light shouldn't shine directly onto a picture. The angle needs to be between 30–60 degrees. Ceiling lights should sit above artwork. If that's not possible, tilt the picture slightly away from the wall so you won't get glare. Light from a lamp can also be used to illuminate a picture.

EXTRA LICK OF PAINT: Lynn's question

 I've got an oil painting with a splatter of white house paint on one corner. It's been stored in the garage but I'd love to hang it again.

To find out what kind of house paint it is (either water-based or oil-based), test by wiping a cotton bud dipped in methylated spirits over the splatter. If the paint comes off on the bud, remove the rest of the paint with methylated spirits. If it doesn't remove it, test with mineral turpentine and remove. If in doubt, see a restorer.

HINT

HOW TO FIX A SHAKY PICTURE FRAME

1: Set up a workspace
Place sheets of newspaper on a flat work surface. Use a thick towel larger than the picture and place it over the newspaper, then place the picture frame on top.

2: Disassemble the frame
Carefully remove the back of the frame, making sure you remove the nails evenly. If there is glass, and you're afraid of breaking it, slide a scraper blade between the nail and the glass, then tap by sliding the hammer along the scraper blade towards the head of the nail. Alternatively, pull the head of the nail with a pair of pliers up the scraper blade so you don't slip and hit the glass. Remove the glass, backing boards and picture, and place them to one side on a sheet of acid-free paper in the order you removed them and in the same orientation.

3: Check the corners of the frame
Look carefully at the corners of your frame. If there are triangular corner supports over the mitred joints, the screws may need to be tightened. Put a dab of water-based PVA wood glue on the inside of the mitred joint before replacing the triangular reinforcing corners. Always square up the corners of the frame using a set square or protractor. If the corners are joined together with a piece of wavy wire, it's a flat corrugated tack which can work loose. Put a little wood glue down the corrugations before replacing the triangular-shaped reinforcing corner and tacking it in place. Use a protractor and set square to square the corners. It's important to do all four corners quickly. Don't allow one corner to dry before the others or you will get warping from the glue.

HINT

4: Allow to dry
Put a piece of plastic over the joins then place a heavy piece of planking or a large tray on top and stack with books. Leave to dry overnight. Clean out any dust in the rebates.

5: Reassemble
Gradually stack your glass, mountings, picture and backing board back in. If you want to use new tacks, use flat push-in framer's tacks. Cover the backing board with acid-free brown paper and use acid-free tape along the join between the backing board and the frame to stop insects, mould and fungus from getting inside.

HINT

HOW TO MOUNT A PICTURE
Having a favourite poster or print professionally framed can be a costly exercise. It's a job you can do yourself, although we suggest doing a practice run first. After choosing a frame to go with your picture, select an appropriately coloured mounting board. If you want to make the picture stand forward, use a darker coloured mounting board than the picture. If you want the picture to recede, use a lighter coloured mounting board.

Items: *Stanley knife*, lead pencil, steel or steel-edged right-angle ruler, pattern maker's wheel, acid-free tape, mounting board and cardboard.

1: Set up a workspace
Place sheets of newspaper on a flat work surface. Use a thick towel larger than the picture and place it over the newspaper.

HINT Continued

2: Frame and glass

Lay the frame face-down on the workspace and place the glass inside the frame. Wedge small pieces of cardboard 90 degrees to the glass between the frame and the glass so the frame won't rattle. Make sure to trim the wedges with the *Stanley knife* so the cardboard is flush, or in line, with the edge of the frame so you can't see it.

3: Mounting board

Make small marks on the edges and in the middle of the mounting board with a lead pencil to fit the picture and frame. Cut the mounting board using a pattern maker's wheel. Put a steel or steel-edged right-angle ruler in the appropriate position and run your wheel along the edge. It will automatically mitre the corner on the mounting board. Also cut the middle of the mounting board so the picture fits. Then assemble all the bits and do a test placement of your picture facing upwards. Lay your mounting boards, surround boards and picture as though they are in the frame, but facing upwards. Then make the actual placement in the frame. Don't glue or tape the picture to the mounting board. If there's any gap or rebate on the inside edge of the frame, keep adding mounting boards until the back is flush. You can also use inexpensive acid-free foam framers' board to fill the rebate.

4: Securing

Put on the backing board and use framer's tacks or small tacks to secure it. Use a framer's hammer or rubber hammer to tap in the tacks, being careful not to jar the glass. If needed, use a spoon cup side towards the tack and tap on the back of it with a hammer. Once it's secured, dip acid-free paper tape in water and lay it across the backing edges to seal. Sponge the area clear of water, trim the excess and leave to dry face down.

LIGHTING

It's important to be able to vary the lighting in the lounge/family room according to the activity being carried out. You need bright lights for reading, but dimmer lights when watching TV. If you don't have enough light, activities such as reading or sewing can become stressful. Table and floor lamps are a good option with dimmers installed on your lights. For relaxing lighting, use lamps with soft bulbs to create a rosy or golden glow. The reason you relax with rosy lighting is because it's like a sunset. For bright lighting, use blue-white light which wakes you up. Many hardware stores and supermarkets now sell bulbs with a range of tints.

FLOORING

It's worth spending money on flooring because you'll have it for a long time. The options are almost overwhelming. The main types are timber, vinyl, cork, concrete, tiles, marble, slate, self-levelling plastics and rubber. Then there are different coverings for floors including carpet, vinyl, silk, rubber, coir and sisal.

CARPET AND RUGS

Our advice is to choose the best carpet you can afford. Carpet can be made of wool, nylon, cotton, silk, mohair, angora, coir, sisal or seagrass. A good combination for carpet is 93 per cent wool/7 per cent nylon—the nylon strengthens the wool fibres so the carpet lasts longer. There are also different carpet piles to think about: cut, loop or shag. Shannon prefers cut carpets because they're easier to clean and care for. Shag carpet has to be vacuumed twice as often and special care needs to be given to the long fibres. If you love shag, get it in a rug because it's easier to maintain.

HINT

HOW TO CHOOSE FLOORING

What to choose will depend on where you live, how you live and your preferences. Timber floors are easy to clean, but can be noisy. Noise can be reduced with a rug, a runner or a polypropylene transparent runner. Heavy furniture near the walkway also lowers the vibration in the floor and stops echoing. Carpet is warmer and quieter, but stains more easily and wears out after about 20 years. Whatever you do, don't choose something over-patterned that will date: go for classic colours and styles. Where you can be bold is in the choice of rugs. Rugs are great because they protect carpet, delineate a space and provide decoration. In zones where kids play, a rug is an extra layer of padding and can be washed easily. Tiles are easy to look after but can be cold and harsh. Concrete floors are a popular choice now but, like tiles, can be a bit harsh. Shannon loves marble floors with lots of rugs.

TIP

Clean sisal with a mixture of wheat bran and vinegar and a stiff broom. Place wheat bran in a bowl and add drops of vinegar until it's clumpy but not wet. Scatter it over the sisal, rub backwards and forwards with a stiff broom, then vacuum.

Common carpet stains

Shannon is often asked how to remove stains from carpet, but many people go overboard with the advice and turn their stain into a swamp: **don't use too much water or moisture**.

Keep these guidelines in mind *before* tackling your stain:

Work out what the stain is made of. Is it a protein, fat, chemical/biological dye or resin/glue?

Unless you know it will work, always do a test patch first. It's a good practice run.

Never spot-clean stains on your carpet within four weeks of it being steam cleaned. Spot-cleaning can adversely react with steam-cleaning chemicals.

Never use excessive water or moisture on carpet. More is not better. If moisture penetrates to the base of your carpet, it will create a further stain when it comes into contact with the jute backing.

Stain-removal solutions are not interchangeable. You can't use advice relating to carpet on your woollen jumper. Every surface and stain is different.

CARPET RESCUE: HOW TO FIX YOUR JUTE STAIN

Does this scenario sound familiar? There's a stain on your carpet. You follow the instructions and then find you've created a bigger stain. What's gone wrong? The problem is you've used too much moisture which has penetrated to the back of the carpet, the jute, and created a new stain. Don't despair. If the area is still wet, place lots of paper towel over it and stand on it. Then treat with a small amount of glycerine applied with a toothbrush. Work in all directions so each part of the carpet fibre is treated. If the area has dried, apply glycerine in the same way. This will clear the jute stain. Then apply the original solution to the original stain. **And remember, more is not better.**

HINT

HOW TO WORK OUT WHAT A STAIN IS MADE OF

If you're not sure what your stain is made of, here are some tell-tale indicators to help you. **1.** Protein stains are darker on the edge. Use cold water and facial soap to remove. **2.** Carbohydrate stains have a darker mark in the centre of the stain. Use warm water and facial soap. **3.** Fat stains spread evenly in a circle and require detergent and warm water to remove them. Use solvents for chemical and resin stains. If there are several components to a stain, remove proteins first, then carbohydrates, then fats, then chemical and resin stains.

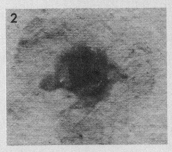

REMOVING STAINS FROM CARPETS

Red wine—use paper towel to soak up as much spill as possible. Sprinkle with bicarb, sponge with white vinegar and dry with paper towel.

Coffee/tea—apply a little glycerine to the stain with a cotton ball, then sponge with white vinegar.

Cooking oil—apply a little dishwashing liquid and scrub with a nylon brush, then sponge with warm water. Dry with paper towel.

Biro—allow some milk to rot in the sun, then apply the rotten milk solids to the stain until the colour rises. Wash with facial soap and cold water.

Orange juice—absorb as much of the juice as possible with paper towel, then sponge with white vinegar. Expose the area to sunlight or UV light.

Acrylic paint—sponge repeatedly with methylated spirits until paint is removed.

Pet hair—put on disposable rubber gloves, wash hands with soap and water and shake dry. Stroke your gloved hands across the surface to pick up the hair.

Urine—blot with paper towel then sponge with white vinegar.

Poo—remove solids, sponge with a little facial soap and cold water, then sponge with a little dishwashing liquid and warm water. Finally, sponge with a little white vinegar.

Mud—dislodge as much mud as possible with a hairbrush, then vacuum. Then use the froth from a bucket of soapy water with a toothbrush and work from the outside to the inside of the stain. Place paper towel over the top and stand on it to absorb the dirt and moisture. Repeat until clean.

TIP

The easy way to pick up solids is with two nit combs pushed towards each other. It slides under the muck and lifts it out of the carpet.

HINT

HOW TO MAKE AN ALL-PURPOSE CARPET CLEANER

Sprinkle a little bicarb over the carpet, vacuum, then lightly wipe a little white vinegar over the carpet with a stiff broom. Leave it to dry, then vacuum. For severe stains, use ChemDry. Spray it over the stain and while wet, scrub with a nylon brush. Apply paper towel and stand on it to absorb the moisture and stain.

HINT

HOW TO CLEAN CARPET OR A RUG

Hire a carpet cleaner at the supermarket. Use half as much chemical as suggested and add 2 teaspoons of eucalyptus oil, 3 tablespoons of white vinegar, 2 tablespoons of bicarb and 2 tablespoons of methylated spirits. If cleaning a rug, hang it over the clothesline to dry: the grass will love the run off.

HINT

HOW TO FIX A RIPPLING RUG

If your rug is rippling because of age, take it outside and place it face down on a sheet on the lawn. Grate $1/2$ bar of facial soap and mix with a bucket of warm water. Sweep the back of the rug with the soapy water and a stiff broom. While the rug's drying, tug it flat. The soap stiffens the fibres in the backing of the carpet and holds it flat.

TIP

If you have fleas in your carpet, place peppermint tea bags or fresh mint leaves and water in a spray pack and lightly spray, then vacuum the carpet. Fleas hate mint.

FURNITURE

Shannon has a favourite comfy chair in her lounge room. And right next to her comfy chair is her little box of goodies—a stash of stuff, which includes everything from nail polish to sewing needles and the current book she is reading. Jennifer loves lounging on the couch, so cushions and throws are part of her accoutrements.

HOW TO CHOOSE A COMFY ARMCHAIR

Often people consider only the look of an armchair rather than the comfy factor. To help you with your choice, follow these guidelines:

When sitting on an armchair, your feet should sit flat on the ground and your knees form a 90-degree angle.

When resting your arms along the armrests, your fingertips should reach right to the end.

The dip at the back of the chair should be in line with your shoulders and the base of your head should be supported by the chair.

The seat well should match your bottom.

If your knees are too high, you can add a cushion to the well of the chair to boost the height. If you don't have a large enough cushion, place a smaller cushion under the existing cushion to avoid the hump effect.

The best way to avoid making the wrong fabric choice when buying an expensive upholstered item, such as a sofa, is to close your eyes when selecting it. Focus just on the feel of the object; don't let your sense of sight overwhelm your sense of touch.

When it comes to choosing the covering, there are many options and it's difficult to say which is better. Select the fabric according to your requirements. If you have children, you need something washable and strong, such as **cotton** or **linen**. We also suggest having slipcovers made from an inexpensive fabric, such as canvas, which can be thrown in the washing machine when grubby. Increase the protection by spraying it with *Scotchgard* after each wash. **Leather** lasts a long time but takes more work to keep in good condition. Make sure you use a good-quality leather conditioner at least once every 3 months. **Nusuede** looks beautiful and, if you don't have to worry about pets or heavy wear and tear, is a lovely surface to sit on. Clean it using a mixture of wheat bran and white vinegar. Place 1 cup of unprocessed wheat bran in a bowl and gradually add drops of vinegar until the mixture clumps together to resemble brown sugar—it should never be wet. Transfer this mixture to a stocking and tie into the toe. Rub backwards and forwards like an eraser to remove surface grime, watermarks and general muck, then vacuum. Store it in a ziplock bag for next use. Some of the new **vinyls** can be very attractive but pens, pencils and all varieties of ink tend to mark them quite easily. Clean with a damp cloth.

TIP

If you have oily hair, protect your chair with an antimacassar or headrest cover. They can be made to match the fabric of your lounge chair. Because they're removable, they can be washed easily.

BAD BIRO: Bernadette's question

Q: I've got black biro marks over a yellow leather couch, but don't really want the bumble bee look. What's the solution?

A: Apply white spirits with a cotton bud and go over the biro marks. When the ink melts, apply talcum powder to absorb it. If any ink remains, do it again. When it's removed, use leather dew to recondition the leather.

> **TIP**
>
> Protect the vulnerable ends of armrests with armrest covers in matching upholstery or *Scotchgard* them.

> **TIP**
>
> In your main relaxation area, make sure each chair or lounge has a place to rest a drink. This could be a coffee table, side table or stool. The coffee table should be at knee height when you're sitting down; if it's any lower, you'll hit your shins. There should be easy pathways between the furniture so that guests don't knock their legs.

DISPLAY CABINETS

Mementos and collectables reflect your passions and should be proudly displayed. Organise your special objects by colour or shape as this is more pleasing to the eye. If you choose to have them lit, the best angle for lighting is at 40 degrees, shining away from the viewer, so that you won't get light bouncing off any shiny surfaces. If you want to show off details, keep objects at eye level. Never place dark colours above pastels because the display will look top heavy—lighter colours are better higher up.

BOOKSHELVES

Many people store their books in the lounge room. If you do, the best way to organise them is by subject, then alphabetically by title or author, whatever is easiest for you to remember. Another organisational idea is to mark out the different areas on your shelves with a silk ribbon hanging over the edge—and you could write what the subject is on the ribbon. Store the most-read books at eye level because they're easier to find and you won't have to bend or stretch when you need them. Large and heavy books should be kept on lower shelves. Only organise books according to colour if you don't read them because you'll never find anything. Don't overcrowd the shelves or they'll look cluttered. Keep books and shelves free of dust and make sure valuable books are kept away from windows so they're not exposed to light or changes in temperature. If there's any damp, keep silicone crystals or sticks of white chalk down the back of the shelves.

TELEVISION

The television needs to be positioned so that light doesn't fall on the screen. It should be placed with the back next to or diagonal to windows or other light sources. If the lounge is arranged in one corner of the room, the TV should be placed diagonally opposite: watching TV sideways isn't comfy. To work out the best height for the TV, fix a piece of wool with *Blu-tak* to the centre of the screen. Sit on the chairs and extend the wool to eye height. The angle of the string should be no smaller than 45 degrees in any direction. Ideally, your eyes should be parallel to the screen so your neck doesn't strain. Flat screens can be mounted at all positions, but make sure your head looks directly at, rather than tilted up, to the screen. When arranging the TV, test the vision from every chair in the room. Test the couches and chairs and add extra pillows to get an idea of how tall people will experience the room; crouch down as though small, so you get the best position for line of sight. Have sufficient cushions for people of all shapes and sizes. If you don't have footrests, have some pouffes, footstools or some really big stackable cushions—Moroccan floor cushions are great for this. A little advanced planning like this and your loungeroom can be your own home theatre without expense.

STEREO

The stereo should be easy to access but not be placed near walkways because you're more likely to bump into it or disturb the mechanism. Angle the speakers, which should be on a stable surface or securely mounted on a wall, to maximise sound. Unstable surfaces or shaky hooks can cause vibrations and buzzing in speakers and can damage them. The rubber ring inside a speaker moves backwards and forwards: if the ring moves to the side, it stretches out of shape and is damaged. Be careful placing speakers and headphones next to the TV, their magnetic fields can affect the picture. Face speakers away from the TV. Jennifer thought her TV was conking out when the colour at the corner of the screen became distorted. It wasn't the TV, it was the stereo speakers interfering with the picture.

Keep the magnets from old speakers: they're really strong and kids love them.

Never place speakers next to glass because the glass will vibrate and hum. Anyone who lives under a flight path will know the effect.

REMOTE CONTROLS

Make sure your remote controls are easy to find. Consider installing retractable cords if yours maddeningly go missing all the time.

COMFY CRAFT

HOW TO MAKE A REMOTE TIDY

If your remote controls always go missing, attach them to something that's fixed. To do this, buy two self-adhesive *Velcro* strips and a good-sized retractable cord. Attach either end of the cord to the *Velcro* strips and fix one end of the *Velcro* to the underside of the coffee table, or a similar convenient base, and the other end to the remote control. Retractable electronic cords with toggles also do the job. Another way to store remote controls is to attach a thick flat piece of wide elastic with several twist pins—which are available at fabric shops—to the arm of a lounge chair. Position the twist pins along the elastic to create the slots where the remote controls will sit.

HEATING AND COOLING

HINT

HOW TO WARM UP THE ROOM

Because it's so easy to flick a switch and turn your heater on, many people don't consider other ways to warm a room. Be aware that glass in windows and doors is a major source of heat transference, so in winter—and summer—cover glass with blinds or curtains. Check the room for draughts. Rattling doors and windows are the most common source of cold air entering a room. You can check for draughts with a lit candle: the flame will bend away from the source of the draught. If the doorjamb is loose, place a felt strip down the jamb. Add a draught brush along the bottom of the door or use a draught stopper (also called a snake or sausage)—these come in a range of colours and styles and can blend or contrast with your other furnishings (Shannon has a fluffy leopard snake! The kids love it). Also look at the vents and get covers for them if too much air is getting in.

Rugs, cushions, throw rugs and other soft furnishings help to warm up a room, too. The position of your furniture affects the temperature of a room as well. If you put it against a wall, it acts as a thermos—cooling the room in summer and warming it in winter—because you're creating thermal mass. If you want a warm and cosy lounge/family room without blowing the heating budget, don't go minimalist in winter.

Keep warm in winter by crocheting a blanket. The faster you crochet, the more coverage you will have and the warmer you will be, so use a jumbo hook and several strands of wool at once. If you prefer to knit, use rocket needles and several strands of wool at once. Wool can be bought cheaply at charity stores. Make your own crochet hooks using wood from a wooden coat-hanger. Break the coat-hanger and smooth the sides with a sharp kitchen knife and sand until roughly cylindrical and smooth.

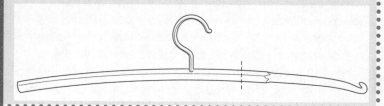

Heaters

We're more aware of our carbon footprint these days and it's worth-while considering other options before putting the heater on. Dress for the season—wear slippers, ugg boots, thick socks or moccasins; put on a jumper or cardigan—and have blankets and throws available. Think about insulation as well. Put furniture across breezeways, use heavier drapes and place furniture against interior walls. Baking meals in winter warms the house as well as your tummy. Then if you are still cold, put the heater on!

There are many different types of heater available. Base your selection on the size of the room, the cost of the heater and the environmental impact.

Heaters can use electricity, oil, gas or solid fuels, such as wood, coal or briquettes. Electric bar heaters give a quick burst of heat but are expensive to run. Fan heaters are popular, but use a lot of electricity and sap moisture from the air. Oil heaters are safe, economical and radiate heat in all directions, but are slow to heat up a room. Timers can be set so that they're operational when you want them to be and many are now fan-assisted, which helps distribute the heat around the room. Gas heaters use a flame and have a ceramic core that radiates heat. They're economical, but because the heat only radiates forward they have to sit against a wall. Many people have reverse-cycle air conditioning, but it uses a lot of electricity. Gas fires, many of which are designed to resemble a log fire, work well for heating large rooms.

Where you place the heater is also important. Be careful with bar heaters: make sure they have an auto-off feature that turns the heater off if knocked over. Keep them away from flammable items.

Make sure the heater you choose has a good grille and grille protector to protect little fingers.

It's vital to teach children from an early age about the dangers of heaters and fire.

Fires

Once they're started, an open log fire is lovely to gaze at and is very comfy, but they can be a lot of work and create mess. To stop the walls from becoming sooty, have a good-sized extended mantlepiece, which forces heat into the room rather than up the chimney. If you're unsure how much heat is going up the chimney, get coloured smoke pellets from the hardware store to track where the smoke is going. Check that the flue is the right size for your fireplace. If it's not, it may need to be altered, depending on its location in the house and where the wind blows. You'll need a professional to help with this.

To work out when it's time to call the chimney sweep, scrape a fingernail on the inside of a cold chimney. If soot flakes off, rather than smears off, it's time for a clean. Excess smoke is another indicator.

Always have a hearth or fireproof rug in front of the fire with mesh firescreens (available at specialist stores). Use suitable tools and have a place for them to rest. Fire irons are useful, practical and fun—everyone loves to poke a fire—and include a long-handled fork for toasting marshmallows. A hob is great for heating hot chocolate.

What to burn in the fireplace

By law, you can't burn green or unseasoned wood. It has to be dry. The harder the wood, the longer it will burn. Start your fire with short burning wood and when it takes, use hardwood. The reason hardwood burns more slowly is because it has less sap. If you keep a woodpile and season your own wood, always cut hardwood when it's green and allow it to season in the stack. Once it's dry, it's impossible to cut.

TIP

Look for timber at council clean ups. Just make sure it's seasoned for at least 12 months. Write the date you collected it on the end of the timber with a pencil (some pens create toxic fumes when burnt) so you know when it's ready. Local timber mills and hardware stores will also have cheap timber off-cuts.

HINT

HOW TO BUILD A FIRE

When building a fire, start with rolled up pieces of newspaper, then in a log-cabin pattern or teepee pattern, lay fine kindling over the top of the newspaper and allow air to circulate. Add small kindling and increase the size of the wood until the fire takes.

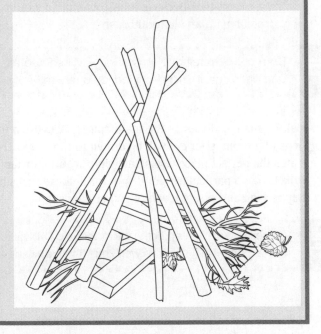

TIP

Once the fire is thriving, create some great smells by throwing a handful of herbs or fruit woods, such as apple, peach or olive, on the fire. Avoid pine because it has a tarry smell. Eucalyptus has a fresh smell but has a tendency to spit and splatter. Whatever you do, don't use wattle because it explodes!

SAP SAGA: Jim's question

 We've got a lovely old marble fireplace, but sap from the firewood has dripped onto the marble and penetrated into it. Can I get it out?

 The best way to dissolve sap is with tea tree oil applied with a cotton ball. Because it has penetrated, you may have to scrub with an old toothbrush.

 Don't use polyurethane on fireplaces. When heated, it bubbles and discolours. It's not designed to cope with heat.

Position mantle clocks on the mantlepiece. Because a fireplace is the focus of a room, your eye will be drawn to the clock. The mantlepiece is also the perfect place to display your favourite ornaments and trinkets. It's a particularly good spot for delicate items because they're high and out of reach of young hands.

 Old-fashioned mantlepieces used to have a cupboard on one side where port, whisky and rum were kept. The fire would warm them!

Fans

Ceiling fans, freestanding fans or desk fans should be positioned to maximise airflow—moving air reduces mould spores, dust and smells. To bring air from the outside in, place the back of the fan towards a window or door to draw in the air. Face the fan towards the window or the centre of the room to get air circulating around the room. Just remember to clean fans regularly because the moving blades create a static charge and dust is attracted to them. Clean with either a feather or fabric duster.

SMELL

Adding aroma—by having fragrant flowers or flowering plants or using fragrant room sprays or candles—to a lounge/family room is lovely, but don't overscent the room because it can increase, rather than decrease, tension and cause headaches! In colder months, spicy potpourri placed near heaters will gently scent the air and make you think of warm puddings. In summer, use a potpourri that includes citrus, pine, rose and lavender.

TIP

Dry some lavender by hanging it upside down in a warm, dark place until the flowers are dry. Wrap the dried flowers in a doily or some colourful paper and put them on display.

HINT

HOW TO PREPARE FOR A BOYS' NIGHT IN

There's no need to feel nervous if your house has been nominated as the location to watch the next football match. With just a few precautions, the risk of collateral damage can be reduced significantly. A key factor is to have the right lighting: you don't want the room to be too light or too dark. If it's too light, they'll turn the lights off and if it's too dark, they won't notice what they've spilled. Scotchgard the carpet, use table protectors on wooden tables and leave lots of coasters lying around—thanks to the blokes having spent extended time at the pub, they'll use them and inadvertently protect surfaces from water marks. Stock the fridge with their favourite beers and non-alcoholic drinks and keep an easy-to-find supply of snacks, which help absorb the alcohol, so they don't raid all your other food. If the snacks have already been prepared there'll be less mess to clean up later. Have a taxi number in large numbers above the telephone.

HINT

HOW TO PREPARE FOR A GIRLS' NIGHT IN

Girls can be just as messy as blokes! If painting nails, dyeing hair or applying self-tanning lotion, make sure you have all the solvents ready—these stains are the hardest to remove! Be prepared for wine spills by having plenty of paper towel, bicarb and white vinegar on hand. Have lots of non-alcoholic drinks available because women absorb alcohol more quickly than men. Have some coffee percolating—the smell will make them head for the caffeine rather than the booze. Shannon has noticed that women prefer using plates to paper serviettes, so have lots of bread-and-butter plates out—and paper serviettes. You'll need some tissues if watching a chick flick on DVD. And if there's a big group of women coming over, warn the neighbours about the noise! As with the blokes, have a taxi number in large numbers above the telephone.

HOW WE USED TO KEEP COMFY FROM *FORTUNES IN FORMULAS FOR HOME, FARM AND WORKSHOP* BY HISCOX AND SLOANE (1944)

To colour billiard balls red: wash the ivory article first in a solution of bicarb. Then plunge for a few seconds in a bath of equal parts water and nitric acid. Remove, rinse in running water, then put it in an alcoholic solution of fuchine and let it remain until it is the required colour. (Shannon still uses fuchine in her workshop for colouring ivory.)

GUESTS

If you have to turn your lounge room into the guestroom when you have overnight visitors, there are some easy ways to make their stay as comfortable as possible. We're talking the whole five-star experience here! Always include a clock radio, lamp and two towels, one for hair and one for body. Have a guest pack of goodies, which includes personal soaps, tissues, paracetamol, *Vaseline*, *Band-Aids* and a small bottle of port—anything they might need in an emergency. Ask if they have any allergies to pets or any special food requirements. Depending on the season, have a fan, heater or extra blankets. Offer to hang up any clothes—use your wardrobe or another space—and let them know where the iron and ironing board are stored. And, so that your morning routine isn't disrupted, discuss when the shower is available. Give them a spare key and your mobile or contact phone numbers. It's also a nice idea to include a street directory or map of the local area. And to top off the whole welcoming, comfy feeling, include some freshly cut flowers in a vase.

CHANGE THE LOOK

If you feel as though your lounge/family room needs a revamp, you can alter the look easily by changing cushion covers and adding slipcovers—which can be made professionally if you're not great with a sewing machine—to your couch or armchairs. Slipcovers help protect upholstered furniture and can be easily changed according to your mood or the time of year. Canvas is ideal in summer, a heavy-weight fabric works well in winter. Have one set in a neutral-toned lightweight cotton or linen for summer and another set in a warm-toned heavyweight fabric, such as felt or tweed, for winter.

In winter, keep a mohair or cashmere throw draped over the arm of the couch ready to use when it's chilly, and snuggle when you want.

THE DINING ROOM

The dining room has undergone a revolution. It used to be a space where diners could enjoy their meal away from the mess of the kitchen, but that's all changed. In one exclusive restaurant that we know of, a dining table has been installed in the middle of the busy kitchen so that diners can see how the food is prepared. It's the same in people's homes: seeing the food being prepared is part of the night's entertainment. In many homes, the dining room also doubles as the place for the kids' homework, the computer or a variety of projects, so storage space in this area is important.

GETTING ORGANISED

Organising the dining room is a fairly straightforward exercise. The basics are a table and chairs. To increase the comfy factor, add a dresser or sideboard to store items, such as plates, cups, cutlery, linen, mats, serviettes, drinking glasses, china and decanters, that are needed to 'dress' the dining table and make entertaining special.

HINT

HOW TO SELECT A DINING TABLE AND CHAIRS

Select a table that suits the room and your dining needs.

If you often entertain large numbers, an extendable table is the best choice, or a table if you're challenged for space. Comfy chairs are a must. Feet should sit flat on the ground and legs form a 90-degree angle. Your back should be 90 degrees to your hips and there shouldn't be any pressure on the back of your knees. It's better for chairs to be slightly lower than too high. When sitting in the chair, your elbows should be 3cm below the tabletop. These chair and table heights make dribbling less likely.

Storing extra chairs can be an issue. You can hang them from her walls, Shaker-style, or use chairs from other parts of the house, such as the office. Jennifer has fold-up chairs that are stored in the cupboard. Shannon uses stools which double as tables in her lounge room. Shannon collects stools and is an advocate of them because they can be used in so many different ways. You can sit on them, rest things on them or stand on them. Put a circle of plywood on top of a stool and you have an instant extra dining table. Put stools side-by-side, place a length of timber on top and you have a trestle. Be aware that bar stools don't have angled legs so you need to use four to create a table.

HINT

HOW TO REMOVE A WATER MARK FROM A SEALED TIMBER TABLE

It's annoying when this happens. The first task is to work out what the table has been sealed with: varnish, polyurethane, shellac or wax. To do this, take a pin or needle, hold it in a pair of pliers and heat it on the stove. Touch the pin or needle to an inconspicuous part of the table and smell the fume it creates. If it smells like burnt plastic, it's polyurethane. If it smells like an electrical fire, it's an oil-based varnish. If it smells like burnt hair, it's shellac. If it smells like a snuffed candle, it's waxed. To repair polyurethane, apply a little *Brasso* with a cloth and rub firmly in the direction of the grain over the mark. It will look worse before it looks better! *Brasso* partially melts polyurethane and allows it to refill the tiny air holes that create the white mark. Shellac, varnish and wax can be repaired using beeswax applied with the back of a piece of lemon peel.

LIGHTING

Light should be directed at the centre of the dining table. Most people like to be able to see what they are eating. If it's at one end, it makes the table feel lopsided and moves the conversation towards the light. If your lighting is not over the table's centre, you could turn off the main light and use a candelabra or candelabra lamp in the centre of the table. Down lighting is ideal because it's easier to see other people at the table. You can shine a lamp up the wall to create soft lighting. For comfort make sure no one is caught in the spotlight! Specialist wall lamps are available as are self-adhesive rechargeable battery lamps. Candles and the occasional coloured light can make a feature light. Billiards lights work really well in dining rooms because you can change their height and the designs can be modern or traditional.

If you are unhappy with your lights, you could change the globes for a different colour tone, add different light shades or you could even hire a lighting consultant to help you place your lights.

VENTILATION

Ventilation is very important in the dining room. If the air is stagnant, unwanted smells will hang around—and really, you don't want to smell curry while eating strawberries and cream! Create better airflow by opening windows or using a fan (you could put a small desk fan in one corner away from the doors to encourage airflow. If you can't get uninterrupted air flow across the room, aim the fan along the wall. This makes the airstream circle the room. You don't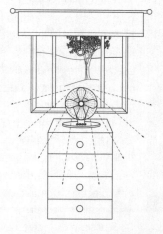
need to have the fan on full blast; steady air movement is better (no one likes eating in a hurricane).

INFORMAL DINING

When dining informally, there are several ways to make it comfy. Set
the table according to the menu. The table can be bare or dressed;
you can use placemats, a casual tablecloth or a throw. Choose
colours according to the time of year, with bright colours
for summer and jewel-like ones for winter, or have a theme.

For barbecues, picnics or outdoor meals, don't forget to arrange
food on platters and place them in the centre of the table for people
to help themselves. Always have lots of serving utensils, such as
tongs, salad servers, forks and spoons. If barbecued meat is placed
on a platter, have a carving knife handy so that people can cut up
meat into smaller portions, if desired. Use brightly coloured paper or
coloured cloth serviettes—coloured cloth serviettes hide greasy
marks better. If using paper plates, make sure they're strong. If not,
use them on top of a plastic plate. Modern paper plates aren't waxed
so tend to flop! You can wash and re-use plastic plates until they
become scratched. After they scratch, use them to support paper
plates, but don't put food on them because they're unhygienic. Avoid
plastic cutlery because it's always difficult to use and often breaks;
it's better to use stainless steel cutlery and wash it up later. Most
importantly have an easy way to cart all your gear to and from the
kitchen: a large sealable plastic container is ideal as it will save extra
time best spent partying.

SEMI-FORMAL DINING

Great company, food and conversation should be the aim of any
dinner party, but how you dress the table is important, too, as it can

TIP

Think before you put items on tables where people eat—even a
handbag may have been placed on something unhygienic!
Don't spread bacteria to the tabletop.

set the mood. Smarten the look of your dining table with a table-cloth—there are many colours and designs to choose from—or use placemats, if you prefer. Think about a centrepiece for the table, but not one that obscures the view from one side of the table to the other. No one wants to crane their neck to be part of the conversation.

Shannon's family loves hosting high tea for semi-formal gatherings. High tea is held in the late afternoon and the best china and silver is used. Tea is served with sandwiches, cakes, scones, petit fours, devilled eggs and cold meats displayed on tiered plates. The top tier of the plate holds scones, the middle tier has savouries and

THE NASAL ENTRÉE

When hosting a dinner party, lay some squares of muslin on each place setting, add a few herbs being used in the meal on top and fold the corners of the muslin to form a flat envelope. When warmed dinner plates are placed on top of the muslin envelope, the herbs release their aromas and stimulate the appetite. Even a simple meal tastes better with strong herbal aromas. Alternatively, if you have an oil-burner or candle in the centre of the table, put some herbs from dinner into the centre of the oil. Your olfactory sense will love it!

COMFY CRAFT

TIP

Sweet flavours shut the palate down and savoury flavours waken it. Start a meal salty, sharp and tangy and end it with sweet and creamy flavours. Sorbet is often used between courses as a palate cleanser.

Shannon's sorbet

Combine 1 pint (500 ml) of water, ½ pint (250 ml) of lemon juice and ½ pint (1 cup) of sugar. Mix and boil for exactly 3 minutes. Freeze in a large bowl stirring once every 10 minutes until it goes fluffy.

sandwiches and the bottom tier holds sweets. High tea should last for one hour, so it's a convenient way to meet someone without it taking up too much time. It is the perfect excuse to take out great grandma's china.

TIP

To make candles last longer, put them in the freezer for a couple of hours before using them. They will have less drip.

WAX WOES: Annabelle's question

Q: We had friends around for dinner and had a lovely night, but when I blew the candle out I managed to also blow the liquid wax all over the tablecloth. How can I remove it?

A: Avoid the problem next time by either using a candle snuffer or by placing your hand on the other side of the flame before you blow it out! To remove the wax from fabric, get some ice, a blunt knife, paper towel and an iron or hair dryer. You may also need some tea tree oil. Place ice on the wax to harden it, then scrape off as much as possible with a blunt knife. Place paper towel underneath and on top of the remaining wax and run a warm iron or hairdryer over the top. The wax will be absorbed into the paper towel. Use tea tree oil on any remaining oily marks.

FORMAL DINING

HINT

HOW TO SET A FORMAL DINING TABLE

You may never host a formal dinner party, but it's still good to know what to do just in case! The table should be set with a white tablecloth and crisp white napery. There are at least three courses and the number, type and order of the courses determine the placement of the cutlery. The implements to be used first are positioned farthest from the plate. Let's run from left to right on the table:

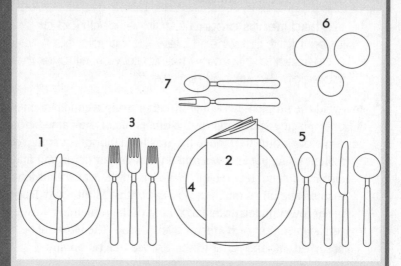

1 bread-and-butter plate with a butter knife on top of the plate;
2 napkin, folded in a triangle or rectangle, placed on top of the bread-and-butter plate. Sometimes the napkin—arranged in

a decorative design, such as a fan—may be placed in the centre of the serving plate. You should be able to pick up your napkin from the top corner, give it one shake and it unfolds effortlessly. It's then placed on your lap. Don't tuck your napkin into your neckline unless you are under five!

3 salad or entrée fork, dinner fork, and dessert fork all with tines pointing upwards;

4 service or charger plate in the centre of the setting;

5 dessert spoon, dinner knife, salad or entrée knife with blades facing left and a soup spoon. A teaspoon is sometimes placed here in case you need to remove foreign matter from your mouth. To elegantly remove any foreign matter from your mouth, place your napkin between your index and third finger, bring the index finger to your nose so the napkin covers your mouth and use the teaspoon in your other hand to remove the stray item. Return the napkin to your lap and deposit the foreign matter inside the napkin. It's very discreet!

6 glasses for water, red wine and white wine served top right of the setting. Champagne glasses and dessert wine glasses are added at the end of the meal;

7 any unusual pieces of cutlery, such as tongs, shell spoons and two-tined forks, are placed at the top of the setting.

8 Plates are stacked at the table in the order they're to be used unless the catering service is limited. If it is, the entrées are brought in ready-made from the kitchen. The order is soup coupe (not bowl), entrée plate and main course plate.

The butter knife is used for spreading butter, not cutting rolls. The correct way to break bread is with your hands. Never apply butter directly from the butter tray to the roll. You should always rest the butter on one side of the bread and butter plate and then apply it to the sections of the roll you have broken off. Don't smear the whole roll.

Teacups are not usually on the table for formal dining. Coffee and tea is generally served elsewhere, or after.

TABLECLOTHS, RUNNERS AND THROWS

Protect dining tables with a table protector with the rubber-side up and the fabric side down. Then place a tablecloth or a throw on top. Tablecloths are great decorators: there are so many colours, styles and fabrics available—from froufrou to minimalist. There are sheer fabrics, such as organza, which allow you to see the table beneath, waxed cloths, laces, velvets, cottons, linens and mohair to name just a few.

For extra flair, use a runner—with or without a tablecloth—on the table. Runners add extra protection to the table for those who like to display ornaments, fruit bowls or candelabras. Or go old-fashioned and use a doily, small tablecloth or cartouche—which is a shield- or lozenge-shaped doily. Table decorations don't have to be placed at the centre of the table. You can use a throw on the diagonal or arrange it in a zigzag shape. To do this, position the runner and fold it at various points on a 45-degree angle along the table.

To make life easier, put mats down to prevent heat marks and use coasters to avoid water marks. Deal with spills and stains as soon as you can.

TIP

Hide scratches on mahogany with raspberry leaf tea. Dampen a raspberry leaf tea bag with water and rub across the scratch. The acids in raspberry leaf tea react with the timber and force tannins to the surface.

TIP

Raspberry leaf tea is also great for cleaning old lace because it gives that aged colour. Boil water in a pot on the stove with a raspberry leaf tea bag, then add the lace. The more teabags you use, the darker the colour of the lace will be. If you get too much colour, boil the lace in white vinegar.

FLOWERS

Remove the stamens from lilies before putting them in a vase because they leave stains. The best way to do this is to place a plastic bag over your hand, then pull the stamens off and into your palm. When finished, hold the stamens in your palm, pull the plastic bag from behind your hand and wrap it over the stamens. Put it straight into the bin. Your hands won't have yellow stains all over them! If they do, wipe with a little kerosene.

Inexpensive oasis blocks (the green sponges used by flower arrangers) make flower arranging very easy and are available from the supermarket. The oasis absorbs green slime and protects vases from scratchy flower stems. You can also buy malleable plastic sacks from florists that are designed to be wrapped around florist blocks and arranged in any shape you like.

Simple flower arranging

A flower arrangement can be as simple as a single bud in a vase or a blossom placed on a plate. To present a single flower so that it won't

HINT

HOW TO MAKE FLOWERS LAST LONGER

Cut flowers will last longer if you cut their stems just before placing them in water and if you maintain the water level in the vase. Do this by adding ice cubes to the vase every morning and night (chilled water also makes flowers last longer). Use the sachets supplied by florists or available from supermarkets.

With **daisies and soft-leaf plants,** trim excess foliage and add a pinch of salt and sugar to the water. This makes the flowers last longer and stops the water from smelling.

To keep **violets** longer, immerse the whole violet in chilled water for about 2 minutes and then place in a vase.

For **roses,** place an old penny, a 1-cent piece or a piece of old copper jewellery in the water. Rescue wilting roses by trimming the stems and filling the vase with chilled water up to the bract or throat of the rose and leave for a couple of hours.

To prevent stems of **native flowers** from going furry, put a small piece of charcoal in the water.

droop, wrap the stem in a piece of wet tissue paper, wrap that in plastic wrap, then use coloured tissue paper or ribbon to decorate.

Arranging flowers for meals

Some flowers—such as nasturtiums, blue borage blossoms, Australian violets, English violets (not African), roses, lavender and any of the fruit blossoms: cherry, apple, pear, orange and lemon—are edible. All have wonderful flavours and colours and are great when used in salads or to decorate cakes and plates. Violets and roses can be crystallised by dipping them in egg white, then rolling in caster sugar syrup and placing in the freezer for 10 minutes. The flowers become translucent and taste yummy. To make sugar syrup, mix 1 cup of caster sugar to 1 cup of water and bring to the boil. Allow to cool a little, then use for dipping while still warm.

HOW TO ARRANGE FLOWERS

Your flower arrangement will be influenced by the shape of the vase and the shape of the flowers.

Posy—For narrow-necked vases, make a posy arrangement. Start with the head of one flower and place it between your thumb and forefinger. Keep adding the flowers in a circle until complete. Hold your fist beside the top of the vase and trim the bottom of the flowers to suit the vase.

Solitary bloom—Create a statement with one large bloom, such as a bird of paradise flower. Place lemons or oranges at the base of a large glass vase. Wedge the bird of paradise between the lemons or oranges and fill with water.

Orb—Place flowers in a line across your sink with the heads stepped down underneath each other. Cut the stems so each one is 5mm shorter than the other. Use greenery, such as camellia or magnolia leaves, fern or fir, and for every second flower add a frond of greenery. Start with the tallest flower at the centre of the vase and spiral outwards. This arrangement means you see all the heads of the flowers. It's perfect for the centre of the table.

Pyramid—Make a pyramid design to sit against a wall. Using oasis as your base, place large greenery at the back to form a triangular frame, add small fronds, narrow dimension sticks or ribbon grass to delineate the top most point. Place long-stemmed flowers pointing to either side to show side points of the triangle then start filling it in with flowers and greenery. Use two parts flower to one part greenery because the latter tends to be bigger. Fill until the triangle is complete.

Ribbon grass is very flexible—like plant wire—and is great to twist into a circle and place at the base of a round vase before adding flowers.

HINT

Glass marbles, pebbles and shells can be used inside vases to wedge flower stems in place. Never drop them directly into a vase or you could crack it. Instead, place them in a tea towel, lower it in and then slowly remove the tea towel.

Flowers for every occasion

Use your imagination—rather than arriving at an occasion with just a bunch of flowers, choose them to suit the event.

For a **new baby,** fill a plastic potty with flowers or teddy bears.

Fill a saucepan with flowers and utensils for a **kitchen tea**.

For **back to school,** use coloured pencils and flowers in a waterproof pencil holder.

Anything that can hold water can be used as a vase.

Use ornaments or oddments in flower arranging. Look in second-hand shops and around your house and see what you have.

Aarrange a series of unusual-shaped bottles or tiny glass juice bottles and stick a daisy in each.

Use different shapes and sizes in bottles to make an arrangement interesting. Use your imagination.

To appear **English** and formal, make sure the flowers are of even numbers and are balanced from side to side.

For a **French** look, have evenly balanced flowers on a diagonal slope.

Go **Italian** and use many flowers in a round or explosive bouquet.

For an **Australian** arrangement, use natives and go spiky.

For a **Japanese** feel, arrange flowers in odd numbers.

Low table runner of flowers

Choose a low flat vase and pack it with oasis foam. Start placing your flowers or foliage in a pattern that pleases you. Shannon likes sinuous lines or rivers of colour. Play with different heights, colours, bunching, textures or bloom size. Group a section with small flowers to make one big flower.

Artificial flowers

These days, many artificial flowers look real. To keep the illusion, make sure you dust them regularly with a soft paintbrush or with a hair dryer on the cool setting. To clean paper flowers, hold them upside down in a paper or plastic bag with 1 teaspoon of salt and shake lightly. Shake off the salt and arrange again. Help retain their colour by keeping them away from direct sunlight and deter bugs by placing 2 cloves in a small green bag that matches the foliage and attaching it to the stem.

THE STUDY/HOME OFFICE

Every home needs an area where administrative tasks are dealt with. A dedicated space is ideal, but not necessary. You just need an area that can be easily converted into an office. It could be a small cupboard, a space under the stairs, the dining table, a large box with a lid or an arm pocket over the armchair. An empty fireplace is a great spot for filing cabinets. Your office could be a shed in the backyard: just make sure you protect it against insects. Jennifer's office is in the attic and because it's separated from the rest of the home, climbing the stairs gets her in the mental space for work. Shannon's study has a fax, printer, scanner, computers, phone, stationery, lamps, filing cabinets and shelving units.

GETTING ORGANISED

The essentials are a table, chair, lamp and storage. Make sure the chair height is adjustable so your shoulders are relaxed and not hunched. The backrest should sit in the small of your back. To work out the best desk height, fold your arms against your body and lean towards the desk: your elbows should rest on the desk. When typing, hands should be as flat as possible. Remove stress from your back with a footrest and save your shoulders by getting up from the desk and moving around every half an hour. If nothing else, look to the horizon to stretch your focal length and help prevent myopia. The height of the computer screen should be 10 per cent below your vertical vision. If it's too low, you risk back problems and eye strain; too high and you'll stress your neck. Your work space needs both ambient and task lighting: a desk lamp is essential. And you need to be able to store your work 'stuff' either on shelving, in a filing cabinet, concertina files or large stackable plastic boxes. The latter are perfect if you don't have a dedicated study space and need to pack the office away. Just make sure in-trays and out-trays are easy to access. Shannon loves a nifty flat file that can be accessed vertically and horizontally, is portable and can hook onto a wall.

> If you can afford one and you have a spot for it, a safe is a great idea for storing important documents, such as birth certificates and passports, and valuables because they are fireproof. If you live in a rental property, portable safes are available.

> Keep a box of tissues, a wastepaper bin and a notepad in the office.

HOW TO ORGANISE YOUR PAPERWORK

There are many ways to organise your affairs. The important point is to have a system. Ideally, store all your paperwork in a filing cabinet, from which you can add to or subtract as needed. If you don't have the space, use portable concertina-style folders or ring binders. Although basic, an old shoe box can be used to store receipts and other items for tax time.

Shannon's husband has developed a system that uses about 10 removable hooks lined up along the office wall. (If you don't have an office wall, you could use the back of a door or the inside of a cupboard door.) Each hook is for a different type of bill, and each bill is secured and attached to a hook with a bulldog clip. One hook is for the phone bill, another for the electricity, the mobile phone, lawn mowing, water rates and so on. The bills arrive and are sorted to the appropriate hook and as the bill is paid, its receipt is stapled to the front of the bill. It means you can see at a glance which bills are outstanding. When the clip is filled, all but the front bill is filed in the filing

HINT continued

cabinet. This system works equally well for incomings, as well as outgoings, which makes doing your tax so much easier. Keeping receipts sorted is another challenge. Not only do they crumple up and look like scraps of paper to be thrown out, they fade in sunlight and with exposure to heat. To deal with them, keep a lidded container near the front door for household members to empty receipts from their pockets, wallets and bags as they walk in. Once a week the container should be emptied and the receipts filed. If necessary, write on the back of the receipts the items that are tax deductible. If you are computer literate and have a scanner, scan images of the receipts and use one of the many image collection software packages to organise and annotate the receipt images. You could then save them on a CD or memory stick. It means that no matter how old or faded the receipts are, you'll always have a legible copy. Make sure you file them by date as well as by subject or content. This makes it easier at tax time and your accountant will thank you for it. Keeping your receipts in order has the added bonus of helping with budget plans—you won't be able to say 'I don't know where the money goes.'

TIP

THE BUDGET

Being financially insecure isn't comfy. One way to deal with this is with a budget. Keep a record of what you spend so you can see the areas in which you need to tighten (or expand) the belt. Write down what you spend, take into account interest rate rises, keep receipts and put them into a spreadsheet on the computer. That way you can plan ahead. The more information you get into a budget, the better. Consult a professional for further advice.

HOW TO MAKE A CORD TIDY

To stop your office from becoming a jungle of cords, buy some plastic piping, which comes in a range of colours, from the hardware store. Cut it down one side, push the cords into the cut slit and the tube will automatically wrap around the cords. All tidy!

TIP

Always have extension cords and power boards with circuit breakers on hand. Store them out of the way with a cord tidy or in a separate drawer.

TIP

It's best to use power boards that have a circuit breaker. They're easy to identify because they have a little red or black button on the side. If you overload them, the circuit is cut and will automatically switch off. To restart, unplug everything on the power board and press the red button. Reintroduce your items one by one until the button engages again and turns everything off. Then you'll know it's the last item that has a short or if the combination is too great. Try testing the last item by itself. If the button shuts off you know you have a short in that item.

HOW TO MAKE YOUR OWN MAGAZINE FILES

Convert old cereal boxes into magazine files. Cut them to style and paint with a good-quality gloss spray or cover in paper and plastic or contact. Always seal them because cockroaches are attracted to cardboard.

HOW TO MAKE YOUR OWN PENCIL CONTAINERS

Take old tin cans, wash in detergent, rinse and dry well in the sun. Paint them; decorate them with contact, diamantes or pasta or cover them with wallpaper that matches your office. To cover cans with scraps of fabric, spray with adhesive, wrap the fabric around the can, smooth out any wrinkles and cut away any excess fabric. Stick on braid or ribbon to hide raw edges. Make as many as you like for different kinds of pens and pencils.

TIP

Sardine cans are great for paper clips or drawing pins, etc. Make sure you wash the sardine cans in detergent and water before using them. If there's any lingering odour, leave in the sun for a day.

CLEANING

To minimise cleaning, always have a coaster for drinks but place them away from elbows. Because there are fixed items on office desks, most people do the edge clean, but it's also good to do a thorough clean. Remove everything from half the desk and clean it, then do the other side. Doing a thorough clean protects your electrical equipment from dust.

The dangers of dust

It's important to keep your computer and other electricals clean and dust free. Dust can create electrical contact between points that aren't supposed to touch which causes arcing or electrical sparks.

Computer

Computers are positively charged and positive ions attract dust. When cleaning the computer, or any other electrical item, make sure it's turned off and unplugged from the socket. There are specialised products to clean computers, but Shannon doesn't think they're necessary for cleaning the casing. For light cleans, use a cloth dampened with water and tightly wrung out. Never use a wet cloth because water can corrode the ports! For dirty surfaces, apply some anti-static CD spray to a cloth and wipe it over all the surfaces, including the venting hole. Never spray anything directly onto a computer. It's fine to use your vacuum cleaner to get at dirt outside the computer but never use it inside the computer because it creates static electricity and could ruin it. You can vacuum the vent holes by wrapping a T-shirt over a vacuum head and gently clearing them. Clean the keyboard by turning it upside down and gently shaking it. You could also use your vacuum cleaner or compressed air in a can applied through a nozzle. Shannon's husband Rick borrows her air-brush compressor. To clean keyboard keys, use cotton buds dampened with a little methylated spirits or water.

TIP

To deter bugs, spray surface insecticide on a rag and wipe over the back of the computer. Make sure you keep computers ventilated by placing them at least 10cm away from any walls. This will prevent overheating.

Mouse

You know it's time to clean the mouse when it becomes sticky and hard to manoeuvre. Newer ones are optical and can't be pulled apart, but you can clean the case by wiping it with a cloth dampened with methylated spirits. Make sure you clean the track wheel. To clean the underside of the mouse, dip a cotton bud in methylated spirits, wipe the slide points that make contact with the mat and dry upside down. Give the mouse mat and the cord a wipe with methylated spirits applied with a pair of pantyhose to get rid of skin cell and sweat build-up.

Fax

Clean the outside of the fax with a cloth dampened with warm water and tightly wrung out. Clean rubber rollers with a little methylated spirits applied with a cotton bud, then clean again with a lint-free cloth dampened with water and wrung out, which will remove the fibres from the cotton bud.

Scanner/photocopier

Clean the outside as described for the fax. Clean the glass with a lint-free cloth dampened with methylated spirits. Clean the buttons with methylated spirits and a cotton bud.

CAN YOU REMOVE A SCRATCH ON AN IPOD SCREEN?
Jennifer managed to get a scratch on her iPod screen the day she bought it. It seems she's not alone, with many users complaining that their screens scratch easily. There's nothing you can do about a scratch. Use a case or protective film to prevent further scratches.

The Kitchen

Kitchens are generally organised around the triangle principle with the sink, oven and fridge forming each point of the triangle. Even though these elements are fixed, there are many other variables and plenty of ways to make your kitchen function better and be more comfy. It needs to work for you whether it's country-style with every utensil on display or a minimalist one with an entirely clear benchtop.

HOW WE USED TO KEEP COMFY FROM *PEARS' CYCLOPAEDIA* 33RD EDITION (1928)

Kitchen tables and shelves may be kept very white and clean if you have this mixture used for scouring: ½ pound of sand, ½ pound of lime, ½ pound of soap. Work the dissolved soap into the dry ingredients, put the mixture on with a scrubbing brush and wash off with plenty of cold water. Lemon juice well rubbed into the kitchen tables quickly removes all grease.

GETTING ORGANISED

Shannon thinks the kitchen is the comfy centre of the home and loves cooking in hers (she even has a commercial-sized fridge!). Jennifer loves cooking when the kitchen and utensils are right. To make the most efficient use of space in your kitchen, store items near where they are used. Put the chopping board between your sink and oven and keep aluminium foil and plastic wrap between the oven and fridge. If there's more than one cook in the kitchen at a time, make sure there's enough work space. The kitchen is an explosion for your senses: sight, touch, smell, sound and taste are all utilised in this room and need to be considered when undertaking your kitchen audit. Here are some comfy considerations:

Benchtop height—unless you're installing new benchtops to suit your height, you don't have much choice as most are set at 900 millimetres. If you get a sore back when chopping, there are other options. If the benchtop is too low for you, use a chopping block with adjustable legs. If the bench is too high, add a table or stool that's at the right height for you or use a step to stand on. If you have a choice, go for a rounded or half-rounded edge on benchtops because it won't hurt as much if you bump into it.

Kitchen nook—if you have space, a kitchen nook is a great addition that allows people to sit, eat and chat while you cook. It could be a small table with a couple of chairs or some stools placed at the end of the bench. Just make sure any coverings on seats are made of cotton so they can be washed easily. If space is limited, consider using an extension table.

Lighting—direct light should be aimed on the preparation areas: where you do chopping (benchtop), cooking (stovetop) and cleaning (sink). Don't have light aimed into your eyes. Other areas of the kitchen need softer lighting so dimmers are a good option. Have a qualified electrician help you change any lighting configurations. A good amount of natural light also makes the kitchen feel more comfy. Many people love having curtains or blinds in the kitchen; if you do, make sure they're washable and easy to remove to clean.

Flooring—if the floor is cold and hard, warm it up with a rug. Make sure it's non-slip, without any curling on the edges and can be washed easily.

TIP

No matter what you've been told, it's more energy efficient to turn the light out if you're leaving a room, even if only for a short time.

HINT

HOW TO CHOOSE LIGHT BULBS

In Australia, incandescent light bulbs are being phased out because they're not energy efficient. At the moment, they are the most popular light bulb and come with a screw base or bayonet cap. They also come in different wattages—more watts means brighter light. You shouldn't use globes at a higher wattage than recommended for the fitting. Globes can be clear or opaque; the latter diffuses light more evenly. The main alternative to the incandescent light bulb is a fluorescent light bulb which can be compact or tubular. Fluorescent lights must be recycled because they contain mercury. Tungsten-halogen globes are also available and provide a more brilliant light. They come in a range of shapes and fittings.

Ventilation—being able to remove smells from the kitchen is very important. There are two main ways of doing this: one is through a window; the other is with an extractor fan. If you have only one window in the kitchen, create a cross draft by placing a fan near the door facing the window. After cooking fish or curries, rinse the extractor fan filter straight away and wipe surfaces with bicarb and white vinegar. A couple of drops of vanilla extract in a warm oven create a homey smell. When cooking food with strong odours, leave a tray of bicarb on the bench while cooking.

Stacking—stack crockery and glassware in an ordered way. It looks neater, is easier to access and is much more comfy.

The best way to stack cups and saucers is the interlocking four method where four cups are placed on four saucers and each cup handle hooks into the bowl of the next cup until the four cups form a circle. It's not ideal, but if you have to stack glasses inside each other, use paper towel between them to stop them jamming.

To stop crazing in good china, place a piece of paper towel between each item.

Accessories—if your kitchen is looking a bit shabby, think about getting some new handles on the cupboard doors. It's a simple change but it can make a huge difference visually. Avoid handles that will catch on clothing or bruise legs.

Personal touches—have a radio, CD player or TV in the kitchen. Whoever cooks gets to choose the music or TV show. Personalise the space with a noticeboard and keep photos, artwork and other things you love on it. If you don't have space for a noticeboard, the fridge is also a great place to display artwork and photos. You could also use blackboard paint on the back of the door—just like a café—and provide chalk for writing lists, menus, schedules or for doodling.

Accidents—always have some burn cream or aloe vera plant and some *Band-Aids* within easy reach. Don't use papaw ointment or *Vaseline* on burns because they make the burn sweat.

WHAT EVERY KITCHEN SHOULD HAVE

When it comes to buying kitchenware, buy the best quality you can afford and be prepared to shop around. Professional catering suppliers are worth a look with good-quality items at reasonable prices; check on the internet as well.

 Glassware—if you have space, have twelve tall tumblers, twelve red wine glasses, twelve white wine glasses, six sherry or liqueur glasses and six short tumblers or scotch glasses. At a minimum, have enough glasses for a medium-sized dinner party including extras in case of breakages. Decanters or carafes are also handy to have. As outlined in *Spotless* and *Speedcleaning*, never put precious glasses in the dishwasher. Over time, the exterior will become scratched leaving a cloudy residue. You may not mind for glasses in everyday use, but you will be disappointed when expensive sets are permanently etched.

 Narrower glasses make drinks taste sweeter because of the way you roll your tongue as you drink. That's why using a straw makes the drink taste sweeter. Using champagne flutes takes the hard edge off dry sparkling wine. Champagne saucers make sparkling wines taste drier.

Crockery—we suggest eight microwave-safe settings for crockery. And even though they may look attractive in the catalogue, it's best not to get silver- or gold-rimmed sets. If you've put anything silver or gold-edged into the microwave, you'll know why we advise against it. It sparks and can cause major damage to your microwave. The edging also fades in the dishwasher. This doesn't mean you can't have precious metal-edged sets like grandma's heirloom, but they should be kept for special occasions only. Keep them on display and clean them every six months or they can craze. Choosing patterns and designs is very personal. There's nothing wrong with having more than one design because you can change the look of a table setting with different designs. For one, keep it simple and sturdy and elegant. Have at least one large serving platter and always have extra tea and coffee cups— twelve in total is a good number.

Cutlery—we recommend stainless steel cutlery for everyday use as other types, such as silver or brass, can affect how your food tastes. Sometimes this is welcome: strawberries eaten from a silver spoon make your tongue tingle! Many house- holds have an everyday cutlery set and a special cutlery set. For silver cutlery, make sure you hand wash it—dishwashers leave blackened marks. Other elements also discolour and corrode silver, such as salt, proteins or acids, so clean them as soon as possible. To get a glass-like polish on silverware, rub with a paste of wheat bran and white vinegar. Put cotton gloves or a pair of old cotton socks on your hands to stop acid from your hands affecting the silver when you clean it. Clean the paste off and polish with a soft cloth. To remove rust marks from stainless steel cutlery, rub with bicarb and white vinegar.

Saucepans—have at least one frying pan with rounded sides for flipping, one heavy-based frying pan for grilling and browning, one small saucepan for making sauces, one medium saucepan for stewing, one saucepan steamer or fold-up steamer, one large saucepan for boiling items such as spaghetti, one cast-iron pan suitable for braising and using in the oven (with no plastic handles) and one wok. Ensure saucepans have good fitting lids and vent holes.

HINT

HOW TO STORE POTS AND PANS

If you've ever seen inside a restaurant kitchen, you'll notice they keep their pots on hooks at eye level. It's really convenient but not an option for most household kitchens. Many people store their pots stacked inside each other from largest to smallest. This saves on space but it's annoying when you have to unstack them each time you need a pot. For this reason, we recommend that pots used regularly should be stored standing alone with their lids on top. The best place to store them is below waist height—that way, if you drop them, there's a shorter distance to the floor and you're less likely to hurt yourself—and near the oven. If you get bugs, rinse the pot before using it. The process of heating the pot will kill any bacteria.

HINT

HOW TO REMOVE A HEAVY-DUTY BURN IN A PAN

If you've got a heavy-duty burn in a pan, try this new solution. Fill the base of the pan with white vinegar and put it in the freezer. When frozen, remove from the freezer and allow to thaw. Then add bicarb and scrub while fizzing. Freezing allows the vinegar to penetrate underneath the stain making it easier to scrub off.

HOW TO REPAIR A POT HANDLE

Strap the handle with butchers' twine then cover the strapped handle with heat-resistant superglue. This forms a seal that is hygienic and non-toxic. It will loosen if washed in the dishwasher or left soaking in boiling water. If this happens, repair again.

Baking tins—have one large baking tin big enough to cook a roast and a medium one. Before buying them, measure your oven and make sure they fit. There's no such thing as a standard-sized oven! You can now buy silicone baking dishes, baking pans, cake pans, muffin moulds and flan tins that can be rolled up and secured with a rubber band. They are light-weight and wash really easily. Have one round or one square cake tin, one muffin or patty cake tin and one baking tray. For people who love to cook, there are many more items that could be added to this list, but these are the basics.

HOW TO REMOVE RUST FROM BAKING TINS

These days, you're less likely to have as many baking tins as grandma, but you may have a friand tin or muffin tin stashed away somewhere. These tins are prone to rust because they're made of mild steel or low-nickel stainless steel which transfers heat quickly. To prevent rust, heat edible kitchen oil, such as vegetable, canola or peanut oil, in them. When cool, wipe out the oil with some paper towel. If it's too late and you've already got rust, rub with a cut raw potato that's been dipped in bicarb. Then protect from further rust by heating a little oil, allowing it to cool and wiping it out with some paper towel.

Knives—buy the best knives you can afford. The best knives have a blade that extends all the way to the heel of the knife handle. Handles should be made of horn, heavy-grade plastic, bakelite or timber and be brass-riveted all the way through the handle. Include a large carving knife, a carving knife with a curved blade, a serrated bread knife, a paring knife and a cleaver. It's best for knives not to come into contact with each other because they lose their edge.

HOW WE USED TO KEEP COMFY FROM *PEARS' CYCLOPAEDIA 33RD EDITION* (1928)

Knife cleaning may be facilitated by taking a strip of old woollen carpet, tack it tightly on a board and sprinkle it with bath brick. This will produce a good polish and sharp edge without scraping the knife.

Utensils—two wooden spoons, a rolling pin, spatula, slotted egg slice, pair of tongs, whisk, large piercing fork, metal skewers, bamboo skewers, can opener, bottle opener, corkscrew (source from a vintner supplier), slotted spoon, large serving spoon, salad servers, vegetable peeler, bean stripper, mandoline, grater, garlic press, potato masher, salt and pepper grinders, colander, set of strainers, measuring cups, measuring jug, small kitchen scale, egg timer, lemon squeezer, 3 microwave-safe covered dishes (preferably glass, china or pyrex), two stainless steel mixing bowls, one salad bowl, six air- and water-tight sealable plastic containers. Check at garage sales and second-hand dealers for older utensils as they can often be of better quality than newer ones and are easy to sterilise before use.

HOW TO MAKE A KNIFE AND UTENSIL HOLDER

You can make a flat holder from canvas or an upright holder from PVC piping.

To make the canvas holder, first work out whether it will sit along a wall or inside a cupboard door. Measure the area making sure you leave enough headroom so the tops of the knives and utensils will fit the space. Measure the canvas so that two-thirds of the fabric forms the body of the holder and one-third of the fabric is folded from the bottom to the middle of the canvas. Stitch sections vertically along the canvas with a heavy thread to create slots for the knives or utensils. Secure two hooks to the area where the holder will be located.

To make the upright holder from PVC piping, work out the number of different pipes you want, their height and colour then have them cut at the hardware store. Secure PVC caps to the bottom of each piece of pipe. Arrange them in a line or unevenly like an enlarged stationery holder. Then glue them into place with PVC glue.

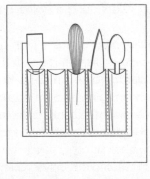

HINT

HOW TO STERILISE UTENSILS

To sterilise metal utensils, add 1 tablespoon of salt to a pot of water and bring to a rolling boil. Immerse the items and leave for 4 minutes. If the pieces are plastic, use a baby bottle sterilisation system available in tablet form from the supermarket. Soak overnight then rinse with boiled water. For wooden items, fill a large saucepan with cheap cooking oil, add the items and gradually heat the oil until just about to smoke: you'll see a blue fume. Leave to cool then wash up normally. This process is also good to seal wooden spoons from stains, such as curry paste.

TIP

Remove rust from utensils by boiling them in a saucepan in cheap cooking oil. Place them in a cold pan with the cooking oil, raise the temperature until blue smoke forms on the oil, then return to room temperature. When cooled, wipe utensils with paper towel.

Trays—are an essential comfy kitchen item. They're handy to transport food and drink and can also be used to store small craft projects or puzzles. If you like to eat dinner in front of the TV, consider using a *Stable Table*.

Appliances—a toaster (with a good action), automatic switch-off kettle (so it doesn't boil dry), juice extractor, electric mix master, hand-held mixer and crock-pot are the basics. There are many other kitchen appliances that are available, but these are the essentials. Never place electrics in water or the dishwasher: it's incredibly dangerous!

You'll feel more comfy if you have a designated spot for tea towels and hand towels—the oven door is a popular spot—so that when you need them you know exactly where they are. If you don't like having them on display, store them over a rail in a cupboard or fix a self-adhesive rail to the side of the fridge. Try to use a hand towel rather than a tea towel when drying your hands to avoid contamination. Always have a spare tea towel in a drawer in case you need one in a hurry.

TIP

Have a storage bag for old plastic bags. The best kind is sausage-shaped. New bags are put in the top end and old bags removed at the other end.

Refrigerator—purchase the best-quality fridge you can afford. It's an investment you'll have for some time. If you can, choose a fridge with stainless-steel interior walls. It's easy to clean and you can see all the way to the back of the fridge. Select a fridge configuration that suits you—with either the fridge on top and freezer at the bottom or the other way around. We both prefer fridges with freezers on the bottom so food is at eye level. Big families may need a separate fridge and freezer. Choose a fridge with auto-defrost because it will save time and effort. It's also a good idea to place good-quality slides under your fridge because wheels tend to dig into vinyl floors and leave rust marks. Nylon slides—available at hardware stores—prevent these markings. Simply place them under the wheels.

Make sure your fridge has adjustable and removable shelving in the doors so you can easily remove them for cleaning. For the body of the fridge, choose grilled shelving over solid ones to allow better cooling and air circulation. Opt for large crisper drawers and keep a thin sheet of foam rubber in the bottom to aid air circulation. Set the height of the shelves to suit your needs. Clean stainless steel with a pair of rolled up pantyhose.

TIP

Leftovers are best stored in glass containers. Plastic containers are absorbent, particularly with oils—because plastics are made with a petrochemical base—that's why your plastics end up looking like whatever was stored in there, be it curry or spag bol!

HINT

HOW TO FIX A FRIDGE SEAL

If you have a damaged fridge seal, your power bills will be higher and the fridge dirtier! There are two types of fridge seals: one is secured with silicone adhesive that looks like a rubber strip; the other is attached by a metal beaded strip that's screwed on. If yours is a silicone seal, seek professional help. Otherwise, buy seals from a hardware store and replace them yourself. Remove the old seal by unscrewing the strip and removing the beading. Clean any rubber marks with damp salt. Measure the new fridge seal against the old fridge seal for size. Immerse the new seal in hot water for about 2 minutes to soften the rubber and make it easier to position. Replace the seal and when you get to the corners, cut a single line through the seal and mitre the inside edges. Don't cut right through to the outside edge. Replace the beading and the screws. Check that the seal is secure by putting a piece of paper in the door and closing it—the paper should be difficult to remove. To make the seals last longer, wipe them with *Vaseline* after cleaning.

TIP

Store fruit that shouldn't be refrigerated in a mesh bowl so air can circulate. Fruit placed at the bottom of a regular bowl ripens (and rots) more quickly.

TIP

FRIDGE TEMPERATURE

Check the temperature inside your fridge with a thermometer. The crisper should be at 4 degrees.

Microwave—most households have a microwave that's only used for reheating and defrosting. They can do so much more! The best way to become comfortable and proficient with your microwave is to read the instructions and then try new things. Shannon cooks a leg of lamb in the microwave! Her trick is to cover it in baking paper. Select your microwave according to the functions you need it for, the space you have and the wattage: 1200 watts is best. If you only use it for reheating, you can get away with having a 400-watt microwave.

Never place metal in the microwave because the microwaves are reflected by it, you won't heat the food and you could blow the element. Glass or microwave-safe ceramic cookware are safest. The best cookware to use in the microwave is glass because you can see how well the food is cooking. Avoid putting plastics in the microwave, even microwave-safe ones, because heat makes plastic fume and can contaminate your food. We met one man who showed us his microwave-safe plastic dish that had a red marking around it from his reheated bolognese. He was horrified to learn that the food had penetrated into the plastic through microwaving. Only use microwave-safe plastic wrap in the microwave and make sure it doesn't touch the food you're reheating.

One of the big errors people make when microwaving is leaving the food uncovered so it dries out. Either cover with baking paper or place a glass lid or plate over the food. Covering food helps with heat efficiency and retains vitamins. It also speeds your cooking. Any foods with a skin or membrane need to be pierced before microwaving or you could end up with a mess. Don't use sealed containers or sealed bottles because pressure builds up and the item can explode.

It's also good to stir food halfway through cooking so it cooks evenly. And you need to allow for standing time as food continues to cook for the length of time it was in the microwave after the bell dings.

Never dry your socks in the microwave! Even if they're clean they'll leave an odour in your microwave, as Shannon found out when an old flatmate used this technique!

Dishwasher—as we mentioned earlier, not everything can be washed in the dishwasher because it's a harsh environment for delicate items. Be careful what you put into your dishwasher. Don't place items soiled with ash, sand, lubricating wax or paint in the dishwasher because they can damage the machine.

If you feel guilty about the amount of water a dishwasher uses, there's some good news. Modern machines are far more water efficient, using about 18 litres of water per normal cycle. This compares with about 6 litres for one sinkful of water and you generally need two sinkfuls to match one dishwasher load. Just remember, the dishwasher is only water efficient if it's full and well stacked.

You can use white vinegar as a rinse aid but only if it has a 5 per cent acid content. Some dishwashers also have rinse-aid dosage settings so you can alter the amount of rinse aid according to your needs. Clean the filter every wash. Check spray arms every 20 washes and unclog with a pointed object, such as a bamboo skewer.

Cockroaches love dishwashers because of the warmth so keep the area clean. Many manufacturer warranties don't cover damage by cockroaches.

Dishwashers break down more than other white goods so it's worth getting a service guarantee. Consult the instruction manual to find out how often it should be serviced. If you've misplaced yours, see if it's available online or ask the manufacturer to send you a new one. It's worth reading.

Don't leave dirty dishes sitting for too long in the dishwasher—you'll create a bacteria farm!

Unload the lower rack first. That way you won't get water drips from the upper rack falling onto dry plates.

Make sure the detergent dispenser is dry before adding detergent or it will clog and leave residue in the dispenser.

MELTED PLASTIC IN THE DISHWASHER: Mimi's question

Q: I use a lot of plastic spoons feeding my young child and wash them in the dishwasher. One of the spoons fell onto the heating element and melted. What can I do?

A: If you can remove the spoon entirely, that's fine, but you have to be very careful with heating elements. If even the smallest amount of plastic remains, it can clog up the moving parts inside the dishwasher. To fix it, you'll need a dishwasher repairer. To remove the burnt smell, run the dishwasher empty on the hot cycle with either a proprietary product for dishwashers or fill the soap dispenser with equal parts bicarb and white vinegar.

The reason why beer goes flat when you pour it into a glass is because detergent residue changes the surface tension of the beer and flattens the bubbles, so make sure you rinse the glass with water first.

Oven—most ovens are gas or electric. Choose one that suits your needs. Gas gives you instant heat and preserves more moisture in food better than electric ones. These days, newer electric ovens can be as quick as gas. Ovens can either be zoned heat or fan forced. Zoned heat means there are three different heat zones in the oven at the same time—the hottest at the top, moderate in the middle and cooler at the bottom. It means you can put different foods in at the appropriate zones according to their cooking time and have them ready to eat at the same time. A fan-forced oven creates an even cooking temperature in the whole oven. Self-contained steam ovens are also available and can be built in or sit on the benchtop.

You can also get self-cleaning ovens which, despite their name, doesn't mean you never have to clean them. Pyrolytic ovens work by heating the oven to 500°C/935°F which turns food into ash and you then wipe it out. Catalytic ovens are based on the absorption of food but you still have to wipe them clean. They both leave a charcoal smell. For remaining muck, clean with bicarb and white vinegar.

When buying an oven, consider the size, shelving options, tray options and door strength. Ovens placed at eye level are easier to access. Read your instruction manual to work out the appropriate settings for the best cooking results.

Don't use your fingers to taste food because it's unhygienic. Use a clean spoon and use it only once!

**HOW WE USED TO KEEP COMFY FROM *PEARS' CYCLOPAEDIA*
33RD EDITION (1928)**

To test the heat of an oven, place a piece of white paper in the oven
and if the heat be too great, it will blacken and burn. If it only turns
a light brown colour, it be fit for pastry. If the paper turns a dark
yellow shade, the oven will be fit for baking the heavier kinds of
cake. If a light yellow, then it be fit for sponge cakes and the lighter
kinds of biscuits.

HOW TO REMOVE FOIL FROM THE OVEN: Rebecca's question

Q: After burning cheese on the bottom of my new
oven, I lined it with foil which I left there for a month
or two. When I tried to remove it, two patches
became stuck to the bottom. I tried to scrape and
scour it off. Nothing worked. Can you help?

A: It sounds like a joke but the answer is salad dressing. Mix ½
cup of white vinegar with ½ cup olive oil and 1 teaspoon of
salt. Apply to a warm but not hot oven. Warm means you can
put your hand into the oven without burning it. Use either a
dishwashing brush or a pair of pantyhose rolled into a ball
and scrub. Vinegar is an acid and helps dissolve grease and
char, oil is a lubricant and salt is a mild abrasive. The mixture
is non-toxic and any leftovers can be used on a salad!

TIP

Many people use talcum powder to absorb fat splatters and stains.
While it does absorb the fat, it creates a new gunk. Shannon's tip is
to lay paper towel over the fat, then scrub with a little dishwashing
liquid. Rinse with water and apply paper towel again.

KIDS IN THE KITCHEN

Kids love being in the kitchen but some safety precautions are necessary. First, keep anything toxic or valuable out of reach. The best strategy is to store them on high shelves. Another easy option if you have very young children is to fix elastic bands over door handles so they can't be opened. This works only until they discover how to remove the elastic bands! Make sure sharp knives cannot be accessed. If the oven is low, install an oven lock. From the age of about five, children can help in the kitchen. Teach them to set and clear the table one item at a time. Give kids their own kitchen utensils, though not sharp knives, so they can share the cooking experience with you. They can rip up lettuce for a salad, shape biscuits and make dough and pastries—kids love doing anything with flour. They can stir things, but not on a high heat, peel potatoes, husk corn, wash vegetables, make cheese on toast and crack eggs into a bowl. It's a great way to share the stories of the day while you teach them some valuable cooking tips.

CLEANING UP

Some people like to clean as they cook, others wait until after the meal. Either technique is fine. If you wait until after the meal, at least stack items as you go. Never allow your washing up water to become too greasy and disgusting. After washing up, use the dishwashing water to wipe down benchtops, cupboards and the sink. Then use a clean cloth or a rolled up pair of pantyhose to wipe off the dishwashing water. Wipe cupboard fronts with a clean damp cloth, then sweep the floor and take out the garbage.

TIP

Before washing up a greasy pan, soak up excess oil with newspaper or paper towel.

TIP

If you have spots on your plates from detergent, add a couple tablespoons of white vinegar to the rinse water.

HINT

HOW TO FIX A BLOCKED DRAIN

Prevent blockages by keeping a guard over your sink waste. If you do have a blockage, or nasty smells, sprinkle $\frac{1}{2}$ cup bicarb down the drain then pour over 1 cup white vinegar and leave for a few minutes. Flush with hot water: just boil the kettle and pour it down. If the blockage remains, try a plunger, or you may have to go under the sink and check the S-bend.

CARING FOR BENCHTOPS

Timber—if timber is unsealed, clean with detergent and water, allow to dry and wipe with a good-quality furniture oil. For surfaces which come into contact with food, use a small quantity of warm olive oil. Some olive oils contain vegetable sediment which can attract fruit fly so make sure you spread it thinly and wipe off all the excess. Use olive oil only on timber surfaces in the kitchen. Olive oil is safe to use around food, but because it attracts fruit fly it's not good to use outside the kitchen. Bicarb and white vinegar will remove any stains, but remember to reapply the olive oil. If you prefer, keep the timber moist and splinter-free by rubbing it with the peel of a lemon.

For sealed timber, sprinkle some bicarb, then spray white vinegar over the top and wipe with a cloth. Be very careful with polyurethane surfaces because if you scratch them, you'll have to reseal them. If you do scratch the surface of polyurethane, wipe it with *Brasso* in the direction of the grain. The mark will become worse before it gets better. *Brasso* works because it partially melts polyurethane. If the scratch has penetrated through to the timber, you'll have to reseal the area which is a big job. If this is the case, seek the advice of a professional.

Laminate—the best way to keep laminate clean is to sprinkle some bicarb then spray with white vinegar and wipe with a sponge. If you get heavy staining with tea or scorch marks, put glycerine on the stain for about 5 minutes, then use bicarb and white vinegar.

HOW TO FIX LOOSE LAMINATE

To repair loose laminate, apply PVA glue and either clamp or weight the area. If using a book as a weight, put plastic wrap over the area first so the book doesn't get damaged. If the laminate is chipped, mix malleable epoxy resin or *Araldite*, place it in the hole, lay plastic wrap over the top and weight the area with a book. Trim any excess with a knife. Then use folk art paint in a matching colour and re-colour.

Corian—clean by sprinkling some bicarb then spraying over white vinegar and wiping with a sponge. Use detergent and water for a polyurethane finish.

Marble—special care should be taken with marble because the surface is porous. Clean with bicarb and one part white vinegar to four parts water. Never put full-strength vinegar on marble because it could react with the lime and eat into the marble. Always rinse thoroughly with a cloth that's been wrung out in water. If the surface isn't sealed with polyurethane or another sealant, use a good-quality liquid wax for marble flooring to make the benchtop less porous and less likely to absorb stains. The way to tell if marble is covered in polyurethane is to put your eye level with the marble surface and

HOW TO FIX CHIPPED MARBLE

To repair a chip in marble, use candle or crayon in the same colour. Melt the candle or crayon with a hair dryer over the chip. Allow it to set then buff it level with rolled-up pantyhose.

shine a light along the top. If the light shines in one uninterrupted beam, it's sealed with polyurethane. If the beam of light has lines and dots, it's unsealed.

Granite—clean with bicarb and white vinegar. If it has a polyurethane finish (see Marble, page 100, for how to check this), keep the surface clean because heat, abrasives, moisture and chemicals can cause it to bubble.

Stainless steel—the best way to clean stainless steel is with bicarb and white vinegar and a rolled up pair of pantyhose. Then rinse.

> **TIP**
>
> To polish scratches in stainless steel, use a damp cloth and a little cornflour. It will polish without scratching. You can also wipe with a pair of pantyhose dampened with a little water and rolled into a ball.

> **TIP**
>
> Keep old tea bags. You can place cold ones on your eyes to reduce puffiness. You can tie the string of dampened tea bags to the tops of your broom bristles and wipe over wooden floors. They clean aluminium beautifully and are also great in garden mulch. The tannin in tea kills dust mites, too!

> **HINT**
>
> ### HOW TO FIX AN UGLY VIEW
>
> When Jennifer was growing up, the next-door neighbours kept a run-down old bus in their driveway which sat right outside the kitchen window. Year after year the bus got rustier and more decrepit. If you have an unattractive view from your kitchen window, install a small glass shelf across the window and arrange glass jars, coloured glass bottles, herbs or other transparent or translucent pieces of kitchen paraphernalia on it. This way light can still get in but the uninteresting view is obscured. Just make sure you can still open the window for ventilation.

RECYCLING

Once you get into the habit, it's easy to recycle. Store items that can be put into a compost heap in one bin and non-recyclable items in another bin. Earthworms are great in compost and can be bought by the punnet on the internet or at some nurseries. They're also great for mulching heavy clay soils.

TIP

Recycle supermarket shopping bags by washing them and reusing them over and over again. They can last from 3–5 years.

KITCHEN FIRES

About 30 per cent of house fires start in the kitchen. Follow these guidelines to minimise the risk.

Never leave the kitchen while food is cooking on a high heat.

Never leave the stove on if you leave the house.

In the event of a fire, don't throw water on burning fat or oil because it will make the fire worse. If safe, try to smother the flames with a saucepan lid, damp tea towel or fire blanket.

Keep a fire blanket in the kitchen.

Don't touch the pan.

Keep flammable items away from flames.

Get into the habit of turning saucepan handles away from the front of the stove so they're not easily knocked.

WHAT TO DO IN CASE OF FIRE

If it's a small fire, put a saucepan lid over the fire and turn the energy source off. This will starve the flame of oxygen. If it's large, ring the fire brigade and use a fire blanket. If you don't have a fire blanket, put a damp (not wet) tea towel over the fire. When the flames have died remove the saucepan from the stove. **Never carry a flame.** If the flame is on an electric element, dump, but don't throw, flour on it. Make sure you dump the flour so that air isn't released too close to the flame.

If you need to evacuate the house, remember the saying, 'Get down low and go go go'. Cover your mouth with a cloth to avoid smoke inhalation and close the door to each room after you leave to delay the spread of the fire.

HINT

HOW TO CLEAN SMOKE DAMAGE

Smoke damage is really difficult to clean. Clean everywhere or the smoky smell will linger! To remove the black marks from walls, brickwork, tiles and other rough surfaces, combine cigarette ash and white vinegar to form a slurry and apply with a brush. To get rid of the smell, you must clean every surface in the room with soap and warm water. This includes hinges, filter pads and the vent on the back of the microwave. Wash all soft furnishings including curtains and curtain rods. Turn the power off and clean every light globe and every light fitting. Clean the back of and underneath the fridge and clean the seals. When cleaning the back of the fridge, unplug it, slide it out and sweep the back mesh with a brush and dust pan. At the base of the fridge is a condensation bucket that isn't removable. Use a sponge to soak up any water, gunk and dead insects. Clean around the stove. Often insurance companies will cover smoke damage and provide specialist cleaners.

FRESHENING UP YOUR KITCHEN

You may not be able to afford a complete overhaul but you can freshen up your kitchen quite easily. Try these tips:

Clean canisters and paint them in a new colour.

Change cupboard door handles.

Buy new tea towels.

Change photos and artwork on the noticeboard.

Add utensils and fruit bowls/remove utensils and fruit bowls.

If you have an oblong dining table, turn it in the other direction.

Change the colours of yor soft furnishings and object d'art to suit the season—use warm earthy tones in winter and bright cool blues and whites in summer.

Rearrange collectables.

HINT

HOW TO FIX LOOSE HINGES ON KITCHEN DOORS
Generally, hinges can be tightened with a screwdriver. If a hinge screw won't fit properly, pack the hole with a match or bamboo skewer cut flush to the frame. Wedge it in, then refit the hinge.

HOW TO FIX A BROKEN DRAWER

First, work out what's wrong with the drawer. Has the runner become detached? Is the base loose? Or is there a problem with the joints? For wooden runners, reattach with wood glue. For plastic runners, buy a new one from the hardware store and install following the manufacturer's instructions. If the base of the drawer is loose, use a furniture stapler, available at hardware stores, stapling beside, not on top of, the existing staple holes. If the glue or staples have become loose on the joints, you can re-glue, but you have to make sure the corner is sitting at 90 degrees. Do this with a protractor or a right-angle set square. When square, run some glue into the corners and clamp it with a 90-degree clamp or by wrapping a piece of butchers' twine around the entire drawer and leaving it for 24 hours.

THE PANTRY

It's always good to have a well-stocked pantry. You won't waste time racing to the shops and you'll always be able to whip up a meal. What you stock in your pantry will be affected by the space you have and your food needs. The basics include flour, sugar, salt and pepper, dried herbs, a range of sauces, vinegars, oils, tinned food (such as soup, tomatoes, tuna or salmon and canned fruit), pasta, rice, dried goods (such as split peas, lentils and pulses), tea and coffee. Always have two tins of soup so you can whip up an easy meal for one or more. It's also handy to keep biscuits and crackers for visitors. Jennifer keeps two of each of the most-used pantry items; that way, as long as you remember to replace used items, you never run out of anything.

Shannon sets up her pantry by food groups with carbohydrates in one spot and proteins in another. She always keeps bay leaves in the carbohydrate section to deter weevils, which live in flour and grain foods, such as pasta, oats, wheatgerm and cereals. Remove grain foods from their packaging (cockroaches are attracted to paper and cardboard), store in airtight containers—Shannon prefers glass—and group together. (If you don't have room for jars, fold over the tops of the packaging and peg or clip to secure.) Tins are arranged together in rows according to food groups, with smaller tins at the front and larger ones at the back and labels facing the front so you can see what they are at a glance. Rotate your tins so newer tins are at the back and older ones at the front.

There's a common belief that coffee beans once opened keep better in the freezer, but the latest advice is to store them in the fridge.

Leave a *Texta* in the pantry to write the purchase date on packaged food. If tins have popped or blown, carefully place them inside a plastic bag before putting them in the bin in case they explode. If labels look old-fashioned, ditch the item.

Keep spare pegs or bulldog clips in the pantry ready to seal packets.

USE-BY VERSUS BEST-BEFORE LABELLING

All packaged food with a shelf life under two years has to have a use-by or best-before date marking. Use-by food can't be sold after the expiry date for safety reasons. Best-before indicates when the food is likely to go stale but may not pose a safety issue. It can still be sold after the date. Bread has a best-before marking with a shelf life of less than a week.

To deal with weevils and moths, wipe the shelves with bay oil, store bay leaves in canisters or wipe shelves with oil of penny-royal, but **don't use oil of pennyroyal if anyone in the house, including pets, is pregnant.**

The Bedroom

Your bedroom should combine personal style with function to create an inviting zone that is quiet when you need it to be and light or dark when you want it. Your bed and pillows should suit you perfectly and there should be a spot for all your clothes and accessories. Even though you spend a lot of time sleeping in this room, it's important that you can close the door and relax here.

HOW WE USED TO KEEP COMFY FROM *FORTUNES IN FORMULAS FOR HOME, FARM AND WORKSHOP* BY *HISCOX AND SLOANE* (1944)

A good bedbug killer is benzene pure and simple or mixed with a little oil of mirbane. It evaporates quickly and leaves no stain. The only trouble is the inflammability of its vapour. Where wallpaper and woodwork in a room have become invaded, the usual remedy is burning sulphur. To be efficient, the room must have every door, window, crevice and crack closed. A rubber tube should lead from the burning sulphur to a keyhole or augerhole and through it, and by aid of a pair of bellows, the air should be blown to facilitate the combustion of the sulphur.

GETTING ORGANISED

Shannon's bedroom is all about comfort—from the super organised wardrobe to the waterbed—whereas Jennifer's bedroom is all about fitting in eclectic furniture, including the set of cedar drawers from Aunty Eadie. The furniture you put in the bedroom will be dictated by the size of the room and the location of windows, doors, built-in wardrobes and fireplaces. It's important not to overclutter your bedroom because it will make it harder to relax in. The one essential is a bed. Other items include bedside table/s, wardrobe, set of drawers, mirror, lamps, chair, bookshelf, blanket box or storage spot and bin. Some people love to have a TV in their bedroom to go to sleep to. If you do, have a remote control or install a timer switch to turn off your TV. If viewing from a prone position in bed, have the TV at a reasonable height or you'll end up with a cricked neck.

Have an inviting corner or a comfy space in the bedroom for a chair or chaise longue. Use it as a quiet spot to read or to rest clothes on, to tie shoelaces or put stockings on.

COLOUR

The colour of your bedroom has a huge bearing on its comfort factor. Pale colours tend to work best and aim for clear rather than muddy colours because muddy ones make the walls look dirty. As a rule, avoid dark colours because they can make you feel depressed and encourage you to sleep in. Dark green can make you sleepy, but you may not always want to be asleep in your bedroom. Red makes you hungry, which is why it's a popular colour in fast-food outlets.

The best way to find out what colour works for you is to spend time in rooms of different colours and shades to see how you feel. When it comes to sheets and bedspreads, choose contrasting colours to the walls. The bed should be the focal point of the room but it shouldn't disappear into the walls.

FLOORING

Choose flooring that feels comfy underfoot. Many homes opt for carpet in the bedroom, even if the rest of the house has floorboards. If you have floorboards, it's easy to add a rug or two. Place rugs next to your bed so there's a soft landing on getting up. If you can't afford to buy a rug, make your own using canvas, calico or old sheets, decorate it using folk art paints and seal it with hairspray. Secure rugs to the floor with double-sided tape so people don't trip over.

HINT

HOW TO MINIMISE NOISE

Sleep can be easily disturbed by noise. Noise is transferred by vibrations and tends to travel upwards in straight lines. To reduce the noise level, you need to interrupt the line and stop the vibrations. Muffle sound by placing heavy objects against the wall. Put pelmets over windows and use heavy curtains, several lightweight curtains or ruffled curtains to help minimise noise. Fluffy items also help cut down on noise. If noise is coming from underneath you, don't lean your bed against the wall. Putting high-density foam rubber squares under the four corners of the bed will also help. Layering carpets and rugs also helps to reduce noise levels. If the noise is coming from above, hang mosquito nets or a parachute from the ceiling or put up some wall hangings. Put felt spots behind picture frames and mirrors on walls to prevent vibration. If there's a space under your bedroom door, block it with a foam brush strip, which is available from hardware stores, and attach to the bottom of the door. If the door rattles, place foam rubber stripping along the door jamb. Clothes and coats hung on the back of the door absorb noise and stop vibrations.

The ultimate in reducing noise levels is double glazing. It is expensive, but very effective. A friend of Shannon's has double glazing and from the inside of the home, you have no idea how much traffic is passing outside. For outdoor areas, such as courtyards, resist noise with tall thin plants, such as yakkas, which baffle the noise but still allow in light.

Never have a loud clock near a bedroom because the continual ticking is irritating.

 Don't have the sound of running water near a bedroom—you'll want to pee all the time.

LIGHTING

You need to have a range of lighting in the bedroom. In addition to the main light, have a lamp beside your bed, which is handy for reading and getting up in the middle of the night. Stumbling around in the dark can be hazardous and you'll be much more comfy if you can turn the light on and off from the bed. It's dangerous to have lit candles in the bedroom—you could fall asleep and cause a fire. If you do use them for a special occasion, remember to put them out before going to sleep.

HOW TO BLOCK THE LIGHT

There are several ways to block light from coming through windows. What you select will depend on the space and your preferences.

Curtains—the darker the curtain, the less light will penetrate. Curtains should be weighted and extend past the window frame. Use pelmets on top of the window to prevent light from seeping in. Another technique is to layer curtains with lighter ones underneath and heavy ones on top or consider having a blind underneath a curtain. Modern curtains can be hung on micro-tracks which allow them to hang more easily.

TIP

If air vents let in too much light, you can buy clip-on covers for them, which allow air to flow but block light and baffle sound. They come in a range of designs and colours.

Blinds—there are a range of blinds including roller blinds, vertical blinds, Holland blinds, Roman blinds and Venetian blinds. They can be made of wood, plastic, fabric or metal and come in a range of colours and sizes. The thicker the slat on venetian and vertical blinds, the stronger they are.

Shutters—are good for noise, light and security. Good strong frames and solid locks allow you to have your windows open and still be secure. They're also good for privacy. For more flexibility in the amount and direction of light, you can install louvered shutters, which are available in metal for increased security. They look like timber shutters, but have a full metal frame and slats.

HINT

HOW TO DEAL WITH MOSQUITOES

The best way to deal with mozzies is to stop them from getting into your home in the first place. Do this by having flyscreens on every window. Screen doors should also be covered with flyscreen. If you still have a problem, install a mosquito net over the bed. You can choose lacy and romantic or bold and modern, or you could dye the mosquito net to match the colour of your room. Children might like their net patterned with camouflage designs, spider webs, flowers or butterflies. Another way to deter mozzies is to add a drop of lavender oil to the light bulb on your bedside lamp or to apply diluted lavender oil over your body.

If you're having trouble sleeping, try this tonic. Inside a clean handkerchief or square of muslin, add 1 teaspoon of rose petals, 2 drops of lavender oil, 1 teaspoon of fresh thyme leaves and 1 sage leaf. Wrap it up, secure with a ribbon and tuck it into your pillow. As you toss and turn in bed, it will release its aroma. It should last for about 3 months.

Make sure the room is tidy before going to bed so you don't stumble over things in the night. Close wardrobe doors so you don't bump into them. Closed wardrobe doors also allow better air movement through the room.

BEDS

Your bed is a very important piece of furniture; a good night's sleep is one of life's greatest comforts. The most common types of bed are: ensembles, which consist of two mattresses, one on top of the other; slat beds with a mattress resting on a wooden slat base; water beds; futons; sofa beds and air beds. The style you choose is a matter of preference. Be particular, though, with the choice of mattress. The

HOW TO CHOOSE THE BEST MATTRESS

The best way to choose a mattress is to take the Goldilocks approach: lie on it, preferably with the person you sleep with. Most bed shops are happy for you to try mattresses out for as long as you need to. We recommend lying on the bed for at least 15 minutes—you shouldn't roll towards each other or away from each other. Shannon suggests wearing trousers in case you fall asleep—you don't want your skirt riding up in public! If you have back issues, consult your health provider before choosing a bed.

spring mattress is the most common type and can be pocket sprung, continuous sprung, open coil sprung, visco-elastic or memory foam, which is based on NASA technology.

HINT

HOW TO CHOOSE A WATERBED

Before getting a waterbed, make sure the flooring in the bedroom is sturdy: they're heavier than other beds! A soft-sided waterbed suits most people and takes away the feeling of being in a swimming pool. Have adequate baffles to prevent slosh and waves. The bag cover that zips to the mattress frame should be strong and double-stitched. When filling a water bed, both you and your partner should check the water level by filling it to where you think it should go and securing the inlet/outlet. Test it when you lie down. If you automatically roll towards each other, you need more water. If you roll away or off the bed, it has too much water. It can take a bit of fiddling! Clean them using the '333' technique: every 3 months, add chemical to the water; every 3 months, pull the cover off and wash it as you would a doona; and every 3 months, wipe in and around the bag and underneath the plastic reservoir. Make sure you dry the area thoroughly with a towel before returning the bedding.

Once you've made your mattress choice, care for it by flipping and turning it regularly so pressure is distributed across the mattress. Place a coloured ribbon or coloured safety pin on each corner so you know where you are in the rotation cycle.

WHERE TO PLACE THE BED

Working out where to put the bed is very important. There are a couple of choices. One way is to align the bed from north to south for magnetic balance. The other way is to locate it so that air flows across the bed, which Shannon prefers. To do this, place the bed

between the window and the door or between two windows so that
air circulates above it. That way, you avoid stale air and mould.
Where you put the head of the bed will depend on whether you're an
early or late riser. Early risers often like to face the rising sun. Late
risers prefer their face in the shade. Strong sunlight or light of any
sort on your head stimulates the chemicals that wake up your brain.
Another consideration for bed placement is where the afternoon sun
hits. If you live in an area where the western wall heats up in the
afternoon, it's best not to position your bed on the western side
because you'll boil in hot weather. On the other hand, if you live in a
cold area, it's a good idea to put your bed along this wall.

Always use a mattress protector because they're much easier to
wash than a mattress. Sheets soak up a lot of sweat, but they don't
stop all the moisture from getting through to the mattress. If the
mattress gets damp, mould grows, which can lead to respiratory
problems, skin irritations and nasty smells. It's anti-comfy.

Air the bed every day to allow sweat to evaporate and to freshen
your sheets. Getting sunshine on the mattress is also good because
UV light kills microbes. To air the bed, simply flip the blankets and
sheets off the bed to allow air and light into the bed. It requires only
10–15 minutes a day.

DUST MITES

It's been speculated that more children are getting asthma because of
dust mites. It's not so much the dust mite as the dust mite poo that's
the problem. The best non-toxic way to deal with dust mites is with
tea. Place 2 tea bags in a spray bottle of cold water and set aside to
steep for 5 minutes. Remove the tea bags, lightly spray the mixture
over your mattress and pillows and allow to dry. Do this weekly.
Another suggestion is to suck a damp tea bag into the vacuum
cleaner before vacuuming. It kills dust mites in the vacuum cleaner
and in the areas being vacuumed.

To tackle dust, hire a negative ion generator from a hardware store. Positive ions are created when inorganic materials rub together or against organic materials. In a home, it means furniture attracts dust and becomes statically charged. Leave the machine on for 1 hour. Use it once a month unless your house is very dusty and then use once a week. One long-term study into childhood asthma found that contact with a bird, such as a budgie, helps to reduce the incidence of asthma. They're not sure why, but researchers speculate that this contact activates the immune system.

TIP

Have a designated cleaning cloth for each room so that you won't spread bacteria around the home. Using old pantyhose or old T-shirts and washing them in the washing machine after each use is an inexpensive and hygenic way to go.

HINT

HOW TO CHOOSE THE BEST SHEETS
Opt for natural fibres, such as cotton, linen or silk, when choosing sheets. The best sheets have a high thread-count, which means there are more threads per square centimetre: the higher the thread count, the softer the sheet. Also consider the quality and length of the thread. The longer threads provide a softer sheet. Egyptian cotton is the best quality but also has a higher price tag. Top-of-the-range silk sheets are measured by momme weight. The higher the momme weight, the better the quality of the silk. Polyester cotton sheets are fine to use, but will pill after a while.

Ideally, each bed should have three sets of sheets: one on the bed, one in the wash and one spare. It's a good idea to have extra sets for children. Sheets should be washed once a week in hot water and hung out in the sunshine to dry. Sunshine is a great antibacterial and the sheets will smell fresher as well!

Some people like to iron their sheets. Shannon doesn't do this because they can get a plastic feel. Instead, hang sheets on the washing line and when dry, swiftly fold them while still in the sun. It gives them an ironed look without ironing!

HINT

MAKE YOUR SHEETS LIKE A 5-STAR HOTEL'S
We've mentioned this before, but it's worth repeating. An easy way to make your sheets feel just like the ones in hotels is to add rice starch when rinsing them. Keep the water after boiling rice and add 1 cup of this rice-water starch to 2 cups of water and stir thoroughly. Add $\frac{1}{2}$ cup of this mixture to the rinse cycle of the washing machine.

HINT

HOW TO CREATE YOUR OWN VACUUM-SEALED BAGS
You can create your own vacuum-sealed bags using extra tough garbage bags. Simply place items in the bag and gather the mouth of the bag into a circle. Put the vacuum cleaner pole into the bag, suck out all the air and tightly seal with six rubber bands. Label the bag so you know what's inside.

UNDER BED STORAGE

Underneath the bed is a great spot to store items you don't use often. Store items in clear plastic containers or use vacuum-sealed bags.

BREAKFAST IN BED

If you're going to pamper someone by serving breakfast in bed, use a tray with a crisp napkin, a tablecloth—don't forget the lovely old ones you inherited from grandma—and a flower. If you're in a spoiling mood, feed them strawberries on a long-handled silver spoon: they'll get a tingle from the silver.

> People often get leg cramps in bed. It is believed that these cramps are caused by a build up of uric acid in the muscle. The best way to stop a calf cramp is to pull your big toe towards your head with your fist. This spreads the uric acid through the muscle quickly. To prevent cramps, drink lots of water. Cramps are caused by many things, including kidney problems, being pregnant, being overweight, or from doing lots of exercise.

PILLOWS

Pillows are another important comfy purchase. They come in all shapes, sizes and fillings. Fillings include foam, latex foam, feather, tea tree, cotton, wool, kapok and blow fibre, a polycarbonate fibre. As with mattresses, select one that feels good to you. A bit of information that you'll be happy to learn is that the cost of a pillow has no

> Select cotton or linen pillowcases and use pillow protectors. Wash them each week in hot water because they tend to get body fat on them.

> If you get marks from mascara on your pillows, remove it with methylated spirits. Prevent the problem recurring by removing mascara from your eyelashes before going to bed!

> If you like ruffled pillow cases, keep them for show pillows because the ruffles can become uncomfortable to sleep on.

HINT

HOW TO WASH PILLOWS

Pillows can be hand washed or machine washed. Check the care label to find out how your pillow should be laundered. Wash using warm water and a cheap hair shampoo or a woolwash. If using a top loader washing machine, there is a knack to washing pillows so they don't become compacted. You need to make sure the pillow doesn't come into contact with the agitator, so wash two pillows at a time. Place them flat along the curve of the washing-machine barrel so that each pillow end meets. Allow the water to fill in the washing machine using the soak cycle, but don't allow the pillows to soak, then rinse right away. Rinse once with shampoo or woolwash and again with clean water. So all up, you've rinsed three times.

Dry pillows flat on a drying rack or on the clothesline. If drying on the washing line, peg a towel over two lines to create a tray. Put the pillow on top and peg it to the towel so it doesn't flip over. Turn and shake the pillow every 2 hours. Make sure the centre of the pillow is dry. Shannon washes pillows once a month, more during summer.

bearing on comfort. You don't have to spend a fortune! If you suffer from asthma, avoid feather and kapok pillows because dust mites breed more quickly in them. Whatever your choice in pillow, use a pillow protector and launder them regularly.

DOONAS

If you can't be bothered washing your doona, at least hang it on the clothesline in the sun to allow the UV rays to kill bacteria and dust mites. There are mobile feather doona cleaning services. Someone comes to your house and cleans the feathers in the back of the truck. A new cover is then added to the cleaned feathers. Consult your local directory for contacts.

HINT

HOW TO CLEAN A DOONA

We've described how to clean doonas in *Spotless* and *Speedcleaning*, but as the topic continues to come up here it is again. Wash them twice a year or even more if you sweat a lot. You can tell it's time for a wash when the fibres are packed down and lumpy or the doona is smelly. Some doonas can be put through the washing machine. Check the manufacturer's instructions first. Others, regardless of the filling, can be washed in a bath or a large sink. Fill the bath with warm water and half a cap of woolwash for a double bed-sized doona. Lay the doona in the bath, then get in yourself and stomp up and down on the doona until you get rid of all the dirt and grime. Empty the bath, fill it again with clean blood-heat water, stomp over it again, then let out the water. For the final rinse, fill the bath again with clean blood-heat water and allow it to soak into the doona. Drain the water from the bath and tread on the doona to squeeze out as much moisture as possible. Take the doona outside and put it on an old sheet. If you don't have a lawn, place it flat over the top of the clothes line. Leave it to dry for quite some time, then shake it and turn it. You need to do this about three times until it's almost dry. Then hang it on the clothes line on separate lines, so the doona forms a U-shape, and peg on the two outside edges to allow air to circulate. Unless you already have a stitched ridge, don't fold it over the line. When it's completely dry, give it a whack with your hand or an old tennis racquet. This fluffs up the fibres or loosens the feathers—and is great stress relief! Put it inside a clean doona cover to protect it against spills and grime.

BEDCOVERS

The bedcover can turn your room into a romantic haven, an inspirational Arabian nights place to dream, somewhere crisp and fresh to get a rejuvenating sleep or a cosy nest to snuggle in.

Bedcovers, throws, quilts and bedspreads can be made of cotton, chenille, velvet, satin, brocade, mohair, linen, wool, silk, polyester, nylon, viscose, rayon, angora or cashmere. A nice comfy decorative touch is to leave a cashmere or cotton throw at the bottom of the bed. Changing your bedcover is a great way to alter the whole feel of your bedroom.

BITTEN BEDSPREAD: Nicky's story

Q: My mother gave me her beautiful brocade bedspread. While it was packed away, the mice got to it. I think they have weed on it. I've restitched the holes with other parts of the brocade, but there's a nasty rusty browny stain on it. Can I get it off?

A: Soak the area in *NapiSan OxyAction* in blood-heat water, then rinse in blood-heat water and hang on the clothesline. Next time, store the bedspread correctly: with acid-free paper and naphthalene flakes or mothballs in a cotton covering.

BLANKETS

Blankets come in many different types, including cotton, waffle, woven wool, wool matt, knitted wool, crochet wool, nylon, mink, polar fleece, silk, felt, cashmere and faux fur. Have blankets in different weights for different times of the year. Have at least one good wool blanket, one cotton blanket and one doona per bed. Jennifer loves curling up under a blanket while watching TV in winter. Shannon has a cupboard full of blankets, many handed down from generation to generation. Her family has a tradition of making blankets for babies and adding to them as the children grow. Store them with camphor to keep bugs away.

HOW TO WARM UP THE BEDROOM

Increase the number of curtains or hang heavier curtains in the bedroom in cooler months. Pile lots of pillows on your bed, add a throw rug or two and put rugs on the floor. Arrange the room so that airflow is restricted and use a draught stopper against the door.

In winter, have a bar heater ready to switch on so you can warm up the room before you get out of bed. Modern heaters have an auto-off switch in case they are tipped over, but still be careful using them. Make sure there are no flammable items nearby and never have a bar heater where a child can reach it.

Before going to bed, put a pair of bed socks in the dryer to warm them up and then wear the warm socks to bed!

Use flannelette or brushed cotton sheets for extra warmth in winter.

Warm a soft-brushed cotton blanket in the dryer and wrap it over your feet when watching TV or in bed.

TIP

If you get cold in the middle of the night, it's handy to have a blanket box at the foot of the bed or an extra blanket somewhere close by.

HINT

HOW TO COOL THE BEDROOM

Put a damp towel on top of your top sheet and lie in a breeze or in front of a fan. You could also hang a damp towel over an open window. The towel draws heat from the air, leaving cool air. Reduce the amount of clutter in your bedroom so that air can flow.

BEDSIDE TABLES

Often it's not until you get into bed that you notice rough elbows or dry lips, or that you've forgotten to remove your earrings. Life will be more comfy if you keep the following essential items in your bedside-table drawer:

Moisturiser—lanolin, Vaseline or papaw ointment.

Lavender oil—for mozzies.

Tea tree oil—for itchy spots.

Pin box—for jewellery.

Tissues—to remove make-up (in case you've forgotten to do it already).

Books and magazines.

Coaster for cups and glasses.

Contact lenses or glasses case.

HOW TO MAKE ACID-FREE DRAWER LINERS
Buy some acid-free paper, which prevents yellowing in clothes, from the newsagent. Fill a spray bottle with warm water, add 1 tea bag and set aside to steep for 3 minutes. Remove the tea bag and add a couple of drops of oil of cloves and some of your favourite perfume, then spray over the paper. This mixture is particularly good for winter woollens and the tannins from the tea help prevent dust mites. Allow the paper to dry, then cut to size and place it in your drawers. Replace once a year.

BEDTIME BASICS

There are some simple ways to make your slumber as comfortable as possible.

Choose comfortable pyjamas. Satin may look good, but it wears like a plastic bag and it's hot in summer and cold in winter. If you love the smooth feeling, choose silk instead. Fine cotton and linen are great fabrics to wear to bed. They breathe and feel good against your skin, particularly if you rinse them with rice-water starch (see page 119).

After showering, exfoliate your skin by placing a stocking over your hand and rubbing it on your skin.

Don't go to bed with wet hair. If you must, put three layers of towel over your pillow first.

Always brush your hair before going to bed to remove dead skin and dust. It's much better than lying in the day's dust.

Help produce the chemicals that put you to sleep by having a glass of warm milk, a warm malted drink or a night-cap, such as port, before bed. Don't have anything high in sugar and avoid nutmeg because they're stimulants. Shannon's favourite is warm skim milk with a tot of cognac. Very relaxing!

Natural pick-me-ups and take-me-downs

Pick-me-ups—nutmeg, wattle seed, chilli, pepper, ginger, coffee, strong black tea, sugar.

Take-me-downs—chamomile, verbena, milk, turkey, chicken, carrots, sweet potato, valerian and kavea (a herb available from chemists and health stores).

WARDROBES

Wardrobes may be built-in, free standing or open hanging and need to be ordered and sorted. If you have a small room, consider installing built-in wardrobes: they maximise storage space and if you opt for a mirrored door, it has the dual function of showing you how you look and making the room seem larger. Make sure the depth of the wardrobe is 3–4cm deeper than the width of a coat-hanger.

TIP

Silicone crystals are effective at reducing damp, but can be quite expensive. A cheaper alternative is to wrap 12 pieces of chalk together and hang them in the wardrobe. It doesn't matter if they're coloured as long as they don't come into contact with any clothes, although I do prefer to use white. The chalk will absorb the moisture and can be dried out again in the sun. Have two sets so you can rotate them.

It's a good idea to tidy your bedroom and close wardrobe doors so you don't bump into them before going to bed. This also allows better air movement through the room.

HINT

HOW TO SORT THE WARDROBE

Shannon organises her clothes by type of garment, length and colour, ordering them by the colours of the rainbow. Make sure your wardrobe rods are high enough so that clothes don't drag on the bottom of the wardrobe. Many wardrobes have tubular rods that are not strong enough. To make it more sturdy, unscrew the brackets holding the rod in place and take it to your hardware store. Have them cut a piece of reinforcing steel to fit inside the tube of the rod. Replace the rod in its brackets and secure. Heavier clothes will now be supported.

TIP

If the edging on your clothes is scratchy, you can buy iron-on satin ribbon. Simply lay it over the offending seams and iron in place. If there's itchy nylon lace, remove it with scissors and replace with cotton lace, sewn on with running stitches.

TIP

Rather than using plastic suit bags, cover clothes you don't wear very often with old pillowcases or wrap them in sheets. Slit the pillow case down one side and cover the item. Fold a sheet in half and pull the coat-hanger hook through the centre of the sheet. Plastic bags, including dry cleaning plastic bags, fume and can damage your clothes by leaving yellow marks. Remove them, and any safety pins or staples, right away as they may rust.

HOW TO DETER NASTIES FROM THE WARDROBE

Combine 2 bay leaves (moth deterrent), 5 whole cloves (kills mould spores and deters silverfish), 1 tea bag (kills dust mites), 1–2 heads of lavender (adds fragrance and deters flying insects), 2 cedar chips (deters different moths), 1 tablespoon of bicarb (absorbs moisture and helps prevent mould) in a bowl. Place the mixture in the centre of a small piece of muslin or cotton voile and tie with string or ribbon. Use a different coloured ribbon so you don't confuse it with your shoe frou. This sachet is also great to use in your linen cupboard.

Men will often wear the same after-work clothes during the week and these can be stored on a valet stand. Shannon's thinking of getting a valet stand because she wears an average of three outfits a day: one for grotty work, one for around the house and another for going out in public.

Rather than expending energy picking up clothes from the floor, have a system in place for dealing with worn clothes. Put them in the dirty clothes hamper straight away or hang them or fold them for wearing again. If you've got very smelly clothes, take them to the laundry immediately—you're not going to feel very comfy with a rancid smell in the corner of your bedroom.

Clean clothes before you store them or they'll go mouldy where dirty.

Fasten buttons and zips.

Guard against moths, silverfish, mould and dust mites by making a sachet for the wardrobe (see above).

WARDROBE STOCKTAKE

If you haven't worn something for 2 years, work out why. Are repairs needed? Are there stains? Is it uncomfortable? Do you dislike the fabric? It's good to take note of these things because the next time you go shopping you won't make the same mistake. Either donate unwanted clothes to charity or sell them to a second-hand shop. Clothes can also be put into long-term storage if you can't bear to part with them. It's good to take note of clothes you love and wear to death and why they appeal to you. If you have a checklist when selecting clothes, you'll end up with a wardrobe you love rather than having buyer's remorse.

SHOES

There are many ways to sort shoes. You can use transparent boxes or cardboard boxes with photos on the end of them so you know what shoes are in the box. Baskets that sit on the bottom of the wardrobe allow shoes to breathe and canvas hanging shelves are also effective.

COMFY CRAFT

HOW TO MAKE A SHOE FROU

A shoe frou helps remove odours from shoes. Combine 2 table-spoons of bicarb (absorbs odours and moisture), 2 tablespoons of talcum powder (absorbs moisture and gives a silky feel), 1 drop of tea tree oil (kills tinea), 1 drop of oil of cloves (kills mould spores) and 1 drop of lavender oil (adds fragrance and deters insects) in a small bowl. Place the mixture in the centre of a small piece of muslin or cotton voile and tie with string or ribbon. Using a punching motion, dust inside the offending shoes. Reuse every time you remove your shoes.

HOW WE USED TO KEEP COMFY FROM *PEARS' CYCLOPAEDIA* 33RD EDITION (1928)

Damp feet give rise to many ailments checking healthful perspiration and causing inequality of blood circulation. Dry stockings and shoes should immediately be put on after there has been exposure to wet whereupon injury to the health will usually be obviated. The chief peril lies in keeping damp covering over the feet when moving about ceases.

HANDBAGS

Handbags are best stored in drawers to protect them from dust. If you can't keep them in a drawer, store flat in old pillowcases.

HINT

HOW TO DO THE BAG TRANSFER

One of the annoying things about changing handbags is transferring everything. An easy way to do this is to place a clean towel on your bed or on a table. Empty the bag's contents onto the towel. Put the new bag to one side and start adding things you want. Dispose of things you don't want. Shake the towel outside: no matter how fastidious you are, there's always debris in the bottom of a handbag. Wipe the inside of your old bag with a shoe frou and store.

HATS

Hats should be stored in hat boxes, on blocks or on a covered shelf. If kept in hat boxes, add a small sachet containing silicone gel or chalk, cloves and bay leaves. This keeps insects at bay and absorbs moisture so that you won't have mould problems. If storing hats on blocks, dust them regularly or cover with cotton or linen (you could even use grandma's old doilies).

The Bathroom

For most of us, the bathroom is the room we rush into and rush out of in the morning as we get ready for another day. But the bathroom can also become the ultimate comfy zone with full pampering potential. Bathroom styles are constantly evolving, but what doesn't change are the essentials of air and light. Look for ways to provide good ventilation and think about function—you don't want to hike great distances from the shower to get to the towel rail, for instance.

How we used to keep comfy from *Pears' Cyclopaedia 33rd edition* (1928)

When a tired feeling arises after some unusual exertion, a little rest should be taken if at all possible. All the garments should be loosened and a quarter of an hour spent in absolute rest with every muscle at ease. After this, a warm bath can be taken with half a pint of toilet vinegar or *eau de cologne* thrown into the water. After the bath, make a thorough friction with a little cold cream and a good soft towel followed by a dash of orris-root powder dabbed on the skin. After dressing again, a delicious sense of freshness will be experienced.

GETTING ORGANISED

As with the kitchen, the essential items of the bathroom are fixed, so you're restricted in the changes you can make to the layout. But there are a huge range of options for accessories such as towels, mats, soaps and decoration. You can revamp your bathroom by changing the taps and fittings or by re-grouting.

TOWELS

There are three kinds of bath towel—terry cloth, jacquard and velour. Terry cloth has looped threads extending either side of the base weave. Jacquard is terry cloth with the loops shortened or lengthened to create a pattern. Velour has cut threads rather like velvet. There are three things to consider when choosing a towel. First, make sure it's 100 per cent cotton—synthetics are not as absorbent. Secondly, make sure the size of the towel is appropriate. It's not comfy being only partially wrapped in a towel. Thirdly, select thick towels with the greatest density or loops-per-centimetre. The quick and easy way to work out towel density is by the 'scrunch' test.

TIP

THE SCRUNCH TEST
Place your hand under a section of towel and close your fist around it. The more loops-per-centimetre there are, the less towel will fit into your fist. The thinner the towel, the more it will fit into your fist. Select the thickest towel.

There's also a difference in the quality of the fibre used in towels. The most expensive are **Egyptian** or **pima cotton**, which have fine, combed threads. The next best fibre, and the most common, is **combed cotton**. The type of cotton used is identified on the towel's label.

Have at least two to three towels per person in your home. One towel is never enough and looks a bit sad on its own on the towel rail. It's also good to rotate your towels so that one doesn't become threadbare.

You must wash new towels before using them. Consult the care instructions for specific details. If the towel produces a lot of fluff after its first wash, wash it again before using. Avoid using fabric softeners on towels, they make the towel softer, but less absorbent because the softeners contain oils—and as we all know, oil and water don't mix. If you have used fabric softener and need to strip it out of your towels, add ½ cup of bicarb to your washing powder in the washing machine and use ½ cup of white vinegar in the rinse cycle in the fabric conditioner slot.

Ensure that your towels are completely dry before storing them and using them. A damp towel is an uncomfy towel! Dampness is also a perfect breeding ground for mould and bacteria. Avoid scratchy towels by washing in bicarb and vinegar as described above.

In winter, warm your towels in the dryer before your morning shower. There's nothing lovelier that toasty towels on a cold morning.

Towels should be washed regularly. If they're hung and aired on towel rails, you can use them for a week—although people exposed to a lot of dirt should change their towels every two to three days. Fresh towels are best stored away from the bathroom because they can get a musty smell from the steam. If you don't have a choice, store towels in a cupboard folded flat, not rolled, to avoid creating a mouldy centre.

Towels can make a great decorator statement because there are so many colours and designs available. They can be embellished, too, with embroidery or braid. If you embellish the towels yourself, make sure you wash the braid before stitching it on to avoid that puckering effect and colour run. Another way to embellish towels is to use old doilies. Cut the doilies in half and sew each half to either end of the towel. You can also have your initials or name embroidered on to towels; his-and-hers style.

There's also decorative scope in how you hang your towel. Fold it as you would a fan, then roll one end towards the centre and wedge it into the towel rail. It will hang like an opened fan.

Make sure you have enough towel rails in your bathroom. There should be one for each member of the house plus space for a guest. If you don't have enough towel rails in your bathroom, use large hooks on detachable racks. If you place the detachable rack over the shower screen, cut a circle from a plastic scourer to fit between the rack backing and the screen so you don't scratch it.

HOW TO STENCIL TOWELS

If you're in a crafty mood, decorate your towels using folk art paint, which comes in a huge range of colours, including silver and gold. If your artwork isn't great, buy a stencil and use it to guide your painting. You could even use an alphabet stencil and paint your name.

FACECLOTHS

Facecloths have gone out of favour in many households. Shannon loves them because they're soft, pick up soap well and exfoliate the skin. Use a different washer for each person in the household and have them colour-coded to avoid confusion. Change them every couple of days.

BATHMATS

The main types of bathmat are cotton, rubber and wood. Cotton ones are easiest to maintain because you can wash them with your towels. Rubber mats leave marks, are difficult to clean and will perish, but they are non-slip. If slipping is a concern and you need to use a rubber mat, make sure you regularly wash and salt the mat, which will prevent it from perishing and sticking to the floor. If you opt for wooden slats, give it a good scrub with soap and water and leave it in the sun to dry or stand it against the wall so mould doesn't develop.

DAM STAINS: Joanne's question

Q: Our porcelain bath is really stained from the dam water. Can it be removed or should we repaint the bath?

A: Use *CLR* or *Ranex* following the instructions on the label, then add equal parts water. Don't repaint your bath, it never looks or feels good! However, you can have it professionally resurfaced.

SOAP

At its most basic, soap is made of fat and ash. When the two combine, they create a mild caustic. These days, there are many other ingredients added to soaps and liquid soaps. Soap has different pH levels—a slightly higher pH level is best for washing hands. Soap used for the body should be pH balanced or neutral. Because different skin types react differently to soap, test soaps until you find one that suits you. They should lather well, be non-greasy and leave your skin feeling clean and dry but not dried out. Shannon loves using a lemon myrtle soap made with vegetable oils, cocoa butter, shea butter, castor oil and a mild moisturising oil.

If possible, allocate a bar of soap for each member of the house-hold. Store them on a holder that allows water to drain away. If you don't have a holder that drains, press grains of rice onto the bottom side of the soap to create a space between the soap and the surface. Rice also makes a great back scrub or exfoliator.

Store unused soap in the bathroom or linen cupboard: it keeps the linen smelling fresh and deters bugs.

Liquid soap has become popular and is a great grease cutter. But many are the same as the detergent used for washing the dishes and can be drying for skin and nails, although formulations are always being refined. Detergent is also used in shampoos with oils added to moisturise the hair. Check the ingredients. Ingredient labelling isn't always listed in order from highest to lowest content on chemical or cleaning products. If fragrance is high on the list, be wary!

Don't throw away unwanted cakes of soap—they can be used to lubricate drawer runners when they get sticky! Or grate 1 bar of soap, add to 1 cup of water, bring to the boil and add $\frac{1}{2}$ teaspoon of your favourite essential oil. When cool, place into a pump pack for the bathroom.

Change soap dispensers or swap shampoo bottles to change the look of the bathroom.

HOW TO DECORATE SOAP

There are many ways you can decorate soap. For that personal touch, engrave the name of your children or guests in cakes of soap using the pointy end of a warm teaspoon. Cut out any image you like, even a photo, damp the back of it with water, place it on the soap and rub it with your finger so there's a thin film of soap over the image. Allow it to dry. The image will stay on for as long as the soap lasts!

For a quick bubble bath, add 1 teaspoon of dishwashing liquid and 1 teaspoon of tea tree oil to the bath while it's running.

LIGHTING

Appropriate lighting is essential in the bathroom. Have good, vivid lighting with the ability to soften it. Many bathrooms have low ceilings so recessed lighting is a good choice. Lots of bathrooms have separate lighting around the mirror so every nook and cranny of your face is detailed. If you want your bathroom to have a furnished look, you can use lamps, but make sure they're installed properly. Electricity and water is a dangerous combination!

Many bathrooms have combined overhead lighting and heating, although some people don't like heat coming from above them. Select what works for you. The important thing is to ensure that heating is always safe.

If you have a dark bathroom, you can install tubular skylights. These are cylindrical in shape and extend from the roof of the home to the light-deprived room. They capture sunlight and swirl it down the tube to the room even when sun elevation is low. These need to be professionally installed.

VENTILATION

Bathrooms should always have a window and an exhaust fan so that moisture and odours can be removed. If moisture remains, mould grows. If you don't have a window then an exhaust fan is essential. It's also a good idea to open the bathroom door as quickly as possible after your shower so air can flow. Keep the exhaust fan on so moisture is removed. When cleaning, use bicarb—it will help dry the room out.

STORAGE

Every bathroom has bits and bobs. The challenge in creating a comfortable bathroom is having these essentials on hand, but in an organised way. You could organise the vanity by allocating one shelf to each member of the family. Encourage users to place their items in one spot only, and return items to that spot. That way you won't waste time searching for what you need. Have a spot for toothbrushes and toothpaste. Shannon uses pen and pencil holders for toothpaste and toothbrushes, which means everyone has their own little tube for sticking their toothbrush in and it prevents the bacteria spreading.

HAIR DRYERS, CURLERS AND STRAIGHTENERS

Your hair might be detangled, but hair dryer, hot curlers and straightener cords often become a tangled mess. If you have space, attach sturdy hooks or claw grips to the wall near the power point and hang them there. There may be space for a hook inside a cupboard, but if you're a bit space challenged, you may have to store the hair dryer in a drawer and plug it in each time you use it. Be sure not to store electrical appliances near steam or under the sink in case there's a water leak.

Electricity and water are a dangerous combination! Shannon stores her electrical products on a traymobile (à la hairdresser) that is located near a power point.

TIP Use some thin foam rubber to line the bottom of your make-up drawer in case of spills.

BATHROOM SAFETY

The main issues to be aware of with bathroom safety are scalding and slipping. If you have children, install childproof taps or have the hot water temperature adjusted at the thermostat. To prevent slips, use non-slip mats. You can even have suction mats put in the base of the shower recess to provide extra traction. **Never leave young children alone in the bath!** Even so-called saftey seats can flip over in the bath.

ADD SOME SPARKLE!

Something very obvious and effective in brightening the bathroom is to thoroughly clean it from top to bottom. Remove any loose items from the room and have a shower, without turning on the fan. The room will be really steamy. Keep plugs in plugholes and arm yourself with bicarb, white vinegar in a spray pack and a brush. Lightly sprinkle bicarb over every surface, then spray with vinegar and when the two fizz, scrub with your brush. Use an old toothbrush to access difficult corners and an old pair of pantyhose on the back of taps. Clean light fittings and scrub the ceiling. Rinse the entire room with water. Finally, clean the exhaust fan. You'll be surprised at the difference a good clean makes.

TIP

If your vitreous bath, toilet or sink has discoloured, fill with water, add denture tablets and leave overnight, then wipe with glycerine. A regular-sized bath would need 1 packet of denture tablets.

A perennial issue for most bathrooms is mildew and mould. The worst thing is when mould penetrates the grout or silicone and becomes impossible to shift. To help prevent mould, make sure the room is well ventilated. If you don't have a window in this room, install an extractor fan. When cleaning, add a couple of drops of oil of cloves to the rinse water to inhibit mould growth. If the mould has penetrated, make a paste of bicarb and white vinegar, apply to an old toothbrush and scrub. Do this a few times. If that doesn't work, you'll need to replace the grout or silicone. If you're game, there's the option of using slugs—they love eating mould. This method was trialled by Martyn Robinson from the Australian Museum. He reckons the *limax flava* is the best variety to use. Make a little house for them in an upturned flower pot. They roam at night and prefer cold rather than warm environments.

BATHROOM FITTINGS

The kind of fittings you have impact on the look and feel of your bathroom. Fittings are expensive, so be careful with your choices and always do your homework first. Go to plumbing suppliers and try out the different options. Second-hand building suppliers often have a wonderful range of antique taps and fittings. Make sure that they are in good working condition or you'll waste your money. Be aware that you can buy modified bathroom fittings. For example, if someone in the house has arthritis, choose lever rather than barrel-handled taps and use special arthritis washers so you don't have to turn the taps as hard. There are organisations that can advise on what's available.

SHOWERS AND SHOWERHEADS

In this era of water restrictions, many homes have opted for water-saving showerheads. These save water because the nozzles are fewer and finer and moisture hits the body in a hotter spray so it's steamier. They can't be used in all homes. If your hot water system is on the wall of the bathroom or in the roof, it's a low pressure system and can't use water-saving showerheads. You don't have to feel guilty because it's already saving water. If you don't have a water-saving system, have a timer in the shower and limit showers to 3 minutes. Another way to save water is to have your hot water service close to the shower so the heated water arrives more quickly. If it takes a while for your water to heat up, keep a bucket in the shower to catch the water and use the water on your garden or in your washing machine.

Tap aerators restrict water flow by over 50 per cent and work by adding air to the water. They come in different sizes and flow rates, are available from hardware stores and plumbing supplies and are easily installed.

If there are black prickly things in the shower nozzle, this is hard-water fur or limescale. Unless you have brass fittings, remove them with *CLR* or *Ranex*. Mix according to the instructions on the bottle, in a bucket or ice-cream container and immerse the shower head in the solution. Leave for a few minutes until the solution is absorbed. Then turn on the shower and watch the black prickles fall down the drain. For any strays, use a needle to unblock the holes. Keep brass shower-heads clean with equal parts white vinegar and lemon juice applied with an old toothbrush. Brass showerheads are generally big enough to scrub the hard-water fur out.

HOW TO FIX A LEAKY SHOWER HEAD

The first task is to find the source of the leak. If it's at the shower arm, tighten the nut or check the washer or O-ring—it may need replacing. The leak could be coming from the sealing washer in the arm joint. Remove it and check the pipes before fitting a new washer. Use some plumber's tape over the thread before replacing.

TIP

If you've got water spots on aluminium frames around showers, rub with cold black tea.

TIP

Freshen up an existing shower curtain by washing it in the washing machine on the cold setting and dry in the sun.

COMFY CRAFT

HOW TO MAKE YOUR OWN SHOWER CURTAIN

Give your bathroom a new look by making and installing a new shower curtain. It's a delicate operation, so do some trial runs first. Handling heat guns or large amounts of glue can be tricky.

1: Assemble items

Buy two sheets of 1mm thick heavy-duty clear plastic sheeting from the hardware store. Have each sheet cut to the size you want the curtain to be. Select the new design—use images from magazines, colourful bits and pieces, plastic butterflies, whatever style or design you want. Have a heat gun or spray-on polythene glue on hand.

2: Create workspace

The workspace needs to be large enough to fit the sheeting. Place newspaper over the area.

3: Construction

Place one of the plastic sheets over the newspaper. Then lay the design pieces over the plastic. Place the other plastic sheet over the top. Apply a heat gun in rapid movements over the entire plastic sheet so the two pieces of plastic fuse together. If you're not comfortable using a heat gun, use spray-on polythene glue. Apply it between the plastic sheets. Have enough space at the top to add holes using a hole punch. Attach curtain rings.

4: Installation

Install your new-look shower curtain!

HOW TO FIX A CLOUDY SHOWER SCREEN

Your cloudy shower screen could be soap scum or glass cancer. The way to tell if your screen has glass cancer is to hold a bright torch on one side of the glass and look through to the other side with a magnifying glass. Glass cancer appears as tiny sparkles in the glass. If it's soap scum, remove with bicarb and white vinegar. If you have glass cancer, the damage is permanent. You can apply goanna oil, which lasts for 3–12 months, but its manufacture has been reduced and it's very hard to source. You can lessen the scratches with sweet almond oil, but will have to reapply it after each clean. There is another solution and that's to frost the glass. You can buy frosting cream from the hardware or craft store and apply it with a brush.

HOW TO FROST GLASS

1: Select or create your pattern

You can apply any pattern, texture or design you like. Either cut your own design into cardboard and use it as a stencilling pattern or create a stamp using a potato. Carve the design you want. Fish or birds are popular in bathrooms.

2: Apply cream

Place your design over the screen then apply the frosting cream with a brush. If using a stamp, apply cream to the stamp and mark the screen.

3: Set

Wipe away any excess frosting and allow to set.

4: Wash

When set, remove the remaining frosting and wash thoroughly.

TILES

If your tiles are looking a bit tired, you can replace them, repair them or paint them. Replacing tiles is an expensive and tricky job and a professional is generally needed. If you only have to repair a broken tile, this is what to do:

HINT

HOW TO REPAIR A BROKEN TILE

There are several products that allow you to repair and touch up your tiles. Aqua Knead-It is an epoxy waterproof filler that comes in a roll form. Prepare a porous surface with sugar soap. Prepare a non-porous surface with mineral turpentine and then methylated spirits. Once the surface is dry, put on gloves and massage the mixture with your fingers until it's a consistent colour. Then forcefully work the filler into the broken tile or bath with your gloved fingers until it's smooth and level. Trim away any excess. Remove any residue with methylated spirits. It will set in 1 hour. Touch up the colour with tile paint.

HINT

HOW TO REPLACE A BROKEN TILE

Remove the grout around the tile edge using a grout rake or a hardened steel point, such as a file. Using a rotary tool with a diamond saw tip, cut an X diagonally on the broken tile. Lever it out from the centre of the tile so you don't break surrounding tiles. Chip any last bits out using a fine sharp cold chisel or nail punch and clean off any old adhesive with a chisel. Apply new adhesive to the rear of the new tile, lock it into place using matches or spacers. Allow to dry and re-grout.

HINT

HOW TO GIVE TILES A NEW LOOK
Tile paint allows you to paint directly over existing clean tiles. Be creative and use a variety of colours. Have feature tiles. As with regular paints, you can buy sample pots to see which colours work best.

Grout
Grout, the stuff between the tiles, comes in a range of colours. One way to cheaply rejuvenate a tired-looking bathroom is by re-grouting.

HINT

HOW TO RE-GROUT
Remove existing grout with a tungsten-tipped grout raker or a hardened steel point, such as a file. Select new grout and mix according to manufacturer's instructions. Wipe the grout between the tiles, remove excess before grout sets and allow to dry. Hey presto, new bathroom!

TOILETS
The toilet is a great invention. When you press the button, it lifts an outlet sealing washer and allows fresh water to flow from the cistern into the bowl, pushing the waste down the pipe into the sewerage system. When all the cistern water is released, the outlet washer drops back into place and water is refilled in the cistern until the float reaches its closed position ready for the next flush.

There are two main cistern mechanisms. Older toilets have a ball float attached to an inlet valve which is linked with the outlet. Newer toilets have contained units for the cistern and it can be more difficult to work out what's wrong with them. Either way, there are particular rules about what you can fix yourself and what you will need a plumber to do. If in doubt, seek assistance. There are some basic things that go wrong with toilets that we'll outline for you.

HINT

HOW TO STOP WATER LEAKING INSIDE THE CISTERN

Remove the top of the cistern and look inside. Don't worry about any gunge—the water here is clean! Your cistern will contain either a ball float hanging from an inlet valve or have a self-contained mechanism, which is harder to see. Some newer toilets have the cistern built into the wall and are harder to access, as Jennifer found out when house-minding. When a pipe became loose and water started spurting into the bath-room, she had to turn the water off at the mains and wait for the plumber to fix it, which is a good reminder to know where your water mains is located!

If you can see a ball float in your cistern, and the water is leaking, it could be a problem with the valve mechanism or there could be a perished washer. To check what's wrong, lift the float. If water stops running, you need to replace the ball valve mechanism. If water is released from the inlet valve, the washer may be perished. Washers are relatively cheap and easy to replace.

Another way to test if your cistern is leaking is to put a little food colouring in it. If coloured water flows into the bowl without being flushed, you have a leak and the washer or ball valve washer needs to be replaced. There are many different washers available these days. Hardware stores have a rack of fix-a-tap cards with guide notes.

If you decide to replace the washer, be sure to turn the water off at the stop tap, usually located on the wall at the base of the toilet. Remove the pivot pin and undo the top of the inlet valve until you reach the sealing washer. Turn the washer over or replace it. If it's still leaking, you may have to replace the entire valve.

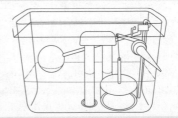

HINT

HOW TO STOP WATER LEAKING INTO THE BOWL

If water flows down the back of the bowl, it could be a worn sealing washer located at the bottom of the cistern. Turn off the stop tap, which is on the wall at the bottom or inside of the toilet. Flush any water. Take out the lifting mechanism and replace the washer. If you can't access the washer inside the cistern, undo the pipe under the cistern and lift out the entire unit.

HINT

HOW TO CLEAN MINERAL BUILD-UP IN THE TOILET BOWL

This can be a big job. Make sure you wear gloves. First, turn off the stop tap and empty the water from the bowl using a cup, then dry with a paper towel. Sprinkle bicarb over the surface. Use a sponge if it's difficult to access. Then use white vinegar in a spray bottle. While it's fizzing, scrub with a brush. If the stain hasn't shifted, use *CLR* or *Ranex* according to the manufacturer's directions. Then turn the water back on.

HINT

HOW TO FIX A BLOCKED TOILET

Children often throw items down the toilet. To retrieve them, try to reach the S-bend with your gloved hands. If you can't reach it, use a plunger to suction the item out. You can also use a mop and plunge it up and down in the bowl. If this fails, you'll need to call a plumber to use an electric eel. If the blockage is caused by faeces, fill the toilet bowl with hot water, leave for 10 minutes and flush. The hot water will break the faeces down. For other blockages, such as tree roots growing through the pipes, an electric eel operated by a professional is needed.

HINT

HOW TO ADJUST THE WATER LEVEL IN YOUR CISTERN

Dual flush systems save water and are better for the environment, but many old toilets do not have this function. To save water, some people place a brick inside the cistern to reduce the amount of water used. Be aware that this can affect the flushing action, so it's not the best idea. You can easily adjust the level of the float in the cistern to alter the amount of water used. Take off the cistern lid. If you have a ball float, adjust the height of the arm to the level you want by bending the arm of the float—the higher the bend, the longer the toilet takes to flush; the less the bend, the quicker the flush time. Make sure that the float doesn't touch the side of the cistern or there will be friction. If you have a plastic arm, there's generally a round screw over the arm which you can turn to change the level. The difficulty is that each mechanism is different and it can be hard to find which bits do what. Be patient, methodical and careful if it's made of plastic because little bits of plastic can fall off and cause major problems.

You may find brown gunge inside the cistern. It's not linked with human waste in any way, but it is a good idea to clean the area once a year. Simply wipe inside the cistern with a pair of old pantyhose.

TIP

If your children continually drop things in the toilet, put some flyscreen at the bottom of the toilet with some string on the side of the flyscreen. Simply pull it up before you use or flush the toilet.

HINT

HOW TO FIX A LEAKING TOILET BOWL

If you have a constant pool of water on the floor, look for the source of the leak. It could be a crack in the toilet bowl. Look at the pipe joining the cistern and the bowl. The black or white rubber may have come loose or perished. Detach the pipe, pull the rubber back, then reattach the pipe and secure or replace the rubber. Check the nut at the base of the cistern. Often there's a removable plastic cover around the nut. Tighten, but don't over-tighten, the nut with a spanner. If it's leaking between the nut and the pipe, you may need to seal between the two with plumber's tape.

TIP

Little boys need a step to use the toilet. Choose one that matches the décor of the bathroom and is light enough for them to put into place themselves. They can often have difficulty with aim as well! To help them, put a ping pong ball at the bottom of the toilet and tell him to aim for it. The ping pong ball won't flush because it's too light and you'll be surprised at how much better their aim becomes!

HINT

HOW TO FIX THE TOILET SEAT

If the toilet seat has become loose, check the nuts and bolts that attach the seat to the toilet bowl. These are easily replaced, if broken. If the seat has cracked, you'll need to replace the entire seat or risk a pinched bottom! Many seats have bolts with concentric heads which you can adjust to move the seat forward.

TIP

Consider changing the colour and style of your toilet seat for a new look.

Toilet discomfort

Concerns about toilet hygiene have been with us forever. Shannon remembers carrying phenyl and wiping it over public toilet seats as an antibacterial. It used to sting when you sat on the seat. The best way to deal with uncomfortable toilet issues is to identify them.

Let the rest of the house know if you're about to spend an extended amount of time in the bathroom, especially if the toilet is in this room.

Make sure extra toilet rolls are within easy reach of the toilet. It's always awkward calling out for extra toilet paper. Can you spare a square?

Many people feel embarrassed about noises when on the toilet. There are a couple of ways to make people feel more comfortable. One is to have an air vent installed with the hum of the motor concealing noise. Another idea is to put a small radio near the toilet.

There are a few ways to cover bad smells. Plenty of sprays are available, but they can smell almost as bad. Create your own toilet spray using 1 litre of water and 1 teaspoon lavender oil in a spray pack. Lighting a match also works to clear toilet odours because it burns methane gas, a highly flammable material and the source of the offending smells, more quickly. If the odour does not dissipate, it means the toilet needs to be cleaned.

Always make sure there is a toilet brush next to the toilet and encourage users to familiarise themselves with it.

Scented candles are a great source of fragrance that also burn methane.

Plants also make a huge difference to the smell of a bathroom. They love moisture and increase negative ions in the room. Rainforest plants are ideal but any indoor plant will work. Just don't choose one that drops a lot of fronds!

Outside toilets were often surrounded by violets, passionfruit, chokos and strawberries because they thrive on poo and methane. The fragrance of violets always overpowers the smell of poo.

UNIDENTIFIED STINK: Margaret's question

 I live on the top floor of a new apartment building and my bathroom drains are really smelly. It smells stale and there's grey stuff under the grill? What can I do?

 It could be a venting problem or accumulated talcum powder. Talcum powder has an absorbent calcium base that becomes smelly grey gunk because it supplies a greater surface area for bacteria and water to stick to. To stop it going down the drain, attach some muslin cloth under the grill and clean regularly. Always vacuum before mopping the bathroom floor. To fix the current problem, flush the drains with ½ cup of bicarb followed by ½ cup of white vinegar. Wait for 30 minutes then flush with very hot to almost boiling water. Wrap a long-handled bottle brush in some old pantyhose and manually scrub the drains. If the problem continues, consult a plumber.

TAPS

The most common reason for a leaky tap is a worn washer and they're generally easy to replace. In days gone by, Jennifer's grandfather turned the leather from old boots into washers. But these days, hardware stores have a massive range of washers to choose from.

The location of the washer will vary according to the type of tap you have. The main types are compression, washerless, ceramic disc and ball-type. The compression tap is the most common and because the jumper valve and O-ring get a big work out, they often need to be replaced, too. To replace the washer, turn the water off at the stop tap or water mains. Drain the pipes. Cover the work area with a rag so you don't scratch the surface. Pull the tap apart and lay out the parts in the order you remove them— this will make reconstruction a lot easier. Fix an adjustable spanner to the body of the tap and turn it anticlockwise. Remove the spindle and remove the jumper valve. Check the washer and any other parts. Check that the seat of the tap is smooth. If not, it will need reseating with a special tool or by a plumber. Check the washer or O-ring and replace if necessary. Once everything has been checked and replaced, reassemble and tighten with a spanner. Open the stop tap slowly and flush the line.

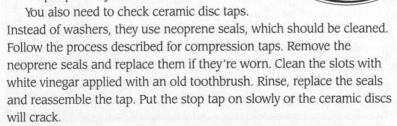

You also need to check ceramic disc taps. Instead of washers, they use neoprene seals, which should be cleaned. Follow the process described for compression taps. Remove the neoprene seals and replace them if they're worn. Clean the slots with white vinegar applied with an old toothbrush. Rinse, replace the seals and reassemble the tap. Put the stop tap on slowly or the ceramic discs will crack.

If you have a ball-type tap or mixer, seek professional help.

BASINS

The older the house, the more likely the pipes will have accumulated gunk in them. Place ½ cup bicarb followed by ½ cup white vinegar down the plughole and leave for 30 minutes. Pour very hot water down the drain. If this doesn't clear the pipes, clean the S-bend, which is located underneath the sink.

TIP

Lower density washers make the tap easier to use but they have to be replaced more often.

TIP

If your sink ring has green discolouration, it's likely you've been using bleach or strong cleaners and not rinsing properly. To remove the green discolouration or verdigris, scrub with bicarb and white vinegar.

HINT

HOW TO CLEAN THE S-BEND

Place a bucket underneath the S-bend to capture any water and gunk. Wearing rubber gloves for grip, unscrew the two big nuts located either side of the S-bend. PVC pipes can usually be removed with your hands. Metal pipes will need a monkey grip, stillson or large adjusting spanner. After releasing the 'S', clean it out by flushing through water. Make sure you use a different tap or you'll flood the bathroom. If there's gunk in the fixed part of the pipes, refashion a coat-hanger into a loop and attach a scourer (cut to size) to the end with string. Work it up and down the pipes to clean out the gunk. Replace the 'S', making sure it's secure or water will leak. Put 1 table-spoon of bicarb down the sink, followed by 1 tablespoon of white vinegar. Leave for 10 minutes then flush hot water down the pipes.

Proprietary products are available to clear pipes, but remember that they're incredibly toxic and can burn your skin. So always wear gloves and goggles and take care.

If the sink is really blocked, you may need to get a plumber. It could be, as friends of Jennifer found, that pipes were congested with decades' worth of hair!

How we used to keep comfy from *Pears' Cyclopaedia 33rd edition* (1928)

To smooth the skin of your throat, cod liver oil is one of the most flesh-forming oils that can be obtained. And once one can make up one's mind to bear with the unpleasant odour, it would be well worth a trial to those who are anxious to develop the neck nicely.

BODIES

The bathroom can be the ultimate rejuvenation and pamper zone. And while there are plenty of expensive products available that promise to turn back the clock, you can make your own great face masks and exfoliators for a fraction of the cost. You may look like an Egyptian mummy, but within the four walls of your pamper zone, who cares?

DEODORANT

Perspiration levels and odours vary from person to person. According to some, a big bearing on this is your diet, in particular the amount of meat you consume. The argument goes that meat is broken down through digestion and releases toxins into the bloodstream, which are then eliminated through areas such as the underarm. Garlic, coffee, onion and alcohol are also supposed to be odour culprits. Some people have acidic perspiration, others have more alkaline sweat. If you have an aversion to underarm deodorants, there are alternatives. Mineral deodorants come as a large crystal block that slow down perspiration and absorb odours. An idea for heavy sweaters is to carry a damp cloth in a zip-lock bag in your bag and regularly wipe under your armpits. Shaved armpits smell less. Wiping a mild solution of hydrogen peroxide or witch hazel to the armpit may help. Rosemary is an antibacterial. Zinc may also help reduce smell.

PAMPERING

Sinking into a hot bath filled with your favourite essential oils is a delightful experience. You may be happy just reclining or you could also 'value-add' with a homemade face mask.

HINT

SHANNON'S FAVOURITE FACE MASK

Make a rough paste with 2 dessertspoons of rolled oats and 2 tablespoons of skim milk. If you have dry skin, add a few drops of olive oil. If you have oily skin, add a few drops of lemon juice. Plaster it on your face and leave until it goes dry, then wash off with water. Your face will feel soft and clean.

TIP

If you take regular baths but don't have a surround shelf, buy a bath rack that sits across the bath—you can even get some with an inbuilt bookstand—or place a small table or chair beside the bath. It's much more comfortable to have items within arm's reach!

HOW TO MAKE A BATH BOMB

Combine 1$^1/_2$ tablespoons of citric acid with 2 tablespoons of bicarb. Add $^1/_2$ teaspoon of dried food colouring and 1–2 drops of your favourite essential oil and mix thoroughly. The mixture should be slightly sticky. If not, add a couple more drops of essential oil and mix again. If it's still not clumping, add witch hazel one drop at a time, until sticky. Firmly press the mixture into moulds, then tap them out onto some greaseproof paper. Leave them to set for 2–3 hours and wrap them in plastic until they're ready for use.

Make your own exfoliator by mixing 1 teaspoon of sea salt with 1 tablespoon of sweet almond oil.

A quick cheap make-up remover is cheap hair conditioner. It won't sting your eyes.

DIY pedicure

Melt soft paraffin wax (available from supermarkets or chemists) in the microwave. After showering, cover your feet with the melted wax and leave for 20 minutes or until hard, then peel off. You'll have lovely soft feet. Paraffin wax is also good for hands.

Massages

For a comfy treat, give someone a massage. It helps to relieve stress, gets the blood moving and feels lovely.

To make an all-purpose massage oil, combine 1 teaspoon of baby oil, 1 drop of lavender oil and 1 drop of tea tree oil and mix well. Peppermint is often used for tired muscles, but if you have sensitive skin, it will go red.

Foot massage

You can even massage your own feet this way! Begin with your fingers placed at the centre of the ball of the foot and work them towards the edge of the foot. This brings blood into the foot so that your feet will feel better faster. Move to the toes and work towards the heel to expel blood from the foot. The technique works well for people with gout. Skin gets thinner with age so be more careful if massaging an older person.

Apply the same technique to your hands.

Back massage

Place hands on either side of the spine and push thumbs upwards along the muscle. Never put pressure on the spine itself or on the base of the skull because it's very tender. Use the heels of your hands along the neck.

Dual massage

You need two people for this technique. Sit on the floor back to back. Place a small pillow between the smalls of both backs and lean against each other in a gentle movement.

HAIR

HINT

HOW TO CLEAN A HAIRBRUSH

You need two hairbrushes for this technique. Place the hairbrushes bristle to bristle, rinse them in warm water with a small amount of white vinegar and rub them against each other. This will remove hair, oils, dust and old skin. Do this every week if you have long hair.

HOW WE USED TO KEEP COMFY FROM *PEARS' CYCLOPAEDIA 33RD EDITION* (1928)

There are many vaunted specifics for the prevention and cure of baldness but none less harmful or likelier to afford general satisfaction than the following cheap and simple application. Whisk up the yolk of one fresh egg and mix therewith an equal quantity of the squeezed and strained juice of chopped and uncooked Spanish onions. Add thereto as much crude cod liver oil in quantity as the two foregoing ingredients make together, and then whisk the whole for fully 5 minutes. The resulting ointment may be perfumed to mask its rather disagreeable odour. Place in a tight receptacle. Rub a little into the scalp patiently every night after first bathing the part well with warm water.

HINT

LACKLUSTRE HAIR

Give your hair some bounce. Beat 3 eggs, add 2 tablespoons of olive oil and 1 teaspoon of lemon juice or, if your hair is dry, orange juice. Apply the mixture to your hair and cover with plastic wrap. Leave for 30 minutes, then wash out, shampoo and condition. To give your hair a really shiny look, wash in shampoo then wash in 600ml of beer. Leave for 30 minutes, rinse in clean water, dry and style as usual. You'll have a mirror sheen!

DANDRUFF

You're more likely to have dandruff if you sweat heavily. Regular washing and clean pillows will reduce its incidence.

The treatment for dandruff will depend on your hair colour. For darker hair, apply a tea of rosemary and water. Add 2 teaspoons of dried rosemary to a pot of boiling water and allow it to steep for 10 minutes. Then apply to your hair. For fair hair, apply maidenhair fern. Add some fern to a pot of boiling water and allow it to steep. Then add it to your hair. If you have a rough scalp, rubbing with coarse salt or brown sugar will alleviate the problem.

SHAVING

Always use a clean razor and choose one you can grip and control well. Always apply a lather of shaving cream before shaving. As a general rule, shave against the grain of the hair. If the hair is particularly thick, shave along the grain first, then against the grain. If you get ingrown hair, regular exfoliation is important. Tea tree oil helps as does increasing blood flow by applying bruise reduction cream. Use a good-quality antibacterial aftershave conditioner.

TIP

If you like to shave in the shower, use an anti-fog mirror. Make one yourself by getting a hand-sized mirror and scribbling soap over it then polishing or spitting onto a tissue and rubbing the surface. Both methods stop steam blocking your view.

Kids

The organisation of a home changes when children come along. You'll find the process less disruptive and more comfy if you make plans before your little bundle of joy arrives. Don't worry: the nesting instinct tends to kick in a long time before you introduce your baby to your home. Even the most undomesticated mums and dads start sorting items for the new arrival. As a rule, the better prepared you are, the easier it will be.

How we used to keep comfy from *Fortunes in Formulas for Home, Farm and Workshop* by Hiscox and Sloane (1944)

For head lice in children, one of the best remedies is a vinegar of sabadilla. This is prepared as follows: sabadilla seeds, 5 parts, alcohol, 5 parts, acetic acid, 9 parts and water, 36 parts. Macerate for 3 days. Express and filter. The directions are: moisten the scalp and head thoroughly at bedtime binding a cloth around the head and let remain overnight. If there be any sore spots on the scalp, these should be well greased before applying.

GETTING ORGANISED

Shannon's baby expertise is based on being a mother, grandmother and carer to many children. Jennifer's expertise comes from being an aunt and a godmother. Having children is like being on a roller-coaster, with the ride much easier if you've got the infrastructure in place. Be prepared to feel both frazzled and fantastic!

Baby essentials include a cot, change table, clothing, highchair and stroller. Light and fresh air are vital: the nursery should be cool and airy, avoiding extremes of hot and cold. Don't use strong perfumes or air fresheners around your baby. All you need to clean the room is soap and water. Since your baby will be spending a lot of time on its back, have some interesting colours in view but don't go overboard and overstimulate them. Soft pastel colours work well in nurseries.

If the baby is disturbed by a noisy household, have a radio or other background noise playing to make them less sensitive to sudden loud noises. It's best for the baby to get used to a bit of noise when they're sleeping or you'll need absolute quiet every time.

Make sure that your baby furniture can be wiped down, which means it should be painted, varnished, metal or plastic. Sealed surfaces can be washed with soap and water. Cane is a good choice because you can take it outside and hose it down.

If you're washing the baby in a large bath, place a clean, plastic clothes basket in the bath, fill the bath to the desired depth with water and place the baby inside the basket. Babies can get very slippery when they are covered in soap and wriggling. This will help you stay in control.

While front packs have become popular, backpacks have the advantage of evening out your body weight. Because the back muscles in pregnant women change as the weight of the baby becomes greater, a backpack helps restore the back muscles.

COT

There are many styles of cot to choose from. Because your baby will be in the cot for up to three years, think about how adjustable and versatile it is. Points to consider:

A strong drop side so the baby can't climb out.

Adequate slat width—wide enough so that a toddler can't climb out or get hands or feet stuck, but narrow enough so that the baby's head can't get stuck between the slats.

Stability—make sure the cot doesn't rock around.

Make sure it complies with safety guidelines. Each state has a Fair Trading or Consumer Department with the latest information.

Be careful where you place the cot. Never have dangly things, including cords from blinds, within reach of the cot or the baby could become entangled. Consider what the baby will be able to reach and whether it's a safety issue. It's also worthwhile installing a smoke alarm in the baby's room, just in case. Keep fluffy toys out of the cot until they're older.

Mattress
Shannon prefers a tea tree mattress for babies up to 6 months old because it allows good airflow around the baby and inhibits insects. After 6 months, the baby becomes too heavy for the tea tree and a foam or inner spring mattress is required. Make sure the mattress fits the cot properly—you shouldn't be able to fit more than two fingers between the mattress and the edge of the cot. The mattress should also be quite firm. Whatever type of mattress you have, use a mattress protector because there are bound to be spills and leaks and it's much easier to clean a mattress protector than a mattress.

Sheets and bedding
Use only 100 per cent cotton sheets—never nylon or polyester. When nylon or polyester gets wet, it creates a moisture barrier and your child

could end up with a rash. Synthetic fibres also hold smells and are harder to keep sterilised. Opt for light cotton blankets, cotton bunny rugs and cotton waffle blankets to cover the baby. Sheets and blankets should always be well tucked so the baby can't unwrap itself and become tangled. As a rule, babies don't need pillows or cot bumpers.

A baby's bed should be aired every day. This means stripping the sheets and blankets from the mattress and hanging them over the edge of the cot. The reason this is important is that babies are very susceptible to bacteria and infection. Babies don't sweat as easily as adults so they have more dead skin cells so wash sheets at least once every 3 days.

If you have creaky floorboards, place a rug on the floor: there'll be less disturbance when you check on your baby.

LIGHTING

Most babies can sleep anywhere and are not too sensitive to light. Parents, on the other hand, are not so good at making their way in the dark. The last thing you need is an injured parent, so don't leave an obstacle course between you and the baby and make sure you have a range of lighting in the baby's bedroom. You want bright lights when needed, and soft lighting during the night, particularly in the early months when feeding is a regular occurrence.

Deter mosquitoes by adding 2 drops of lavender oil to a 250 ml bottle of baby oil, then massage this over the baby's skin. Never apply lavender oil directly to the skin because it's very concentrated. This applies to all essential oils.

BABY MONITOR

There are many baby monitors to choose from. If you have a large house, a baby monitor is essential, preferably one you can clip onto your belt. Baby monitors should be located near the cot so that you can hear any change in the baby's breathing. Just be careful there are no cords in reach of the cot.

CHANGE TABLE

The ideal bench height of a change table is to the height of your elbow, so that you won't have to bend and strain an already sore back. Make sure the change table is padded and use a securing strap so the baby doesn't roll off. Never leave a baby unattended on the change table. Always have a hand on them, even if they're strapped in. Everything you need for changing the baby should be within easy reach. Have a disposal system, such as buckets and bags with ties for old nappies. Buy bags that are environmentally sound and lightly perfumed.

Cloth versus disposable nappies

There's an ongoing debate about whether cloth or disposable nappies are better for the environment. Results vary depending on whether you include the impact of using just the nappies or if you also include the production of the nappy, such as growing the cotton and the disposal of the nappy into landfill. There is no easy answer. The University of Queensland looked at the issue and their findings suggest that disposable nappies use more energy, land area and solid waste but cloth nappies use more water. The researchers suggest that regardless of what type of nappy you choose, think of ways to reduce your environmental footprint.

Cloth nappies with liners are better for nappy rash because more air flows through them. The key to minimising nappy rash is to change the nappy regularly. Papaw ointment is a great soothing balm for sore bottoms.

Dirty cloth nappies should be kept in a sealed bucket. Always shake solids into the toilet before placing in the bucket. To disguise the smell, absorb nasty odours and release a pleasant fragrance, combine some bicarb, sage, thyme and 2 drops of lavender oil and place this mixture near the bucket. Never overfill a nappy bucket because waste will run down the side of the bucket and onto the floor.

ACCIDENTAL ADDITION: Melissa's question

 I never would have done this if I'd had enough sleep, but I accidentally put a disposable nappy in the washing machine and dryer. How can I fix the melted mess?

 Clean the inside of the washing machine by placing pantyhose over your hand and wiping. To fix the dryer, empty it and wipe the drum with glycerine on pantyhose. Thoroughly clean the filters of both washer and dryer. Shake all the affected clothes thoroughly before rewashing them.

WASHING

Baby skin is very sensitive so it's best not to use regular washing powder on clothes or bedding. Instead, use pure soap flakes or specifically designed nappy products. The important part of washing is rinsing—you want to remove as much washing powder from the items as possible. If needed, rinse twice or add a tablespoon of vinegar to the rinse water.

If using a dryer on baby clothes, iron these items as well. Iron steam is hotter than dryer air and will kill more bacteria, which means less likelihood of nappy rash.

To work out how safe a room is, get onto your hands and knees as though you are the baby and see what trouble you can get into—then double it!

STORING BABY CLOTHES

Baby clothes can be passed from baby to baby, almost becoming treasured heirlooms. So looking after them properly is important. The clothes must be completely clean before storing or mould or mildew will grow on them. Use acid-free tissue paper between each layer of clothing to prevent yellow spots. To remove yellow marks, use *NapiSan* and warm water and soak overnight for cottons and linens, or cheap shampoo and lemon juice for wool and silk.

Don't buy baby clothes with buttons along the back because they're uncomfortable to lie on.

Canvas shelving units are a great option for storing baby clothes because they allow good airflow.

HIGHCHAIRS

Be prepared for the highchair to become covered in your culinary creations! When choosing one, consider ease of cleaning, safety and durability:

Never leave a child unattended in a highchair.

Make sure it has a three-strap harness—the tray is not enough (the baby may slide underneath it).

The wider the tray, the more food it will catch.

Make sure the base is sturdy—the legs should be splayed 10 per cent wider than the top of the chair so it doesn't topple over.

Make sure the locking mechanism is sturdy;
keep little fingers away from moving parts when setting the tray;

Keep highchairs away from walls so the child can't push the highchair over;

Make sure it's comfy to sit on with adequate padding or cushioning.

HOW TO MAKE A SOFT SEAT COVER

COMFY CRAFT

This versatile seat cover can be used in many locations, including shopping trolleys. Buy some cotton quilt fabric and cut it into a rectangle 30 x 20cm in size. Make a cut in the middle of the shorter end on one side for the legs. At the other end, sew a long strap of the quilting fabric and attach Velcro to either end. This strap will wrap around the baby and across the front of the chair/trolley/pram. The Velcro means you can secure it and relocate it.

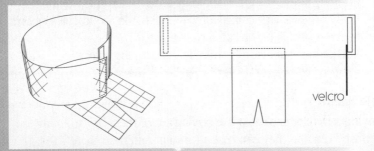

velcro

TIP

If your child creates a huge amount of mess when eating, place a flattened garbage bag under the highchair.

TIP

Each time you prepare vegetables for yourself, cook extra, puree, place in an iceblock container and freeze. Once frozen, transfer cubes to a zip-lock bag and return to the freezer, ready for use when needed (use instead of tinned baby food).

TIP

When your child is ready to drink from a glass, provide some extra grip by wrapping elastic bands around the glass.

HINT

HOW TO GET RID OF THE DUMMY

So many parents feel conflicted about using dummies. The argument against the dummy is that it changes the shape of a child's mouth. The argument in favour is it could be the only thing that stops your baby crying. Then there is the issue of breaking the dummy habit. Here are some suggestions:

Gradual phase out—scale back dummy use to bed time only, then substitute it with a bottle of cool boiled water.

Sabotage—cut the tip off the rubber so it doesn't suction as well.

Fantasy story—tell them Santa needs the dummies for the baby reindeer or that the dummy fairy is coming to collect them. Leave a treat in place of the dummy.

Self phase out—wait for them to outgrow the dummy.

STROLLERS

Buying a stroller is almost like buying a car: there are so many to choose from and they can cost a fortune. And then there's the prestige factor! We're about practicality, so consider these features before purchase:

Strong and stable.

Able to be opened and closed easily.

Good steering—a stroller with a bar across the top is easier to manage than one with two single handles.

Adjustable wheel action—look for locking actions on the wheels so you can manage different terrains and spaces.

Check the brakes.

Comfy seating with recline option and seat belts.

Suspension—to make the journey smoother.

MOULDY STROLLER: Murray's question

 Q: I left the stroller in the boot of the car and it's now mouldy. Can it be fixed?

A: Allow 1kg of salt to dissolve in 1 bucket of warm water, then apply it to the stroller with a stiff brush or broom. Leave it to dry without rinsing; as it dries the salt will form a crust. Then brush it off with a stiff broom and the mould will come off with it. To prevent mould, add a couple of drops of oil of cloves to the water.

AS BABIES GROW OLDER

From about the age of 3, it's time to think about moving from the cot to a bed. It's also time to get your child into good organisational habits. If you start them early, it will become part of their routine and you won't have a constant battle with them about tidying their rooms. Kids need room to sleep, room to play and room for their clothes and toys.

BEDROOMS

Older children's bedrooms should be an imagination paradise. Let them choose their own pictures for their walls. Have a blackboard, whiteboard or noticeboard to express their creativity. Rather than sticking pictures and posters to the wall with *Blu-tak*, let your child select their favourite pictures and frame them. The picture could come from their favourite book, from their own hand or even from the computer. There are many easy-to-install picture frames available including *Perspex* ones with corner clips. Change the pictures as often as you or they like.

BEDS

When your child can climb out of a cot, it's time to move to a bed. Kids' beds should be firm with a soft top. The firm base keeps their spines straight and the soft top stops them from getting sore on the pressure points. Create a soft top by placing a 1cm thick sheet of foam rubber over the mattress. A lamb's wool covering is also good. Because both are washable, they're good for children with allergies.

TIP

Keep a chair beside the bed for reading bedtime stories.

What to do about bed-wetters

Many things can affect bed-wetting. One reason could be that the bladder may not be fully formed, particularly in boys. Never harass a child who wets the bed—no one wants to wet the bed. Some suggestions for dealing with it include:

Go for a walk half-an-hour before bed so fluid is pushed through the kidneys more quickly.

Don't drink before sleeping.

Put plastic underneath the sheets.

I there are continuing problems, seek medical help.

Bedding

Use 100 per cent cotton sheets and doonas and get creative with colours and designs. Kids love their beds and the doona cover should reflect their passions be it space, fairies or fish. You could even have several doona covers.

KIDS' CLOTHES

Uncomfy kids are cranky kids. Small children cannot tell you when something is uncomfortable, so feel the clothing with the backs of your hands. Roll your hands around the inside of new garments. Anything that is scratchy, itchy or rough can then be dealt with. Fix scratchy seams with iron-on hemming tape. If there's lace on fabric, it's generally overlocked with nylon thread not bound. Use cotton binding over rough areas. Because kids' skin is more sensitive, make sure your washing machine is efficient and removes as much of the washing powder as possible. Doing an extra rinse with a small quantity of white vinegar to strip out washing powder will help.

HOW TO CHOOSE CHILDREN'S CLOTHES

There's a huge range of children's clothing to choose from. To save your wallet, choose clothes with elasticised waists, tie backs and plenty of hem on skirts and trousers that will grow with children. Select clothes with deep armpits because tight sleeves restrict movement. If children want to wear tight clothes, make sure it's made of stretchy fabric that gives. Apart from *Lycra*, synthetic fibres tend to be more rigid with less room for growth. Stick to natural fibres where possible—they're easier to keep clean (and kids cannot be stain free!). Make sure long sleeves have a cuff that can be elasticised to take up the slack with fast-growing arms. Kids love colour so allow them to choose their three favourites and try to stick to that colour palette so you can mix and match.

HOW TO ORGANISE CLOTHES

If your children are posting toast into the DVD, they're ready to learn how to put clothes into drawers. Help them organise their own clothes by applying labels to the outside of drawers with the name and picture of what's in that drawer. They could even do drawings themselves. Make it a game, not a chore! And make sure you have plenty of space to store clothes: don't just stuff them into drawers.

Here's an example of how to sort a girl's clothing into easy-to-access categories: ballet and swimming gear, shorts, school stuff, socks, undies and nighties, summer shirts, winter shirts, skirts, trousers, heavy winter clothing, accessories.

Make sure hanging hooks are within reach so children can access them for hanging up clothes. Place shoes on the bottom of the wardrobe so children can reach them. Keep a rack there if possible.

HOW TO FIT CHILDREN'S SHIRTS
To select the right-sized shirt, measure from armpit seam to armpit seam and hang it in front of the child across the chest line. There should be at least 2cm extra on either armpit.

TIP
On winter mornings, place school clothes over a rack in front of the heater. Your children will dress more quickly and be more comfy.

KIDS' SHOES
Ideally, children should have four pairs of shoes, including one pair of well-supported sandals with instep and ankle buckles to allow for growth, one pair of strong trainers with plenty of toe room, one pair of strong leather shoes with room for growth in the toes and a pair of slippers that they are able to put on themselves.

HINT
HOW TO FIT CHILDREN'S SHOES
Small children aren't very good at telling you when shoes don't fit well. A way to work out if shoes are too tight is to put dark socks on the child's foot then dust the inside of their shoes with talcum powder. When you remove the shoes you will see where the pressure points are. When buying shoes, take an old pair of white socks and place some carbon paper inside the sock, carbon-side down. Then try the shoes on. The carbon paper will leave marks on the socks to show how tight the fit is. If the marks are even, the shoes fit well. If there's heavy marking in particular areas, the fit is tight and blisters will form. Wash the socks in milk to remove the carbon ink.

TIP
Many children hate having shoes fitted so take their favourite toy to distract them.

HOW TO MAKE A CAP RACK

No doubt your child has a range of caps and hats that are difficult to store. Make your own storage with some strong ribbon, braid or cord. Attach clothes pegs at even distances along the ribbon, braid or cord, knotting them as you go to keep them in place. Attach to a curtain rod or on the back of the cupboard door—anywhere that you can hang it really—then attach hats and caps to the pegs.

HOW TO CUT A CHILD'S HAIR WHEN THEY WON'T STAY STILL

Before putting your long-haired child into the chair, explain what you're about to do and why. Couch it in practical terms, such as 'See how your hair is falling into your eyes, let's fix it!'. Have a mirror so the child can see what's happening. You could also try telling the child that their hair can be given to the birds to put in their nests. Scatter the just-cut hair over the grass. Kids love the idea that they're giving something to nature. Make sure you tell them that you are the only person who is allowed to cut their hair or there may be lots of self-cutting and some large donations for the birds!

DESKS

No matter what the age, children need a desk so that they can write, read, colour-in or just play on. If they're old enough to walk, they're old enough to have a desk. Plastic desks with chairs at a suitable height are perfect and should be kept where kids play. It will help stop your child drawing on the carpet. Protect the area under the desk with heavy duty plastic sheeting, which is the perfect washable surface. (You can also protect other parts of the house, including the dining table, with plastic sheeting.)

Teach organisational strategies early. Have a large calendar in their room filled with invitations to parties, thank you notes, chores for pocket money, homework and assignment dates with completion stamps or stars to show them when each job is done. At the end of each month, count up the difference between chores and stars and give bonus points, pocket money, treats or outings. Most kids enjoy filing systems so encourage it and make those bonus points fun. Besides the obvious advantages to your kids, you may start to enjoy it yourself.

Doing homework together is a good idea. Children absorb more when they have someone to communicate with. It also keeps you up-to-date with how well they're doing academically and you might learn something as well!

HINT

HOW TO ORGANISE TOYS

Step into most children's rooms and you're confronted by a mass of toys. The challenge is how to store them all. Shannon is a big believer in clear plastic boxes with lids. She's also a big believer in the child sorting out which toys live in which boxes. Because the container is clear, they can see what's inside. But as with the clothes drawers, it's handy to have a label and picture on the outside of the container. It's a good organisational device and gets your child into good habits. Do the task together and make it a fun event. You can use all sorts of cupboards, but avoid stacking toys on bookshelves because when they're full, they fall off. Don't keep large lockable containers in children's rooms in case they get stuck.

Spray the inside of schoolbags and backpacks with *Scotchgard* for that inevitable squashed banana problem. If you have to deal with squashed banana, wipe with glycerine, leave for 20 minutes then wipe out. For banana sap, use tea tree oil.

ACTIVITY CORNER

Many parents have lost the art of keeping children entertained. There are many fun tasks and activities to keep children engaged and happy.

Under the age of 2, the simplest things will keep them entertained. Jennifer knew of one toddler who, despite being surrounded by every toy you could imagine, loved playing with coloured pegs. Saucepans and a wooden spoon are popular. You could put rice into a plastic bottle to make a shaker. There are many items around the home that can become playthings—just make sure they're not small enough to get caught in tiny throats!

From the age of 2, children become keen to explore their world. Bug and tadpole catchers are great. Buy one or make your own using a clear jar and a lid with holes punched into it. Run string around the indentation below the thread on the jar, and wrap it over the top of the lid to create a handle. Just make sure you explain why children are not allowed to shake the jar. Building blocks such as Lego are fantastic: they learn to use their hands and see how things connect.

Children love songs and stories and being involved. Add their names to their favourites. You can even have personalised story books made or create them yourself on the computer. Print out the story and use a big darning needle and wool to stitch the pages together to create a book. If you use staples, cover them with heavy duty sticky tape so children can't scratch themselves.

If your child is old enough (and not likely to get it caught in their throats) make your own popcorn and flavour it. Add herbs, spices or stock cubes to the oil and warm through before you turn the heat up and add the popcorn. Hire a DVD, pull the curtains shut, put the popcorn in beach buckets and you've created an instant movie theatre. Hot chips are another popular treat.

TECHNOLOGY

Technology is such a big part of our world now. Kids need to have access to it, but shouldn't be overloaded by it. Generally, the first piece of technology they'll use is a stereo with a cassette or CD player. These are available with large buttons for easy use. Increase their exposure with toys that use basic computer skills, such as 'speak and spell', kids' karaoke and music machines. They can then advance to small electronic games designed for children.

When your child is ready to use a computer, you can get keyboards especially for them with big buttons with pictures, faces and symbols rather than just letters. It's a great reading aid and they learn to associate by pictures and alphabet. Try asking for advice about choosing games from your local school or computer·shop. Choose age-appropriate and theme-appropriate games for your child. They have ratings for a reason! Many games are not appropriate for small children. Have a net nanny or filters installed on the computer so children don't wander into inappropriate sites. Be honest with them about the real world and teach them how to make informed choices.

COMFY CRAFT

THINGS TO DO WITH MUM AND DAD

● Laminate your children's drawings, paintings or pictures. Ask your children to choose their favourite paintings and turn them into placemats or drink coasters. ● Make teepees from canvas and bamboo poles. ● Make dolls from homemade dough and create spaghetti hair with a garlic crusher. ● Teach your children how to knit, sew or crochet.

HOW TO MAKE YOUR OWN PAINTS

Mix ½ cup cornflour with 2 cups of water in a saucepan, bring to the boil and cook until it thickens. Allow to cool, then add food colourings

HOW TO MAKE PLAYDOUGH

Sift 1 cup of plain flour, ½ cup of salt and 2 tablespoons of cream of tartar into a saucepan, gradually add 1 cup of water and 1 tablespoon of vegetable oil and stir until smooth. Add a few drops of food colouring and 2 drops of oil of cloves and cook over a medium heat, stirring constantly, for 2 minutes or until the mixture comes away from the side of the pan. Remove the pan from the heat and leave until it's just warm. Knead until it's soft and form into a ball. Store wrapped in plastic wrap or a plastic container (the oil of cloves and salt prevent it from going mouldy). Even though it looks like a lolly, kids usually won't eat it because it tastes awful. If they do like the flavour, it is non-toxic.

HOW TO CREATE A DRESS-UP BOX

Use old clothes of your own, pieces from op shops, garage sales or hand-me-downs. Keep old scarves, petticoats, shoes, belts, hats, ties and add them to the box. Dad's old shirts make perfect kings' coats. Make some props: spray paint a circle of paper gold to make a crown. Ask children to make up a story to go with their dressing up and have them act it out. Food can be organised with the theme they choose. To stop children flying off the roof when playing Superman, tell them there is only one magic cape that can make them fly and it's busy.

COMFY CRAFT

HOW TO MAKE BREAD SCULPTURES

Put a protective plastic sheet down on the floor. Get a loaf of fresh white bread and cut off the crusts. Combine 5 slices of fresh bread ripped up into small pieces, 1 teaspoon of salt, 3 drops of oil of cloves and 1 teaspoon of warm water in a bowl. Get the children to squeeze and squeeze and squeeze until the mixture looks like plasticine. You can add food colouring at this point. If you do, wash the kids' hands in white vinegar to remove it. Have a small bowl of water on hand and get the kids to shape the mixture into whatever they want. Once the creation is complete, tell them to dip their fingers in the bowl of water and then rub it over their sculpture to give it a shiny surface. Put it in the oven on the lowest temperature possible. The length of time it takes to cook will depend on how much mixture you have and how thick it is. You'll know it's ready when it's completely dry and is a very light tan colour. On average, it takes 1 hour for every 5mm in thickness. Once it's ready, remove from the oven and leave it to cool. You can paint it, varnish it, do whatever you want with it.

COMFY CRAFT

HOW TO MAKE BEADS

Follow the recipe for making bread sculptures and roll the plasticine-like mixture into round beads. Pierce a hole in the centre of each one with a bamboo skewer. Leave the bamboo skewer in the beads while baking in the oven to keep the holes clear. Remove skewers and create any jewellery you like.

HOW TO BUILD A PIXIES, FAIRIES, GNOMES AND ELVES LETTERBOX

Go to a craft or hardware store and buy a packet of coloured matchsticks and a bottle of Aquadhere or wood glue. Place a piece of paper on the work surface, show the children how to line up the matchsticks next to each other until they make a square and squeeze over some glue. Make 4 square sections for the walls and, using the same technique, make 2 rectangle sections for the roof. The roof needs to be big enough to open so little letters can be sent and received. Allow to dry. Paint the matchsticks with a mixture of 1 part Aquadhere or wood glue and 1 part water to seal.

Put the letterbox at the bottom of the garden and encourage the children to write letters to the pixies, fairies, gnomes and elves. Each day they can check the letterbox to see if the pixies have written back. There could be letters about how important it is to clean your teeth in the morning and why it's good to clean up your room, or they may contain news about how many pixie parties there have been and who was there. This encourages reading, writing and tidying the room.

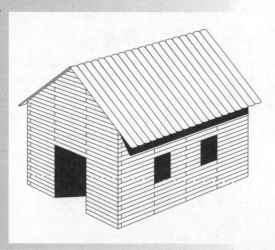

HOW TO MAKE CHRISTMAS DECORATIONS

This activity will encourage children to eat stone fruits and create Christmas decorations. Tell them to keep the stones from the fruit they eat, wash them and leave them to dry on the windowsill. Thread dried cherry pips with a bodkin needle (sharp strong needle) onto lightweight cord, heavy cotton or fishing line and paint. String them together, wipe them with vegetable oil or varnish and hang on the Christmas tree. For apricots and peaches, split the seeds down the centre and remove the kernel, leaving two hollow shells. Find some old Christmas cards and cut out images you like. Rub the outside of the shell with oil, paint or varnish. Put glue at the bottom of the inside and fix the pictures in the cave. You could even glue on a little cotton wool for Santa's beard. Glue a loop of ribbon to the top and while the glue is still wet, dust it with glitter. It's ready to hang.

HOW TO MAKE YOUR OWN GIFT-WRAPPING PAPER

Get 2 sheets of waxed paper large enough to wrap the gift. Lay 1 sheet of waxed paper on the table, then make your design on top of it. You could use leaves, pictures you've cut out, coloured cellophane, ribbons, glitter, paper stars, whatever you like as long as it's flat. Place the other layer of waxed paper on top and heat with a hair dryer. The wax will stick to form one large sheet. If wrapping items, such as fabric, use tissue paper first.

HOW TO MAKE FRIDGE MAGNETS

Use the method described for making bread sculptures. When they're ready, use Aquadhere to glue a small plastic magnet, available at craft and hardware stores, to the back of the creation, then stick them on the fridge.

HOW TO MAKE FAIRIES WITH OLD CICADA WINGS

Cicada wings don't rot and make great wings for fairies. Collect the wings, get 2 pipe cleaners and a piece of tulle. Twist 1 pipe cleaner in half and create a loop at one end for the fairy head. Make 3 twists for the body, leaving 2 loose ends for the legs. Bend the leg ends to make fairy feet. Get half a pipe cleaner and twist it once around the middle section to make the fairy arms. Wrap tulle around the middle, gathering it in at the waist to make a little skirt and attach it with glue or sticky tape. Glue a pair of cicada wings at the back, spray with hairspray and dust with glitter while the hairspray is wet. There's your fairy!

HOW TO CREATE MOULDS

Making moulds keeps children busy for hours and they can make a copy of anything they like, including their own hands. You need 1 bag of dental moulding material called *Alginate* (available from dental suppliers) and 1 bag of casting plaster. Get a plastic container and use equal quantities of *Alginate* powder and water and mix thoroughly and quickly. Place whatever you want to mould into the mixture and hold it still for about 2 minutes. You'll know when to remove it because the *Alginate* changes colour. When this happens, take the item out and leave for 5 minutes. Have another bowl with casting plaster mixed to the directions on the packet. When it's ready, pour it into the *Alginate* mould and leave it to set until hard and dry. Remove the *Alginate* mould and you're left with a copy of your item, which you can paint and varnish. They make great gifts or decorations to place on top of gifts.

HOW TO MAKE YOUR OWN PENCIL HOLDERS

Save old tin cans, wash them out, remove the labels, then spray paint them to remove sharp edges. Create your own label using words and drawings to aid learning. Keep pencils, pens, crayons, chalk or anything you like in them. They're stackable and unbreakable.

HOW TO CREATE YOUR OWN PLAY RUG

Get an old strong sheet or a length of canvas and cut it into a large square. Stitch, glue or iron on a hem around the sides. Attach a curtain ring to each corner and add 2 pieces of cotton tape to two of the rings. Design your own play rug and decorate with a box of felt-tipped pens, fabric paints or folk-art paints. You could draw a map of a town, fields, lakes, rivers or castles. Paint on some winding roads, a playground or an aquarium. Spray both sides with waterproof spray. It's very portable, creates an instant play area, protects the carpet and is easy to pack up quickly: simply pick up the rings on its corners, tie them together and it's a bundle that can be hung up. If you use folk-art paints to create your rug, allow them to dry and then turn it over and iron it to make it waterproof.

HOW TO CREATE A BUSY BOX

Create a busy box by collecting used paper towel rolls, egg cartons, pegs, pencils, odd bits of felt, glue, scissors, braid, scraps of fabric, wool, glitter, feathers, cardboard and old wrapping paper and put them in a box. When children say they're bored and have nothing to do, tell them to grab the busy box and make something. Add items to it regularly so there are new things to create.

HOW TO MAKE YOUR OWN NO-SEW RAG DOLL

COMFY CRAFT

Use scissors to shred some old cotton garments into rags. Get
2 pairs of heavy stockings (not pantyhose) or leggings in any
colour you like. Stuff the ends of the four stockings with the torn
rags and tie off tightly to the length you want for arms and legs.
Then knot the rag doll legs together and continue to knot. Do the
same with the rag doll arms and join all the ends and continue
to knot until the body takes shape. Leave one of the stocking tops
to form the head. Stuff this part with rags and tie off. Use wool on
the top for hair. Use coloured felt-tipped pens to make a face.
Dress in dolls' clothes or use a handkerchief as a sarong.

PLAY DATES

When children reach school age, it's great to organise play dates.
Begin a rotation with other parents. It's important for your child to
interact with other children: it helps them learn about manners and
how to get along with other people.

AFTERNOON SNACKS

Have children prepare simple foods that they can organise on plates
themselves. Make sandwiches and add some quirky bits like a sultana
smile on peanut butter. Make a platter with strawberries, apple,
carrot, tomatoes, banana, orange quarters, mango and watermelon.
(Many children are allergic to peanuts and strawberries, so be careful
when friends come over.) Make a salad. Carrot, zucchini and celery
sticks, sliced mushrooms, broccoli florets and dips such as hummus
or guacamole are great, too. Use cachous—the silver ball-bearing
shaped sugar balls—to decorate buttered bread or milk arrowroot
biscuits. Fairy bread is always a hit, but make sure you use butter or
the colour from the hundreds and thousands will run. Be careful with

MILKSHAKES

Half fill a jar with a sealable lid with milk. Add flavouring and ice-cream. Screw on the lid and shake until there are bubbles. Remove the lid, pop a straw in and it's ready to drink.

coloured drinks: make sure the contents are natural or you may have a tribe of hyperactive kids on your hands.

FAMILY ACTIVITIES

Being comfy is also about being happy at home. And a great way to be happy is to share experiences. Shannon often takes her family on what she calls the 'Wonder Walk'. The idea is to get a sense of wonderment and look at things differently. The way it works is to break the walk up from landmark to landmark and focus on something new each time. For a stretch, look only at the ground, then look only at the sky and see what pictures you can create in the clouds. One thing you can never talk about on a wonder walk is work.

Other family outings include a trip to the beach, a picnic, an afternoon in the park, window shopping on a hot summer's night to get a walk and cool off, an outing to the movies, bird watching, bike riding, bushwalking, backyard cricket, planting a herb garden, building something, such as a dog house, bug hunting or visiting the local library or an art gallery. There are many things to do and lots of them are free.

The Laundry

There's nothing quite like clean clothes to give you that comfy feeling. If you've got your laundry sorted, then you won't be spending more time than you need to cleaning clothes! A laundry should be a bright, airy cheerful place to work. Rips, missing buttons, holes and any other minor repairs should always be completed before washing or those minor repairs could become major ones. Always have a good-sized bin in your laundry for all the lint and rubbish that accumulates in pockets.

HOW WE USED TO KEEP COMFY FROM *PEARS' CYCLOPAEDIA 33RD EDITION* (1928)

Cream of tarter is the bi-tartrate of potash and can be used with lemon juice as a diuretic or to whiten linen.

GETTING ORGANISED

Many laundries are designed by people who don't use them, which is why they're often just a washing machine and dryer behind a cupboard door. How are you supposed to fold clothes in a cupboard? If you have a choice, opt for a good-sized laundry that is airy, has a sink, lots of bench space for baskets, easy-to-clean surfaces and good lighting. Ideally, you want a space for spot removal, washing, drying, sorting, folding and ironing. Because there's a lot of lifting and bending in this room, having a small table and chair or a stool will make it easier for you. Also, an efficient laundry keeps the rest of the house clean because you're not transferring fluff.

STORAGE

If you don't have a cupboard in the laundry, invest in a set of shelves-on-wheels to store detergent, stain-removal products, pegs and the iron. They offer storage and provide an extra work surface as well. If you have a very space-challenged laundry, attach some hooks or a hook-on shower- or laundry-tidy to the back of the door to store items.

Laundry baskets

Laundry baskets can be plastic, cane or wicker. Never have a basket that is too big to lift when full. Plastic ones are light, come in a variety of colours and are easily cleaned with a little dishwashing liquid on a damp cloth. Cane baskets are popular but wear more quickly, take less weight and, because they're unsealed, collect mould. Wicker baskets are rarely made these days but Shannon loves them because they are durable and substantial and last for generations! Wash them with salt water applied with a cloth every 2 months. When not in use, store all baskets upside down or on hooks on the wall so they don't collect dust.

Keep a hand towel in the laundry because your hands will get wet and it will save wiping your hands on your clothes! Also keep a cake of *Solvol*, the soap with pumice, in the laundry so that very dirty hands can be washed there rather than in the bathroom sink.

VENTILATION

It's important for the laundry to be well ventilated or you'll get some nasty smells. If you don't have a window in your laundry, make sure that the dryer is vented to the outside. These can be constructed with narrow ducting, even if the dryer is located on an interior wall: just make sure the ducting is above the height of the dryer because hot air rises. You may need specialist help for this.

If your dryer doesn't have an outside vent, place an open weave, commercially available filter bag over the back vent hole. It must be cleared every use or air-flow will be blocked. When you take it off, remove the lint and dust, wash the bag under running water, wring the water out then place it back again. The bag collects the fluff that would otherwise end up on the wall.

SOUND

Washing machines and dryers can be noisy. Minimise sounds by placing sponges (the ones you use in the kitchen) under the corners where they come into contact with the floor. This will reduce the echo and stop your washing machine or dryer walking across the floor! If your laundry is in a cupboard, insulate the area by attaching 5mm-thick foam sheeting along the walls with spray-on adhesive. Make sure the doors enclosing the laundry are solid and can be closed shut.

COLOUR

In order to tackle stains, you need to be able to see them, so the lighter the colour of the laundry, the better. Choose bright and fresh colours. Shannon likes white.

SINKS

Have the biggest sink that you can find in the laundry. Ideally, choose one that can fit a bucket inside it. Shannon prefers stainless steel sinks. Cement ones can wear and catch on clothes. Porcelain and plastic sinks can discolour. Choose metal over plastic plug holes because they seal better and use proper fitting plugs so water doesn't drain away when you're soaking clothes or washing by hand. Many laundry sinks have an extendable telescopic tap, which means you can top up water in the washing machine or fill a bucket without having to hoist it up and over the sink. Check yours!

HOW TO MAKE A BROOM AND MOP TIDY

COMFY CRAFT

Purchase an 'S' hook from the hardware store, lie it flat and sideways along a wooden surface—such as the back of a door—and secure it by hammering 'U' staples into place. Hang brooms in the 'S'. To secure to a wall, use the appropriate rawl plug for your wall type.

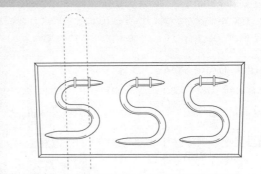

WASHING AND DRYING

Washing machines and dryers are marvellous inventions, but, because they're so easy to use, some of the finer points to looking after your clothes have been forgotten. Keep these principles in mind:

Wash at the lowest temperature that does the job. Consult the garment label. Only cotton and linen can handle very hot temperatures.

Remove stains before washing clothes. If very dirty, soak before washing.

Don't overload the washing machine or less dirt will be removed.

Know the different settings on your dryer because heat can shrink cottons, woollens and delicates. Woollens are best dried flat in the shade or on a padded hanger.

Always button shirts and stand collars up before you wash them. This holds the seam lines straight and makes folding and ironing easier. If you don't stand the collars up, you're more likely to get fraying. Hang shirts on a coat hanger rather than pegging them to the line to retain the shoulder line.

FABRIC CARE SYMBOLS
Be aware that these vary from country to country.

WASHING

95 95° cotton wash—maximum and most effective temperature

60 60°

40 40°

40 40° with bar—synthetics wash

40 40° with broken bar—wool wash

hand wash only symbol

chlorine may be used

do not use chlorine

IRONING

hot iron

warm iron

cool iron

DRY CLEANING

must be professionally cleaned

do not dry clean

DRYER

may be tumble dried

dry on high heat setting

dry on low heat setting

do not tumble dry

SORTING YOUR WASH

Before you put your clothes into the washing machine, you need to sort them. Begin by sorting into different fabric types: you don't want to wash delicates with towels, then separate whites from colours. If the household is large enough, further separate the colours. After sorting, check pockets (a stray tissue is a disaster in the washing machine), close zippers and do up buttons.

> **HINT**
>
> ## HOW TO TEST FOR COLOURFASTNESS
> If you have new clothes and you're not sure if they're colourfast, test an inconspicuous part of the garment: immerse a cloth in white vinegar and wring out, place it over the garment and iron it. Colour will transfer to the cloth if it's not colourfast. Alternatively, dampen a white cloth with white vinegar, wring out and pinch it over an inconspicuous part of the garment. The colour will transfer if it's not colourfast. Always be extra careful with red clothes!

The ideal order for washing is to begin with whites. Then wash all reds, including pinks, burgundies, browns, oranges and red-shades of purple. Because these colours are more likely to run, wash in cold water then wipe the inside of the washing machine straight after washing to capture any colour residue. Then wash greens and blues. Then any black items. Finally wash heavily soiled clothes.

Know how long it takes for your washing machine to go through its cycle so you can plan your routine around it.

FRAGRANCE FLARE-UP: Tina's question

 I'm allergic to the fragrances used in washing powder. I've tried washing with bicarb but the washing comes out grey. Is there an alternative?

 Make your own washing powder with pure soap flakes. It doesn't have any added perfumes or fragrance. Combine 1 tablespoon of pure soap flakes, the juice from 1 lemon and 2 tablespoons of bicarb in a 500ml jar of warm water and mix well. This will last for three loads of washing.

Washing towels

If you hang towels on the clothesline, wash them first because they take the longest to dry. If using a dryer, wash them last because they take the longest to dry and will delay drying your other items.

REMOVING STAINS FROM CLOTHES

Unless specified, soap refers to facial soap, not laundry soap.

Banana—wipe glycerine over the stain and leave for 15 minutes, then wash normally.

Beer (including dark beer)—paint a paste of *NapiSan OxyAction* and water on the stain and leave for 15 minutes, then wash normally.

Beetroot—wipe glycerine over the stain and leave for 15 minutes, then wash normally.

Bird droppings—wash normally.

Blood—wash fresh bloodstains in the washing machine on the cold setting. If you can't put it through the wash, use soap and water. For old blood stains, use cold water and soap and vigorously rub the stain against itself.

Carrot—wipe with methylated spirits or white vinegar and hang the item in the sun. Carrot stains respond to UV rays.

Chewing gum—harden the gum with ice and cut as much off as possible with scissors or a blade. Then apply tea tree oil with a cotton ball, sprinkle over talcum powder to absorb it and work the remaining gum out by rubbing it in circles. White spirits also works.

Chocolate—clean with soap and cold water, then clean with soap and hot water.

Chocolate ice-cream—clean with soap and cold water, rub with an old toothbrush, then wash normally.

Cooking oil—soak up as much oil as possible with paper towel, then apply a little dishwashing liquid and a little water and apply more paper towel.

Coffee/tea—for fresh stains, use glycerine applied with a cotton ball, then wash in washing powder. For old stains, use glycerine, then white spirits and detergent.

Deodorant—apply white spirits to the stain before washing. For stiffened armpits, apply a paste of *NapiSan Plus*, leave for 15 minutes and put into the wash.

Egg yolk—use facial soap and cold water first, then washing powder and warm water.

Fruit juice—wash the stain in mild detergent or white vinegar and hang in the sunshine to dry. UV light breaks down fruit colouring. For stone fruits and fruits with a high tannin, treat the stain with glycerine first.

Grass—use white spirits before washing in washing powder.

Grease—apply detergent to the stain and rub with your fingers to emulsify.

Hair dye—use white spirits or kerosene, or hairspray if you get to the stain immediately.

Ink/ballpoint pen—apply rotten milk or white spirits to the stain. Use glycerine first on red ink.

Lipstick/make-up—apply white spirits with a cotton ball.

Mascara—sponge stain with methylated spirits, then blot with paper towel.

Mayonnaise—massage a little dishwashing liquid into the stain and wash normally in cold water. The massaging is important as it emulsifies the oil and makes it water-soluble.

Milk—wash normally on the cold cycle.

Mud—for red clay mud, apply white spirits then wash. For black mud, wash in the washing machine.

Nail polish—use acetone, not nail polish remover.

Paint—for water-based paint, use methylated spirits. For oil-based paints, use turpentine.

Rust—use *CLR* or *Ranex* or lemon juice and salt.

Sap—apply white spirits or tea tree oil.

Shoe polish—use methylated spirits applied with a cotton ball. Alternatively, use eucalyptus oil applied with a cotton ball.

Soft drink—treat as though it's a fruit stain because soft drinks are coloured with vegetable dyes.

Sunscreen—massage a little dishwashing liquid into the stain, then wash with warm water.

Sweat—make a paste of *NapiSan Plus* and water, leave it on the stain for 15 minutes, then wash in the washing machine. To prevent the mark, experiment until you find a deodorant that works for you. Everyone's body chemistry is different so some people will need a deodorant and others will need an antiperspirant. Make sure your underarms have dried before putting clothes on.

Tar—apply baby oil, kerosene or white spirits.

Urine—wash normally and dry in sunshine.

Vomit—wash normally and dry in sunshine or use *NapiSan*.

Watermelon—becomes alcoholic very quickly causing a smell. Sponge with white vinegar and sprinkle over bicarb to remove the stain and the smell.

Wax—place ice on the wax and scrape as much away as possible with a blunt knife, then use white spirits and talcum powder.

Wine—for new red wine spills, absorb as much moisture with paper towel, then apply a little white vinegar. For old red wine spills, apply glycerine, then sprinkle over bicarb and detergent. Alternatively, apply methylated spirits. For white wine stains, both old and new, use white vinegar.

HOW TO MAKE WOOLLENS FEEL WONDERFUL

The best way to avoid scratchiness in your woollens is to wash them by hand in blood-heat water using cheap shampoo and hair conditioner. (Cheap shampoo and conditioner are preferable because they are made with fewer perfumes and fruit oils.) You need only a little shampoo—the size of a 20-cent coin is enough for a regular-sized jumper. To rinse, use half as much hair conditioner and add a couple of drops of lavender oil to the rinse water to deter moths and silverfish. You can use your washing machine if it has a woollens setting, but use cold water only. To avoid shrinkage, make sure the wash water and rinse water are the same temperature. Woollens should be dried flat on a drying rack or on a clean towel. Never store woollens unless they're completely dry or they will get a musty smell.

HOW TO KEEP COTTONS SOFT

Cottons can be slightly scratchy because a lot of dressing is used on them. The best way to remove this dressing is with hot water and ½ cup bicarb with the washing powder. Add ½ cup white vinegar to the rinse water (put in the fabric conditioner slot).

HINT

HOW TO WASH TRAINERS
This is not suitable for 100-per-cent-leather trainers but is fine for leather/mesh trainers. Pre-wash the trainers with soap and water, putting extra soap inside the shoe, and scrub with a small scrubbing brush or tooth brush. Place the trainers inside a pillowcase and tie closed. Put into the washing machine, adding heavily soiled items if you have any and wash on the warm setting. Dry them in the sunshine or place the trainers, still in the pillowcase, into the dryer and use the cool setting so the rubber doesn't melt.

HINT

HOW TO SHRINK OR STRETCH LEATHER SHOES
To shrink shoes, hold the shoe over a boiling kettle so the steam fills the shoe. Leave for 3–5 minutes, then place the shoes in the sunshine to dry. They'll shrink by half a size. To stretch shoes, hold the shoe over a kettle for 3–5 minutes, pack the inside tightly with newspaper or paper towel and dry in the shade.

HINT

HOW TO WASH KID GLOVES
Wash in mild, soapy, blood-heat water. Press between 2 cloths or towels to remove moisture and wear them while drying. This keeps them supple and soft.

TIP

If you've run out of shoe polish, use lemon juice and polish with wool. The lemon juice breaks down the lanolin in the wool which coats the leather. This is not a permanent fix because the leather will dry out. As an alternative, use *Vaseline* on a cloth.

HOW WE USED TO KEEP COMFY FROM *FORTUNES IN FORMULAS FOR HOME, FARM AND WORKSHOP* BY HISCOX AND SLOANE (1944)

To clean canvas shoes, use ½ ounce of soap cut in small pieces, 30 ounces of water, ½ ounce of alcohol, 1 ounce of soda, ½ ounce of liquid ammonia and 3 ounces of white chalk. Mix and paint on the canvas shoes.

HOW TO WASH A TIE

Always wash ties in cheap shampoo and blood-heat water. For greasy stains, add a little extra shampoo to the spot, then rinse with clean water and dry flat in the shade. Iron with a damp cloth over the top.

Refresh a silk tie by wrapping a damp piece of cloth over the plate of the iron and steaming over the tie.

SAUCE SPILLAGE: Tony's call to Shannon

Q: I was at lunch and spilled HP sauce on my tie. It's not a good look! What do you suggest?"

A: Apply white vinegar, then hand wash in cheap shampoo and blood-heat water. Rinse in blood-heat water and dry flat in the shade.

> **HINT**
>
> ### HOW TO WASH SOCKS
> To thoroughly clean socks, place a cake of soap inside the sock all the way to the toes, shake under running water, remove the soap and then place the sock in the washing machine. Never wash socks inside out because dirt is on the outside of the sock, not the inside.

> **HINT**
>
> ### HOW TO WASH SOFT FURNISHINGS
> Cushion covers generally use non-colourfast fabrics and need special care. If they don't have a care label on them, treat them as though they are made of silk. To wash them, use blood-heat water and a small amount of cheap shampoo, then rinse in blood-heat water. Place the cushion flat in the shade to dry. When pressing cushion covers, always use a cool iron and a clean cloth between the iron and cushion cover. Don't use starch on cushion covers because they won't mould to the shape f the cushion.

Caring for polyester

The best way to keep polyester crease-free and supple without that plastic feel is to remove it from the clothesline or dryer before it's completely dry. Air dry in the shade for the final dry. Never allow it to become bone dry in the dryer or it will shrink and go hard. If you do use the dryer, put a cotton or linen tea towel in with the garment to stop it from overheating.

CHOOSING A WASHING MACHINE

There's a lot of discussion about which kind of machine is better: the top loader or the front loader. Both have pluses and minuses, so do your homework before purchasing. Shannon prefers a top loader because she can see inside the machine and there's less bending. She also prefers white interior drums to stainless steel because stainless steel drums can rust if certain chemicals are used. Front loaders, on the other hand, take up less space and are more water efficient. The other consideration in choosing a washing machine is how many revolutions there are per minute for the spin cycle: the more, the better. Make sure the washing machine has an accessible lint filter. Purchase the biggest washing machine for the space: you can alter the water level depending on the size of the load; overloading a small washing machine will wear out the motor more quickly and will not wash your clothes properly.

Take time to read the operating instructions for your washing machine. Find out how many kilograms of dry clothing and wet clothing make up a minimum water level wash load and for how long the spin cycle runs. Establish whether you can run the spin cycle separately, which is particularly useful for removing excess water from hand-washed garments, such as woollen jumpers, before drying.

Another important factor in the efficient operation of your washing machine is to make sure it's positioned on a flat surface. This will save wear and tear on the machine because the drums and belts will move in exactly the axial orientation they were designed to. To check the area, you'll need a spirit level. Place the spirit level north, south, east, west and diagonally on the machine. If they are not level, vary the feet until they are. If you have non-moveable feet, put a heavy waterproof board under the entire washing machine so that all four feet are covered. Then put a chock, such as a folded kitchen sponge which absorbs vibrations, under the board until it's all level. Never chock only one foot because the vibration of the machine can knock it off.

TIP

If you use liquid washing detergent, transfer from the refill pack to the bottle using a plastic funnel.

HINT

HOW TO GET A MUSTY SMELL OUT OF THE WASHING MACHINE

When moisture is trapped, mould forms and the seals on washing machines are the perfect environment for mould to thrive. To clean your seals, wrap a tea towel over a knife. Sprinkle a little bicarb over the tea towel, add a little white vinegar and work the blade of the knife into the crevices of the seal. In a spray bottle, add 1 litre of water and $1/4$ teaspoon of oil of cloves and spray into the same crevices. Oil of cloves kills mould spores.

Fixable problems with the washing machine

If the machine fills with water but the agitator doesn't work, the belt drive needs to be replaced. If the water doesn't empty, it's a pump or plumbing problem. If it doesn't spin, it needs new bearings. In each case, call a professional. Something you can replace yourself is the hose. These are available from a hardware store or an appliance centre. You'll know it's time for new washing machine hoses or seals when you get black spots on your clothes.

CHOOSING A DRYER

There are two main types of dryer: vented or condenser. Vented dryers work by circulating hot air through clothes to dry them. Condenser dryers work by removing moisture through latent heat. Choose whatever suits you. Just make sure the dryer has a safety trigger so it won't catch on fire. Fire authorities recommend that you don't leave a dryer on if you're not at home because they can catch on fire. That's why the safety trigger is so important.

Shannon avoids machines that combine the washing machine and dryer in one because if it breaks down, you can't wash or dry.

Fixable problems with the dryer

If the dryer stops producing heat, the element is damaged. If it stops spinning but still produces warm air, the belt drive needs to be replaced. If the dryer needs to be reset all the time, the filter is clogged or the fuses are worn. In each case, call a professional.

Always ask the repairer to explain what was wrong so you'll know for next time. It also guards against overcharging.

MAINTENANCE

It's best to buy a washing machine that has a lint filter because it increases the washing efficiency. Clean the filter every two washes or after washing red items. In a top loader, the filter is located either on top of the agitator or in a little bag on the side of the drum or you may have an automatic lint cleaner which means you don't have to clean it. In front loaders, the lint catcher is usually near the door or at the back of the machine. Consult the instruction manual to find out the configuration of your machine.

You'll increase the life of your washing machine and dryer if you have them serviced every 12 months—and you'll reduce those awful downtimes when the dryer or washing machine aren't working properly. Keep information about the service near the machines for future use. Ideally, build a relationship with your maintenance provider. If they know there's going to be ongoing maintenance on your machines, they'll be more likely to keep a stock of necessary parts.

TIP

To dry trousers more quickly, hang them from the bottoms of the legs over two lines. Get the cuff of one trouser leg and peg it to one line so the inside and outside leg seams are lined up. Peg the second leg on the next line in the same way. This holds the trousers in a funnel shape that draws air up through them to dry them faster.

HINT

HOW TO HANG GARMENTS ON THE CLOTHESLINE
It's important to hang clothes as flat as possible on the
clothesline so that there's minimal creasing. Shannon's mum
taught her to repeat the phrase 'I hate ironing' while hanging
out the clothes to remind her to hang them as flat as possible!
Hang each item by the strongest section of the garment. Trousers
and skirts should be hung from the waistband. If not on coat-
hangers, shirts should be hung from the tails and pegged on the
side seams. You'll have less ironing if the shirts are buttoned up.
Woollens are best dried lying flat on a white towel (to avoid
colour transference). Towels should be hung over the line in half
so that the edges sit against each other: they'll take longer to dry,
but will be fluffier. Hang tablecloths, sheets and doona covers in
a 'U' shape between two lines to avoid creases. Hang T-shirts
from the armpits. Hang undies from the waistband side seams.
Hang socks from the tops so you don't get holes in the toes.
Don't leave linen, silk and lace on the clothesline when windy
because the fibres can knot.

IRONING

CHOOSING AN IRON

An iron should be light, have steam and dry functions, a variable
temperature, visible water reservoir, steam burst and water spray and
automatic switch off. Shannon also prefers a cordless iron because
there's less drag on your arm. Non-stick *Teflon* irons have become
popular, but are harder to keep clean, scratch easily and leave a
bigger scorch mark if you have the wrong temperature setting. You
can buy silicone covers for irons and while they may glide over
clothing, you can't always use the steam function with them.

CHOOSING AN IRONING BOARD

It's worth buying the best ironing board you can afford: cheap ones don't last and can be annoying to use.

Ironing board checklist:

Easy release mechanism.

Lightweight.

Flat surface.

Variable height.

Slides or wheels for storage.

The padding underneath the ironing board cover can be made of hessian or *Teflon* padding. *Teflon* is better because it reflects heat back through the board and makes ironing quicker. Hessian tends to harbour bacteria because it creates a hot, moist atmosphere. If there's a musty smell when you iron, it's time to replace the hessian padding. Wash ironing board covers in the washing machine. Change them once a year.

HOW TO IRON

First, consult the care label on the garment to find out how hot the iron should be. It's a good idea to begin ironing clothes that require the least amount of heat and work your way up—that way you avoid scorching your clothes. No clothes look good with iron marks on them! As a general rule, iron the least important part of the garment first because you're more likely to crease that part as you move the garment around. Iron the most important part last—the most important part is what people see the most.

If you're in a hurry or can't be bothered to iron, try the bachelor's ironing technique. Hang the garment in the bathroom while you're showering. When you put it on, the heat from your body will interact with the slightly damp garment and creases will disappear. Of course, it's not as good a finish as ironing can achieve. Another way to smooth your clothes without using an iron is to fill a spray bottle with 1 litre of water and $\frac{1}{2}$ teaspoon of lavender oil and spray it over your clothes before you put them on. Shannon loves using this technique: it removes creases and it keeps mozzies and flies away!

Always iron in the direction of the grain, rather than on the cross.

The steam jets in your iron may become clogged with mineral deposits. Clean them by filling with equal parts white vinegar and water. Let the mixture sit for 1 hour, then empty it out and rinse with clean water.

SHIRTS

Is there a definitive way to iron a business shirt? Jennifer casually asked several people for their ironing techniques and uncovered an incredible level of passion on the topic. Everyone believes their technique is correct and has arguments to support their view. The big dispute lies in whether you iron the collar first or last.

Andy (taught by the family ironing lady, Mrs Donnelly)—iron the collar first, because, unlike the rest of the shirt, it doesn't crush. Next iron the cuffs, arms and the yolk, then iron the entire body of the shirt starting with the right panel.

Tony (taught while in the British Army)—iron the yolk first, then the back, the sleeves, the front and the collar last.

Lou—iron the collar first and last.

Jason—iron the back of the collar, then the yolk, then inside each cuff then the outside each cuff. Iron both sides of the arms, then iron the body of the shirt, starting on the front left-hand side and working around. Jason is big on steam.

And finally, **Shannon's approach**—iron the back of the shirt first, including both sides of the yolk and over the shoulders, then iron the sleeves front-side up from the seam line down to the cuff. Iron the inside of the button and buttonhole tabs, then the outside of each shirt front, always pressing the pocket from the bottom to the top. Iron the cuffs, then iron the back of the collar. Hang immediately on a coat-hanger.

> Many blokes get their business shirts laundered professionally. It is a convenient option, but be aware that the detergents are harsher and the temperatures higher than those used at home so your shirts won't last as long.

MELTED MESS: Tom's question

 I ironed a shirt that had some nylon in it and, as you can imagine, the nylon melted and became stuck all over the iron. Can I get it off or do I need to get a new iron?

 Make sure the iron is cold. Apply some bicarb to the nylon mark, then spray some vinegar over the top. When fizzing, scrub with some pantyhose, then wipe over with a little glycerine. Before using the iron again, make sure you clean the jets by pushing steam through them.

Trousers

Hold the trousers from the bottom cuffs so they hang and line up the seams, stitch line to stitch line. Shake the trousers and run your hand down the middle of the legs so they straighten. Place the trousers on the ironing board with the cuffs closest to the wide end of the board and the waistband at the pointy end. Fold the top leg in half towards the waistband and fold again from the knee to the waistband so the inside surface of the lower leg is displayed. Run the iron along the inside seam, up the inside panel and then iron the front panel. Repeat on the other side, then iron the whole length on the outer side. Finally, place the waistband of the trousers over the pointy end of the board and iron.

HOT IRON: Chris's call to Shannon

 Q: I have two pairs of reasonably expensive trousers that I have marked with a too-hot iron. One is brown rayon/nylon, the other black rayon/polyester/lycra. Is there any hope?

A: Unfortunately, if the fibres have been charred then parts of the fibres are missing, not just stained, which will appear as a distinct colour difference. If, however, they are only singed, you can remove the stain by wringing out a cloth in a 3 per cent hydrogen peroxide solution. Lay the cloth over the scorched stain and iron with a cool iron. If the mark comes out, it's a singe, otherwise it's permanently charred. Be careful when setting the iron temperature: more heat doesn't iron the garment faster.

Skirts

The technique used will depend on the kind of skirt you're ironing, but generally, place the skirt inside out over the pointy end of the board so the hem is closest to the square end. Iron the seams first, ironing from the zipper at the rear or side of the skirt moving it towards you from the hem to the waistband. Work around, then iron all the way around the outside of the skirt. Finally, iron the waistband.

FOLDING

T-shirts

These are better folded than ironed. Hold the T-shirt at the sleeves and tug sideways to remove peg marks, then pull down from the shoulder. Place the T-shirt face down on a flat surface, fold the shoulders towards the centre back, then fold the bottom towards the top. Always remove T-shirts from the clothesline when they are just dry. Don't leave them to bake in the sun because they'll become scratchy and out-of-shape.

Knickers

Hold knickers by the waistband, laying the gusset flat. Fold one side towards the centre, the other side towards the centre, then fold the gusset over the two. Never fold knickers in half because it wears out the gusset.

Socks

Smooth the heel, place your finger on the seam and fold in half. Fold both socks over in one motion so the heel line is on top.

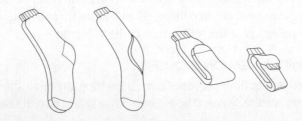

DRY CLEANING

Some fabrics require dry cleaning because water can swell or shrink fibres and affect dyes. Dry cleaning uses liquid chemicals, such as perchlorethylene or white spirits, to remove dirt. Here are some things to consider with dry cleaning:

If there's a stain on your garment, let the dry cleaner know so they can spot clean it. Stains are much harder to remove once heat has been applied.

If clothes have a sour smell after dry cleaning, go somewhere else.

Remove the plastic from the dry cleaner as soon as possible to allow the fabric to breathe. Plastic is high in acid and can leave yellowing marks and cause garments to sweat.

Remove pins or staples because they can rust into the fabric— and rust is very difficult to remove. Ask dry cleaners to use nylon staples or pegs instead.

MENDING

The fact that new clothes come with spare buttons and thread suggests some people still know how to do basic mending. Don't throw those spare buttons away, keep them in a button box. If throwing out worn garments, cut the buttons off and store them in your button box—you never know when they may come in handy.

MEASURING A HEM ON TROUSERS

You will need help from someone else to position the pins. Stand in the trousers with shoes on. The trousers should reach to the base of the toe line (where the shoe upper touches the sole of the shoe at the toe). Place the first pin at the centre-front of each trouser leg, then pin both centre backs, then remove the trousers. Use a ruler or straight edge to line up other pin points. Place the first 4 pins in this order. Front, rear, inside seam and outside seam. Mark the remaining points with chalk, then fold and pin halfway across the fold. Press the new hem into position with an iron. Chalk the line. Then fold to the chalk line. Fold the top of the fabric over to create reinforcement, then press with an iron. Place pins at the top and sew your hem. Herringbone stitch is recommended.

SEWING A HEM

Sewing is not as hard as you might think. The most common stitches to use are herringbone stitch, running stitch and slip stitch. Here are some basic techniques:

Herringbone stitch

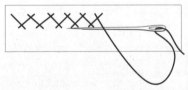

This stitch is strong without causing puckering. Start with 3 back stitches over 4 threads. That means you run the needle and thread over the starting spot three times across four threads. Make a stitch 5mm along the fabric, then stitch backwards so you create the effect of a fish skeleton.

Running stitch

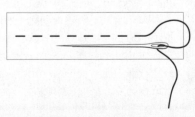

This stitch will show, so use coloured thread to make a feature of your sewing or use a perfectly matching thread to make the stitches disappear. Run a threaded needle through the hem and fabric and weave from one side to the other.

Slip stitch

Make a back stitch between the fold of
the hem and the body of garment, then
make a vertical stitch, sliding the
needle in the fold of the hem towards
you. Make another small backstitch
5mm along the hem, then slide the
needle in the fold of the hem towards

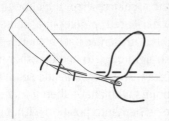

you. The stitch lines up with the fibres of fabric and is best for trousers.

Emergency hem

A safety pin can be used to temporarily hold up a hem until you can
get out the repair kit. Carry some double-sided tape, or Hollywood
tape, in your handbag for emergencies. Another option is to use hem
tape—a fabric strip with an adhesive—which can last for up to six
washes. When it comes to repair time, stitch directly over the top of
the tape and use it as reinforcement.

TIP

To remove a hemline when you're letting down clothes, apply
white vinegar with a cloth on the outside and inside of the
hemline, then iron with a warm iron.

HINT

HOW TO MAKE AN EXTRA DART

Put the garment on inside out and evenly fold the fabric where
you want it to be tighter. Put a line of pins down this point making
sure you place the darts evenly on either side of the waistline.
Check that the side seams are evenly aligned. Use a running
back stitch or a sewing machine to put the dart in place. You
can also use this technique to reduce the cup size of a blouse.

HOW TO FIX A TEAR IN A DRESS

First, use matching cotton to reinforce the edge of the tear so that it won't fray by making tiny running stitches every second thread around the entire edge of the tear. Then start the needle from the back of the fabric and stitch the fabric together as though you are threading a lace on a shoe. Alternatively, use iron-on Vylene—a great emergency patch fabric—which is very light, fine and lasts for 3–4 washes. Cut a section, apply it to the back of the tear and make your repair stitches over the top of it.

For a three-cornered tear, apply iron-on adhesive on the underside of the patch so that it's flat and reinforce the fabric with tiny running stitches.

  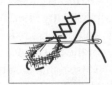

HOW TO PUT A HOLE IN A LEATHER BELT

Place a metal kitchen skewer on a stove until hot. Hold the belt over a ridge at the kitchen sink and push the hot skewer through the belt. Using a hot metal skewer means you don't end up with a shaggy edge to your hole and you don't stretch the leather out of shape.

To repair a hole in a jumper, reweave using a bodkin. A bodkin is a large needle with a slightly rounded point that won't tear the wool.

SEWING ON BUTTONS

For buttons with 4 holes, sew diagonally each way 10 times then do a
back stitch into the fabric behind the button. If the fabric is thick,
wind the thread around the back of the button 12 times then
backstitch 3 times. This raises the button so that when you place the
thick fabric over the button, it doesn't pucker.

WEDDING DRESS RESCUE: Sally's question

Q: My mother got married in the 1960s in a beautiful
dress which became part of the kids' dress-up box.
It's made of silk and covered in mould and dirt
spots. Can it be rescued?

A: Try this solution: get a large lidded box and half fill it with
clean kitty litter. Place a piece of plastic over the kitty litter
and punch small holes across it. Then place the dress on top
of the plastic. Place the lid on the box and leave for 3 days.
This should absorb the moisture that is causing the mould.
Hang the dress in the sunshine and brush the mould with a
stocking toe filled with coarse salt. This acts like a big eraser.
The salt will help prevent further mould spores.

HINT

HOW TO DARN A SOCK

Use matching or contrasting cotton or wool and thread onto a
needle. Make a running stitch around the hole to prevent it from
fraying. Place a darning egg—if you don't have one use a boiled
egg or a light bulb—in the sock so that you have a curve edge to
follow. Starting from one side of the hole, weave to the other side,
pick up a woven stitch and weave back to the other side of the hole.
Do this in both directions until the hole is completely covered. To finish
off, weave the thread away from the hole for about 2cm and cut. Do
not back stitch or knot as these make uncomfy lumps in your socks.

HINT

HOW TO SHORTEN A SLEEVE
Unpick both stitch lines along the join between cuff and sleeve. Place the cuff on the wrist in the required position over the top of the shirtsleeve. Put a line of pins around the shirt sleeve where the cuff touches it. Remove shirt and cut, following the line of pins and allowing sufficient seam to fit into the unpicked cuff line. Pin and stitch—by hand using a running backstitch or with a sewing machine—the cuff in place.

TIP

Everyone should have a quick-unpick: a double-pronged implement with one side that's very sharp and cuts through stitches very quickly.

HINT

HOW TO REPAIR LACE
For an instant lace repair, apply spray adhesive to medical gauze and press it across the back of the lace. When you come to do the repair properly, stitch the gauze into the lace and it becomes reinforcement. Always keep old lace because you never know when you may use it again.

TIP

If you don't have a needle threader on hand, use a piece of fuse wire.

TIP

If you get a ladder in your stockings while you're out, repair it using a piece of your hair as thread. You should always carry a needle in your handbag.

TIP

To straighten wool that's crinkly and out of shape, wrap it around a large piece of heavy cardboard, such as a cereal box, hold it over a steaming kettle until the wool is damp but not wet, leave it to dry on the cardboard and then roll it into a ball ready to reuse.

TIP

To cover up moth holes in clothing, embroider a grub rose or a little flower over it. One of Shannon's sisters saves embroidered logos such as penguins or crocodiles to stick over holes.

TIP

To clean a leather jacket, wipe it with soft cloth and Vaseline.

TIP

Labels on the inside of clothes are generally very uncomfortable and scratchy. Shannon removes hers. If you wish to resell your designer label clothes when you've finished with them, save the labels. That way you can replace the label when you're ready to sell the clothes. Care labels can also be scratchy but contain useful information. Either trim the edges of the label to remove the coarse edge or cut the label off and stick it into a book in case you need to consult it for washing instructions.

LINEN CUPBOARD

When Shannon is feeling miserable, she sorts out her linen cupboard. This is a great form of therapy because the items feel, look and smell lovely and it's very satisfying when the cupboard is neatly organised.

A linen cupboard should be in a dry, cool, airy place. Choose solid

doors with a vent rather than glass or open doors because linen is
affected by sunlight. If you don't have space for a linen cupboard,
create one using flat packs available from hardware stores.

Fold sewing fabric flat and store it in the linen closet to keep it
bug free. Never store medicine in the linen cupboard because the
smell will leach into your linen. Store antique linen in acid-free tissue
paper or in clean old pillowcases. All linen should be stored as
though it were antique because one day, it could be!

To sort out your linen cupboard, begin by laying down acid-free
shelf-liners.

HOW TO MAKE SHELF-LINERS

Buy some acid-free paper from a newsagent. Fill a spray bottle
with warm water, add 1 tea bag and leave for 3 minutes.
Remove the tea bag and add a couple of drops of oil of cloves
and some of your favourite perfume or essential oils, then spray
over the paper. Allow the paper to dry, then cut it to size. Replace
shelf-liners once a year. You can also make your own paper
lace to dress the edges of rough shelves. Place some butchers'
paper or some other acid-free paper over the shelves with a
portion hanging over the edge and cut scallops along them.

Store excess soap in the linen cupboard to scent the linen and keep
bugs out. Don't forget to add cloves, lavender, bay leaves or camphor
to deter silverfish and moths.

How you arrange your linen cupboard is determined according to
your needs and desires. You could store tea towels here or in the
kitchen. You could sort sheets by sets or types. The important thing is
to have a system so you can find what you need when you need it.
Keep the most-used items at the easiest access spot. Hone your
folding skills to maximise shelf space and decrease the wear on the

fabric. Rather than folding items over and into each other, fold them backwards and forwards in a concertina pattern. For example, with a towel, fold it in half lengthways, then fold it in half across. And rather than folding it to the centre and then folding it over again, fold the top over and the bottom under to form a zigzag. Either end of the towel will be exposed.

HINT

HOW TO FOLD A FITTED SHEET

Folding fitted sheets used to drive Shannon crazy until her mum showed her this technique. Lay the sheet down inside out so that the elastic is on the top and the seams are showing. Slide one hand inside each corner peak on one edge of the sheet with your forefingers in the peaks. Point your forefingers at each other and flip one wrist over the other so you have 2 layers of fabric on one hand with the seams lined up. The outer section is the right way out, not inside out anymore. Do the same on the other end and you'll have a flat side with the elastic showing but the seam no longer showing. Face the edges towards the centre so it's nice and smooth and the elastic forms an internal frill. Then fold end-to-end with the elastic hidden inside.

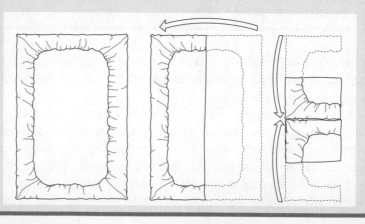

HINT

HOW TO FOLD PILLOWCASES, TEA TOWELS AND TOWELS

Fold pillowcases into sixths rather than eights. Make one fold line down the centre of the pillowcase, then fold one end in by a third, then fold the other end to the other side by a third. Fold tea towels into eights. Fold towels into sixths. These are the sizes that fit best on a standard shelf. If your shelf isn't standard-sized, organise the folds accordingly.

HINT

HOW TO FOLD SHEETS AND TABLECLOTHS

For tablecloths and sheets, fold in half and half again. Then fold one end to the centre, turn it over and fold the other end to the centre. That way you never have more than four layers of fabric. It's easier to store, puts less pressure on the fibres and it's easier to put on the bed. If items are left folded in the cupboard for a long time, turn the fold to the other side to remove pressure on the fibres.

HINT

HOW TO STORE BLANKETS AND DOONAS

Store them in acid-free bags or old pillowcases. If space is at a premium, you can use air-expulsion bags, dry cleaning or garbage bags with the air removed. Fold blankets and doonas according to the size of the shelf using the fan pattern—this means you won't get bulk at one end—then place inside the bag.

Outside

In some homes, the outside is the new inside! The distinction between the two zones has become blurred and in the warmer months, traffic flows seamlessly from one area to the other. Your outdoor area could be landscaped by professionals with elaborate decking, stonework and plants or you may have a handkerchief-sized patch of lawn. The good news is you don't need to have a huge outdoor area to enjoy it. Furniture can be as simple as a bench made from an old door placed on two sturdy stools. Throw over a cloth and it's a dinner table. Throw over a blanket and it's a cubbyhouse. It can even be the score table for cricket, football or basketball games. However you decide to use this area, we have plenty of comfy tips.

How we used to keep comfy from *Fortunes in Formulas for Home, Farm and Workshop* by Hiscox and Sloane (1944)

To remove moths and caterpillars: mix 200 parts of venice turpentine, 1000 parts of rosin, 140 parts of turpentine, 80 parts of tar, 500 parts of lard, 240 parts of rape oil, 200 parts of tallow and spread over the areas affected by insects.

GETTING ORGANISED

Your outdoor area can be used for many different functions. In addition to hanging out the washing, you can create a workspace, a picnic space, a sporting field, a playground, a magical garden, an oasis, an entertainment area and somewhere to recharge the batteries. Some of these uses will overlap, but some will need to be quite separate.

A good first step is to do a landscaping plan. Use a sheet of graph paper and draw the outline of the house, driveway and other fixed markings. Think about where the sun shines at different parts of the day and what kind of effect you're after. If putting in a shed, place it on a level surface, preferably cement. Never put metal directly onto dirt because you can get white ants and bugs. Notice if the wind is an issue. Then get advice from a nursery about which trees or plants work best according to the sun, shade, water usage and wind protection you want. They'll also give advice on water-saving solutions, such as mulch and crystals. Think about colour and fragrance. Shannon loves fragrant gardens with herbs, bush violets and boronia planted along pathways, because, as you brush past them, they release a fragrance. Natives also make huge sense in the Australian climate, but choose the right natives for your climate and soil type.

TIP

Find out what grows well in your neighbours' gardens and use that as a starting point.

COMFY CRAFT

HOW TO MAKE A MAT WITH A SCOURER

Attach a scourer to the corner of a copra or rubber mat with some strong twine and a bodkin (a needle with a rounded point). The scourer helps remove stubborn dirt from the bottom of shoes.

SUN AND SHADE

In working out how to use your outdoor zones, think about sun and shade. There are days when you crave sunshine, but in the heat, you want to retreat to the shade. Umbrellas and shade cloths can help vary the amount of sun you allow into an area. If, on the other hand, your backyard, for instance, doesn't get much sun, you can place a mirror at the bottom of a water feature. You can't keep fish in it because of the heat, but it works well for increasing the sense of light. Underwater spotlights are another option.

If trees are the reason for your shady garden, think about cutting back some of the branches, if it complies with council regulations. If there is an issue with a neighbour about excess foliage, politely raise the issue with them. They could be unaware that their hedge turns your kitchen into a dungeon by early afternoon. You may be able to cut some small 'windows' in the hedge so light can get in but privacy isn't disturbed. They may be happy to install lattice with a vine that lets in more light.

LIGHTING

Outdoor lighting has the dual purpose of illuminating the area and providing security. The ability to see outside in the dark is important for safety, even if you only use decorative lighting on the edges of garden beds, pathways or steps. There are a range of options including spotlights, solar-powered lights and sensor lights from which to choose.

Lighting is very important when entertaining outside, too. Be careful with spotlights: they can make guests feel like bunnies caught in the headlights on high beam. Instead, think about using them as an uplight and position them so that light bounces up a tree or along a wall. That way no one has to look directly at the hot spot. Fairy lights are great—you can string them on trees, around doors, windows and verandahs and even hang them from the clothesline.

To create mood lighting, use votive candles in small glasses. They can be hung from trees as long as the flames can't touch leaves or branches. Make sure the sides of the glasses are high enough so the candles can't be blown out by the wind. Jennifer went to a party that had many Chinese lanterns lit by candles hanging in the backyard that created a beautiful effect.

HOW TO MAKE YOUR OWN PAPER LANTERNS

Buy paper bags in different colours and buy sand from toy stores, hardware stores or garden supplies. (Don't go to the beach and take some because it's illegal.) Place the sand in the paper bag, fold back the top to make a cuff to the height of the sand and wedge a tealight candle in the sand—**make sure the flame and paper don't come into contact**. The light from the candle glowing through the paper bag creates some surprising colour mixes: brown paper bags tend to glow orange, blue bags glow jade, yellow looks almost white and white can look olive.

COMFY CRAFT

Another way to decorate the outdoor area for entertaining is to use coloured light bulbs. Choose red for wild, blue for ethereal and pink for fairy parties. When hanging lights overhead, make sure that they are hung at a height so the tallest person can raise their hand and not touch it—the gesticulation factor has to be taken into account.

A swimming pool can become part of your decoration statement. At Shannon's niece's twenty-first birthday, holes were cut into sheets of polystyrene foam, tealight candles were placed inside the foam and flowers were used to decorate and cover any exposed foam. This gorgeous floral island was then floated across the pool. Source polystyrene from rubber supply stores. Wrap tree trunks in tulle or foil and spray paint them gold or any colour you like. It creates a reflective surface for light and is an elegant decorative touch.

WORKSPACE

The best kind of workspace is a shed or garage with built-in shelves and a workbench. If you don't have a dedicated shed, don't worry, it's easy to create a sturdy benchtop and make a place for your tools. One of the simplest ways to do this is to obtain portable weather-proof cupboards. These cupboards on castors are made of enamelled metal and have doors at waist height. They are lockable and safe to leave outside. You can get lightweight plastic, but it will deteriorate under the sun.

> Look out for old tin chests available at second-hand dealers or at council clean ups. They last for years and can hold a huge amount. If storing them outside, paint with rustproof paint. If you stack them they take up less floor space. Attach a label so that you know what's inside.

An easy way to keep a workspace tidy is to use a groundsheet. Make one yourself: get an old sheet and mix equal parts water-based paint and water, then paint this over the sheet to make it waterproof. When working, weight the corners of the groundsheet with something like a pot plant. Make sure there's a facility to wash your hands. This could be as simple as a bucket with water in it. Have towels and rags handy in case there are any spillages. When working, clear items away once you've finished using them so they won't get damaged.

> Never work with grease when washing is on the clothesline.

TOOLBOX

You can't expect to be comfy if you don't have a toolbox. In our travels we noticed a bright pink toolbox designed especially for women. You could lash out and buy something like that, but it's very easy to make up your own. Shannon has an exhaustive array of tools so she always has the right tool for the job. The essentials include:

Screwdrivers—both Phillips head and flathead in a variety of sizes with non-conductive handles (some of the cheap ones are conductive);

Hammers—tack hammer for light work, ballpein hammer, claw hammer and lumpy hammer, heavy and soft;

Pliers—needle-nosed, electricians pliers;

Side cutters—for cutting wire;

Stanley knife—and extra blades;

Rulers, levels and set square;

Fasteners, screws, nails and bolts—you can buy a set of oddments from hardware stores;

Shifting spanners—small and large;

Drills—small hand-held electric drill and bits;

Saws—hacksaw and Japanese saw for small jobs.

Involve the children by getting them their own toolkits. **Always remember, safety first!**

UNWANTED MANURE: Fiona's question

 My husband stained his jeans and shirt with cow poo. How do you get it off?

 Mix *NapiSan Plus* with just enough water to make a paste the consistency of butter. Paint it over the stain and leave for 10–15 minutes, then place in the washing machine. Hang out the items in sunshine—it will break down grass, a key part of a cow's diet—to dry. For any remaining stains, apply white spirits with a cotton ball.

PICNIC SPACE

Break the household routine! Instead of going out to a park or beach, create a space for picnics in your garden. The picnic could be held at a table or on stretched-out rugs. The food can be anything from simple salads to more complicated fare. The great thing about a picnic at home is the toilet and bins are never far away!

If you decide to position your picnic on the lawn, make sure you have a suitable groundcover. Include a good-sized tablecloth that's easy to wash—and increase the comfy factor by adding outdoor cushions. Always have an umbrella or other shade cover on hand and don't forget the insecticide and sunscreen. And, of course, you'll need cutlery, china and plastic ware.

If you buy a pre-cooked chicken, have it cut at the shop—they have special shears for the job—it will save you a lot of hassle.

A backyard picnic is the perfect venue for eating messy fruits, such as watermelon and mangoes. There are no issues spitting the pips out on the lawn! Other waste isn't as easy to dispose of so have a garbage bag within easy reach. It's also a good idea to keep a bucket of water handy for carrying dirty dishes back to the kitchen. That way they're already rinsed!

For any kind of picnic, always take a chopping board for people to sit their glasses on.

Music is often a welcome addition to a picnic. Make sure it's only background music and keep the volume unobtrusive. You want to be able to have a conversation and you don't want to irritate the neighbours!

TIP

Never wear white trousers at a picnic.

SPORTING FIELD

Who doesn't have fond memories of playing backyard cricket? The
ability to turn your backyard into a sporting venue is important for
children, but given that there are lots of objects being thrown around,
take steps to guard against breakages. Protect your windows and
garden with a sporting screen. These look like a flat trampoline and
are easy to put up, pull down and store away. Another organisational
factor to consider when creating the sporting field is having a place
to store equipment. Not only does it mean the area is kept tidy, you
won't get a trail of dirt through the house. Use plastic containers, if
away from the sun, or metal containers, if in the sun.

PLAYGROUND

If you're creating a play area for kids, make sure it's safe. It should be
enclosed and use equipment that has passed Australian safety
standards. When standing next to a slippery dip, a child should be
able to reach the base of the starting platform with the tips of their
fingers standing on tippy toes. An area with a sandpit is great for a
playground. To deter cats, bury some mothballs around the edges or
paint under the lip with *Vicks VapoRub* or cover it when not in use.
Large shell-shaped containers, available from toy stores, are handy
for this and can be converted into a paddling pool. **No matter the
depth of water, children should never be left unattended.**
Never overload the area with so much equipment that there's no
room for the kids to run around.

COMFY
CRAFT

HOW TO MAKE A TYRE SWING

If you have a strong tree, find a secure branch and tie over two equal lengths of hemp rope (as thick as your thumb). Get an old tyre from your local garage, scrub with a heavy salt solution: 1kg of salt to a bucket of water. In a narrow area, attach rope to two points on the tyre and secure either side to the nearest sturdy wall or fence. It will only swing in one direction. If you have a larger area, tie through the tyre. Make sure there's sufficient space in the yard to swing around. To make a soft swing, use two inner tubes. Tie each rope to an inner tube in a figure of eight loop and knot it in the centre to make a seat.

MAGICAL GARDEN

Most people respond well to a bit of greenery in the backyard. If you
have children, give their imagination some space by having at least
one corner of the garden that is wild. We don't mean wild as in
unkempt, but wild as in a place where butterflies and other natural
delights can be found. Kids are enthralled by wildlife, especially
insects and birds. Shannon has a spot in her garden with a fairy path
made of pebbles and a fairy letter box. If you don't have space for a
garden, create one with pot plants: there's less weeding and you can
change the look of the area with some simple rearranging.

When planning a garden, sit down and think about what you like.
Take a walk around your neighbourhood and see which gardens
appeal to you. If you have a small garden and want to make it seem
bigger, add a *trompe l'oeil* (a mural designed to trick the eye into
seeing something that isn't really there) or place mirrors along one
wall, although make sure that they are not in direct sunlight because
the sun will shine in your eyes. When placing a mirror on a wall,
angle the top of the mirror from the wall by 15 degrees, so that the
sun can't bounce onto the mirror and into your eyes. Soften the
mirror effect by arranging pot plants in front.

Statues and sculptures are a great decorative option. Think about
using found objects such as an old bucket or plough—just make sure
people won't injure themselves on it.

TIP

Avoid gravel pathways. They may look attractive but are very
impractical and hard to walk on because they have an uneven
surface and need to be topped up. The gravel also travels into
the garden and house.

INSECT-REPELLING GARDEN

You can use herbs to deter insects, such as bees and flies. In a spray bottle of water, add 1 roughly crushed garlic clove or 1 large chilli sliced lengthways or ½ a sliced onion. Spray it over areas of the garden that attract bees and flies. Add mint leaves to the bottle for extra repellent properties. Spray the garden with chamomile tea—it's a good all-round insect repellent for plants. Plant basil, pennyroyal or tansy around the barbecue area to ward off mozzies. Grow tansy, garlic and marigolds under fruit trees to inhibit insects attracted to fruit. For the vegetable patch, plant garlic and marigolds: snails hate garlic and are attracted to marigolds, so they'll stay away from other plants. Another effective insect repellent for plants is to combine 4 cigarette butts with 2 cups of water in a spray pack. Be careful spraying this around children.

TIP

To get rid of caterpillars, mash some dead caterpillars in water and spray the mixture over the area. The smell of dead caterpillar makes other caterpillars think it's a dangerous area for them.

HERBS FOR THE PANTRY

Grow some herbs you can use in your pantry! A bay tree is easy to grow and you can use the leaves in cooking and for lining pantry shelves to deter moths! Mint is a great insecticide and is lovely as a tea. Thyme and sage, when added to tea, help soothe a cold. Garlic deters snails. Lavender deters insects, including mosquitoes. Lemon thyme is also a versatile herb. Rosemary is easy to grow and is beautifully fragrant.

After a hard day in the garden, rub papaw ointment into your hands and put disposable rubber gloves on for 10 minutes. It will soften calluses and draw any prickles out.

If you want to keep birds away from fruit trees, hang old CDs in them. The flashing movement and light is confusing and because they're round, birds think they could be the eyes of a predator.

OASIS

An essential part of an oasis is a water feature. It doesn't have to be huge: you can create a reflecting pool by filling a beautiful bowl with water and pebbles or with water and a few floating flowers. Add a pinch of salt to stop the water from going green, unless, of course, you want the green. If you have a pool, you could turn that into your water feature.

Moving water increases the negative ions in the air and helps generate oxygen so you're more likely to feel relaxed when around water. Think carefully about where you place your water feature. If you put it in the centre of the garden it becomes the main focal point—making the rest of the garden disappear—and may take up space that you could use for another function.

Avoid a concrete garden. Not only is it boring, it's psychologically hard on you. Be as minimal as you like but consider some shade and some sunlight. If you don't have a lawn, use comfortable chairs with padding—you need to be able to relax.

Jennifer bought a hammock in Thailand after whiling away many a relaxing hour near the beach. Hammocks can be freestanding or slung between trees or posts—and you can use them as a shade

cloth. If you have space, daybeds also provide a delightful spot to
enjoy the oasis in your backyard. Outdoor lounge chairs can be
further protected by a canvas covering. Make benches more comfy
with padded cushions that extend all the way along the bench.
Store them when they're not in use or they'll get manky. If you don't
have much storage space, keep them in a covered plastic container
underneath the table. If you're after a more robust covering, use
cushions made from sailcloth. Back cushions can be hung from a
wall using eye hooks that have been fastened to the wall. Never use
normal hooks because they can be dangerous if someone leans
against them.

ENTERTAINMENT ZONE

It's great to smell a barbecue in action. These days, barbecues can be
very sophisticated and expensive—with some barbecue areas having
preparation areas, sinks, fridges and dishwashers. Choose a barbecue
to suit your needs and be careful when installing it:

Always leave an appropriate distance between the barbecue
and anything flammable.

Check the gas cylinder for rust and make sure the connec-
tions are secure before lighting.

Make sure the barbecue is on a level base and is sheltered
from wind gusts.

Never store a petrol drum beside the barbecue.

If you're having an open-flamed barbecue, check fire restrictions
beforehand. Never place a barbecue right in the middle of the party

COMFY CRAFT

HOW TO TURN YOUR *HILLS HOIST* INTO A MARQUEE

The *Hills Hoist* clothesline can take up a big part of your backyard, but rather than see this as a hindrance, turn it into an asset. It's very easy to enclose two ends of the clothesline with one piece of lightweight canvas. Simply measure the width of one side of the clothesline, and the length ground-to-ground over the line. Once you've purchased the canvas, place it over the clothesline. Then spray paint the canvas in any colour or design you like (the spray paint stiffens and waterproofs the canvas and freezes it into place). Attach ties to the canvas and secure it to the clothesline. If it's windy, use tent pegs along the bottom of the canvas so that the clothesline doesn't spin around. Put guy ropes or ocky straps

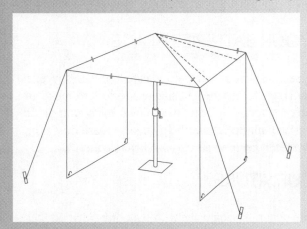

on the bottom of the canvas and secure to a tree or the house to give yourself a larger shade area.

because you won't be able to get away from it if it's too hot. Instead, place the barbecue where wind will blow the heat away.

Keep the area around the barbecue clean and dispose of excess ash on the garden or compost. Ash is alkaline and makes compost work faster.

SANGER STAIN: John's question

I was in charge of the barbecue and managed to drop a sausage on unsealed pavers. What can be done?

Because sausages contain protein, use facial soap and cold water first. For any remaining stain, mix 1 cup of plaster of paris to 1 teaspoon of detergent and place it over the stain. When it dries, brush it away.

Before barbecuing, sprinkle some sand on your pavers to absorb any oil, then sweep it up after cooking.

RECHARGE-YOUR-BATTERIES SPACE

If you meditate or exercise in your backyard, create a private space by hanging sheets from your clothesline or using shadecloth to make an enclosed space. Erect a screen of plants to cut down the sound of the neighbours and help with air pollution (the plants decrease dust from the road and act as a filter, keeping air on your land cleaner).

OUTDOOR FURNITURE

Timber settings—are generally expensive with teak or hardwood the preference. You'll extend the life of your setting if the wood is sealed. Keep this in mind when choosing the lacquer: the lighter the lacquer, the more sun damage you'll get. It's the opposite for paints with lighter paints causing less sun damage because light surfaces reflect heat. Heat is transferred through dark colours and makes the timber hotter and hotter causing it to shrink and warp. Choose the right colour paint or the sun could char the timber.

Glass tables—are popular for outdoor settings, but they are more fragile and are difficult to keep clean, so use a tablecloth in case items are dropped.

Some plastic furniture—is really well-designed for outdoor use. As a rule, the darker the furniture, the less likely it will be affected by UV rays. When choosing plastic furniture, take the heaviest member of your family with you and have them sit in the chair. They need to feel comfortable in it and it needs to be able to take their weight. It's best not to store plastic furniture outside because it breaks down in the sun.

Metal-framed settings—are very strong and durable. They generally have a glass top or polyurethane surface. Keep them covered to protect them.

Wrought iron—is the Rolls Royce of outdoor furniture. It's very practical but heavy. Wrought aluminium or cast aluminium combines the appearance of wrought iron without the weight. Clean with detergent and water and a broom. Spray paint each year with a good outdoor paint. Change the colour and get a whole new look for the backyard. Tie cushions to the chairs for comfort.

Outdoor loom—uses a polyurethane finish over wicker or resin.

Keep cushions in a shed, in the house, under the house, or, if there's no space, in a plastic roller box under your outdoor table. Outdoor chairs with attached cushions should be kept under cover or, if kept outside, rested on an angle. Wash cushions after it rains because they'll collect mildew. Add a couple of drops of oil of cloves to the rinse water to inhibit mould.

WIND CLIPS AND TABLE WEIGHTS

There can be a moment of panic if you're eating outside with a table-cloth covered in sumptuous food, and there's a gust of wind. Protect against random gusts by using wind clips or table weights. Clips are either plastic or metal and slide over the top of the tablecloth against the edge of the table. Table weights attach to the edge of the table-cloth and weigh it down. They are often decorative and can be themed to suit the occasion, such as a birthday party, or the season, such as Christmas.

HOW TO CUT A HOLE IN A TABLECLOTH FOR AN UMBRELLA

COMFY CRAFT

It's a bit difficult to use a tablecloth when your table has an umbrella protruding from the middle of it. So here's the best way to cut a hole in the tablecloth so you don't have bits of fraying cotton. Position the tablecloth on the table and draw on an outline of the circle where the umbrella sits. Cut a small hole in the centre of the circle with a pair of scissors, then make 1cm incisions—like rays of the sun—from the hole to the outline of the circle. Fold the triangular pieces over to the wrong side of the fabric, trim, if necessary, and place iron-on hemming tape over the top. If the tablecloth is linen or cotton, apply a hot iron. If it's synthetic, use a spray-on adhesive rather than hemming tape. No fraying!

UMBRELLAS

Umbrellas are best left up so they don't hoard bugs. If they are down, keep them wrapped in a cover. To clean canvas umbrellas, put 2 cups of table salt or swimming pool salt in a small bucket of water and apply to the canvas with a brush or a stiff broom. Allow to dry then brush off the salt.

HOW TO CLEAN MILDEW ON CANVAS

Add 1kg of table salt to a bucket of water. Sweep it on with a broom, leave it to dry and then sweep it off with a stiff broom. Add a couple of drops of oil of cloves to a spray bottle of water and lightly mist the canvas to inhibit mould.

CLOTHESLINES

Hanging your washing outdoors is by far the best way to dry it— sunshine is a fantastic antibacterial and whitener. There are many clothesline options. Some homes still have the classic Australian icon the *Hills Hoist* in the backyard, but retractable lines are also popular, as they are easy to store away when not in use. When choosing a clothesline you want the biggest space between the lines so there's plenty of room for air to circulate. If the lines are too close, the washing won't dry. Choose plastic over metal lines because they're easier to clean and replace. Avoid nylon cords because the sun breaks the nylon down and it becomes jagged and may snag the clothes. Don't place the clothesline under trees or you'll cut down on sunshine and increase the risk of resin stains from sap and falling leaves. Clothes dry 5–6 times faster on a windy day, even when it's a cold day, so try to position your clothesline to take advantage of breezes. Keep your *Hills Hoist* well oiled otherwise hoisting will become tough on your arms.

Have something for the clothes' basket to rest on while you're hanging out the washing. Clothes' basket trolleys work really well and they are also handy for wheeling shopping from the car. Store pegs in a drainable peg basket, which is particularly important with wooden pegs. Plastic pegs are preferable, but don't leave them pegged to the line because exposure to sunlight will break them down. If you have an outside table, keep it clean so that you can use it to fold clothes on as you remove them from the line. This will save time—you won't need to refold items before you put them away—

and make ironing easier—you won't have a hideous crumpled mess in the clothes' basket to tackle.

> Use one section of the clothesline per family member. That way, when you remove their clothes, they can be stacked in one basket for them to sort and iron.

Have a clear pathway to the clothesline (brushing through under-growth can dirty your clothes). Always wind your washing line down when pegging or unpegging to save your back. Many people become lazy and don't wind the washing line up or down, but winding is good for the mechanism. If it's sticking, add a little sweet almond oil. The ideal pegging height is just above the top of your head. That way you can walk under the line yet still reach it comfortably.

DECKING

The best decking is constructed with seasoned wood. If yours hasn't been sealed, it's a good idea to do this! Not only does it extend the life of the deck, it prevents leaching and the growth of mould. The distance between the boards should be at least the width of a match-stick so that water can drain but high heels won't be wedged. If you plan to spend a lot of time in bare feet on your deck, keep the colour as light as possible so you don't burn your feet—dark colours are hotter. Create a non-slip surface by adding 1 cup of sand to 1 litre of paint. For areas with huge wear and tear, put down mats, rugs or *AstroTurf*. *AstroTurf* comes in an array of colours—just make sure you have the edges professionally heat-sealed or it will fray. Putting down a softer surface also means that if things are dropped, they're less likely to break.

OTHER SURFACES

Concrete is best unsealed otherwise it can be very slippery when wet. Paint it any colour you like. If choosing **brick paving** or **paving tiles**, choose smaller tiles. The bigger the tile, the more likely it will break. There's no need to cement the tiles in unless you want to. Packing them with sand is very effective. **Quarry tiles** need to be kept very clean because they show mould. Never have glazed tiles outside— they're slippery and an accident waiting to happen. **Vitreous terracotta** repels water and grime and isn't as slippery as glazed tiles.

> **TIP**
>
> To remove sap from decking and pavers, rub with tea tree oil and a broom. If it won't shift, apply glycerine first and leave for 20 minutes, then apply tea tree oil.

PATHWAYS

A pathway provides a safe walking surface and is helpful in preventing damage to your lawn—and your shoes—by guiding traffic in a specified direction. Avoid putting in pebblecrete paths which are very slippery, no matter the conditions. If using stepping stones,

> **HINT**
>
> **HOW TO CLEAN A MOULDY PATHWAY**
> There are several ways to clean a mouldy pathway. Check first by scrubbing the area with water and a nylon broom just in case it's accumulated dirt! If it is mould, and there's a garden nearby, sprinkle over some bicarb and white vinegar and scrub with a nylon broom. If there's no garden, add 1kg of table salt to a bucket of warm water and scrub with a nylon broom. The pool-cleaning product, Algene (a non-chlorine algaecide) also works well, but don't use it if there will be run off to lichen or ferns. Algene won't kill shrubs.

choose cement pavers. The best size to use is 500 x 500mm. You must keep pavers clean so mould doesn't build up. Be creative in how you position them.

GUTTERS AND DRAINS

Make sure gutters and drains are clear and unobstructed. When leaves collect in gutters, they hold moisture in one spot causing rust and corrosion. To clear a blocked gutter, you will need gloves, a ladder, a bucket and a butcher's hook. Climb the ladder and attach the bucket to the ladder with the hook. Always keep one hand on the gutter or house and never lean off a ladder. With your free hand, remove waste and place it in the bucket. If you're worried about biting insects, use tongs. If you constantly have leaves in your gutters, install a dome mesh guard which causes most leaves to fall over and onto the ground.

Climbing plants should be kept away from gutters or they will block them. Clip them regularly to keep them under control. Climbing plants also play havoc with wooden surfaces by increasing moisture and rotting wood.

To clear a drain, put $^1/_2$ cup of bicarb down the pipe, then pour in $^1/_2$ cup of white vinegar and leave for 20 minutes. Flush with boiling water straight from the kettle. If bicarb and vinegar don't work, use coat-hanger wire to move the obstruction. If the object won't shift, you'll need to get a plumber with an electric eel.

Check that the grill covers on your drains and grease traps are in good condition. If grill covers are more than 10cm wide, bolt them into place so children can't get stuck down them.

To get rid of possums, apply creosote to the beam ends in the roof of your house or combine olive oil and chilli powder and sprinkle it around the gutters. Many people apply napthalene to deter possums, but don't apply this to timber or absorbent surfaces because it's flammable.

WINDOWS

HOW TO REPAIR A BROKEN OR CRACKED WINDOW

If your sport screen wasn't put up and your aspiring Aussie cricketer smashed a ball through a window, it can be fixed. The easiest way is to get a glazier to fix it for you. But you can do it yourself if you're of the handy persuasion. This technique applies to timber frames. Aluminium ones are trickier to fix, so it's best to get professional help.

First, mark the old glass with an X using strong masking tape and secure any loose shards of glass. Measure the distance between the rebates for the size of the replacement glass. Remove the timber beading from around the glass, marking each piece of beading so that you know which piece goes where. Remove any putty. Remove linseed putty with warm linseed oil heated in the microwave. Never use a heat gun on glass because it will crack it. Carefully remove the glass wearing gloves and dispose of it. Clean the rebate until all surfaces are cleared. Check that the replacement glass fits. Then apply putty to the internal face of the rebate. Place the new glass in position and gently push it into the putty. Tidy up and replace the beading.

HOW TO CHECK FOR SHARDS OF GLASS

Place a lit torch on the floor so the beam goes across the floor. Any remaining shards of glass will sparkle in the light.

HOW TO FIX A FLYSCREEN

Flyscreens are an essential part of the average Australian house. While some people don't like the look of them, if it's a choice between aesthetics and being bitten by mozzies or bothered by flies, most sensible people choose to install them. It's best to completely replace rather than repair flyscreen, but if it's a small hole and you want to repair it, you can make a patch. Cut a square of matching flyscreen and place it over the damaged area. Either sew a running stitch around the square with matching poly-cotton thread or apply craft glue to the edges to keep it in place.

To replace flyscreen in an aluminium frame, buy flyscreen 1 1/2 cm larger than the edge of the frame. You'll notice there's a plastic lining in the groove between the edge of the frame and the wire. This is called beading. Remove this with a screwdriver. Then remove the old or damaged flywire and place the new flywire over the area. Replace the plastic beading using a screw-driver to work the beading back into place, making sure that the flywire is evenly stretched across the frame as you go. Then use a bedding wheel to roll the bead in. Cut off excess wire with a sharp knife or scissors.

COMPOSTS

Composts are both great for the garden and to stop adding to landfill. Choose an isolated part of the garden for your compost. Use plastic containers available from your council, or get wire mesh or wooden slats. For a quick and simple do-it-yourself compost, fill plastic shopping bags with kitchen scraps for composting, such as fruit and vegetable scraps, and tie the handles together. Sit the full plastic bags in the corner of the garden in the sunshine. Six weeks later, you'll have compost. Simply cut the plastic and the material is ready to spread on your garden. UV rays have killed bacteria and any weeds. If you place the plastic bags on top of weeds, it will kill the weeds at the same time, as Shannon found when she used this technique. Tie it off tight so that pests can't get inside.

PETS

Before advances in flea control, most pets lived outside. This is not the case these days, with many pets enjoying a pampered existence.

HOW TO WASH A CAT

If your cat lives inside, it needs to be bathed. Wrap a tea towel over the cat's head—the darkness calms it—and front feet—so that it won't be able to scratch—and secure it firmly. Use pet shampoo with a couple of drops of oil of pennyroyal (**don't use if you or your cat is pregnant**) added to deter fleas. Clean the cat's back with a pet brush, then wrap the tea towel over the cat's back legs and wipe the front with a washer, going from front to back. Don't use a brush. Pamper the cat afterwards so that it has a positive association with washing.

HOW TO TEACH A DOG TO LIKE HIS BATH

If there was an Academy Award for most sulking performance during a bath, Jennifer's family dog would have been in the running. Toby hated having baths and would whimper and shiver throughout the ordeal. If your pooch is similarly dramatic, make being washed a positive experience by creating a play zone. This could mean getting in the bath with your dog and playing while you wash it. Make sure you use warm rather than cold water, gentle soaps—and keep soap away from the dog's eyes—and pat and cuddle the dog.

TIP

If your dog has eczema, put 1 teabag and a sprig of mint in the warm bathwater. It relieves the itching and helps deter the mite carrying fleas, which causes the skin problems. This treatment is like a health spa for puppy dogs.

TIP

To loosen matted hair on dogs, use detangling sprays designed for humans. If you need to cut the matted fur—rather than cutting across the chunk of hair—snip from the skin to the end of the hair, from the centre outwards, so the mat is split in half. That way, you don't end up with a hacked pooch.

YOUR COMMUNITY

Building community is an important part of feeling comfy in your neighbourhood. Here are some tips to get your street talking!

Patronise your local shops. Small corner stores are a great place to meet people in your area, hear about what's going on and get the goss.

Organise a street party. Approach your local council for advice on how to do this. Place a flyer in letterboxes, organise a meeting and delegate tasks.

Instigate a semi-regular barbecue in a local park. Just pick a day, such as the first Sunday of the month, and everyone can BYO.

Have a street garage sale.

If you have children, encourage the kids to get to know each other. If you don't want to have an open house for kids, you can have an open garden for kids.

Get involved in the local school.

Drop a Christmas card in everyone's letterbox.

Do the Wonder Walk (see page 191) in your own street. Ask neighbours about their gardens and compliment them if you like it.

Tackle a local issue or join a local group. If your local park is a mess, organise a cleaning bee. The council may offer some support. Join the local Landcare branch or another environmental group.

Ask the elderly in your street if they need anything from the shops. Ask them about the history of your area.

Be helpful: pick up a newspaper that's been out all day or take out bins on bin night.

Have a street spring clean. Help neighbours with projects, such as cleaning leaves out of gutters.

Do tai chi in the park.

Take a continuing education course at the local high school.

Leave a present for the garbos and the postie at Christmas. Say hello and thank you when you see them.

Speak to the council and find out what's happening locally.
They organise lots of events. Be a part of them.

Try and be involved and get others involved too. Don't wait for
people to come to you, go to them.

NEIGHBOURS

In these days of late-night supermarket trading, the need to borrow a
cup of sugar from your neighbours is less likely. It's still a good idea
to get to know your neighbours because a friendly neighbourhood is
a happy neighbourhood. If you are on good terms with your neighbours, they're more likely to watch out for your house, keep an eye
on activities in the street and keep you informed of local goings-on.

If you're new to a neighbourhood, break the ice by asking about
garbage night or when the postie comes. If there are plants hanging
over the fence, find out if your neighbour likes them or not. If your
children go to the same school, organise a car pool. If you're having
a garage sale, invite neighbours to join in. You could even sell half
your junk to them! If you're having a party, notify neighbours or invite
them. Even if they don't want to come to the party, they're less likely
to complain. Be aware of noise. Ask neighbours if they can hear noise
from your property. Ask if your chimney smoke affects them. If you
make too many biscuits, share them.

Let your neighbours know when you go on holiday. They may be
happy to collect your mail—otherwise, you can ask the post office to
hold your mail—and keep an eye on things for you. And, of course,
offer to do the same for them if they go away.

If you're unable to resolve an issue with your neighbours, see if
your local council has a mediator. They will try and broker a solution.

HOW TO KEEP AN EYE ON ELDERLY NEIGHBOURS

If you have an elderly or unwell neighbour and they live on their own, establish a form of communication so you know if they need help. One suggestion is that they open a certain curtain or blind each day. If it hasn't been opened, you know to check up on them. Check if they need anything when you head to the shops.

Travel

Every now and again, you'll need to venture from your comfy home and stay elsewhere. Generally, travelling is an exciting prospect, but there is an art to travelling well. We'll look at smart packing and getting that checklist sorted. Reduce the turbulence with these comfy hints and tricks and make your travel experience as smooth as possible, no matter what the mode of transport.

HOW WE USED TO KEEP COMFY FROM *PEARS' CYCLOPAEDIA 33RD EDITION* (1928)

Hysteria: A morbid condition indicated by flatulancy and the feeling of a lump or ball in the throat causing a sense of choking or suffocation. Involuntary laughing and crying proceed the hysterical fit in which the patient tosses about violently and is liable to self-injury. A fit of hysteria very often ends in the sufferer going off into a stupor or coma and sometimes this state is reached without preliminary signs. Hysteria is a curious ailment to deal with, being a nervous affection which feeds upon itself and stimulates many diseases. It is always best to exhibit no sympathy with the patient, who is generally a female, but throw cold water upon her face, apply ammonia to her nostrils and administer antispasmodics.

PACKING

Travelling—and packing—is much easier when you have the right luggage. Choose the appropriate size and style for the adventure. We both love luggage with wheels and an expandable section for new purchases!

The most important element to packing is preparation. Avoid the last-minute scramble of shoving random items in the bag or you'll find yourself at your destination missing something vital. The first thing you need to do is work out what to take. Even if you can wash regularly, have at least three sets of clothes for different temperatures and occasions. If you're going away for a week, have one outfit per day. If away for longer, have one outfit for every two days for up to ten days. For extended stays, have one outfit per day for a week. It is essential that you pack clothes for a variety of temperatures, no matter what the season. You shouldn't need more than ten outfits. Always include something dressy and something casual. Whether you are male or female, pack a sarong because it is so versatile: it can be used as a blanket, sheet, picnic rug, shawl, bathrobe, towel, skirt or, with the right jewellery and knotting, an evening gown! Pack predominantly plain clothes, rather than florals or patterns, in colours that coordinate because they're easier to mix and match. And make sure you have suitable underwear to match your clothing. Always include an extra set of underwear and socks and a light cardigan that's easily accessible. A cardigan saved Jennifer in London when she was stranded at the train station and, even though it was summer, it was freezing. If you're heading to a cold climate, have one lightweight outfit in case there's a heatwave. Shannon's trick is to use skivvies and pantyhose to layer under clothes if there's a cold snap. They don't take up much room and mix and match with everything.

For 2 weeks prior to your departure, check the temperature at your destination. Also check the projected weather forecast for the time you'll be there. It's easy to do this online.

TIP

Place your sleeping gear or the first outfit you'll wear on top of the bag so it's easy to access. You may be too tired to unpack when you arrive at your destination.

HINT

HOW TO PACK A SUITCASE

The first rule of packing is to lay clothes as flat as possible, not to fold them up too much. The more folds you make, the more room you take up—because each fold creates a new bubble of air—and the more creases you create in your clothes. Don't roll socks in a ball instead, fold them flat (see Laundry page 215). You can also pack socks into items that might break. Fold clothes to fit the size of your case and put the most important part of the garment in the case first. So, when packing a shirt, lay the shirt face down and flat into the suitcase—with the collar against one side of the case and the tail hanging over the other side. Fold in the sleeves at a 45-degree angle so they're not creased. Then flip the shirt tail into the case, creating as few folds as possible. If you want to wear the shirt straight away, put a layer of acid-free tissue paper over the shirt. This is how shirts used to be packed and how some shops still package them. Place the most fragile items, such as toiletries, in the centre of the bag to protect against breakages. Shannon packs her shoes in an old pillow case so dirt doesn't transfer to the clothes and shoes are easy to remove from the case all at once.

TIP

Always include extra plastic bags and zip-lock bags. Have a soft nylon foldable bag in case you need extra luggage space. Always leave a gap in your suitcase for purchases or use a bag that's expandable.

THE SPONGE BAG

Pack a washer, a small bath towel, a disposable razor, tea tree oil, lavender oil, sunscreen, *Vaseline* or papaw ointment, *Band-Aids*, safety pins, a nail file, scissors, a mini-sewing kit, sticky tape, paracetamol and any other medication you may need. Always have a roll of toilet paper. Seal all liquid containers in their own separate zip-lock bags then pack in another bag. The double protection means less leaking in the case of breakage.

Have 3 metres of twine or cord and six pegs. If you're staying in a hotel and need to wash something overnight, you can erect this line in the shower and peg your wet items to it.

To protect fragile items, blow a balloon up inside the item and tie it off. Then wrap the item in bubble wrap. This technique keeps the pressure even inside and outside the item.

EXCESS BAGGAGE: Annette's question

 I travelled interstate recently and my luggage ended up covered in chilli oil that had broken in someone else's bag. The smell is revolting.

 Use vinegar to break down the oil and the smell, then apply talcum powder over the top. Leave for a few minutes and vacuum.

CHECKLIST

Have a list of things you need to complete and take with you for the trip. Tick them off as you go.

Passport, ticket and itinerary.

Travel insurance.

Money and credit cards.

Money belt—buy one with internal vertical zips. It's easy for you to use but hard for thieves to get at.

Keep jewellery to a minimum or take costume jewellery.

Keys and address book.

Make sure any sharp implements are not in your carry-on luggage.

Speak to someone who's been to the destination before—it could be a friend or travel agent. Find out what you need to know before you go. Preparation is important.

Have mail collected at the post office or organise for someone to clear your mail box. Put newspaper subscriptions on hold.

Install a light timer so your house isn't in darkness while you're away.

Make sure you have an emergency contact. Leave travel details with someone you can trust and can contact in an emergency.

Check prescriptions. Not all prescription drugs are legal in all countries so have a letter or script from your doctor. Some countries won't have the drugs you need so stock up before you go.

Check for travel warnings.

PLANES

Always check what you can and cannot take on board an aeroplane
as it changes regularly—you could be saying goodbye to your
favourite knitting needles or your Swiss Army Knife forever! In
Australia at the time of writing, only 100ml per container of drinks,
creams, perfumes, sprays, gels and toothpastes are allowed on board
and have to be kept in a resealable transparent plastic bag no larger
than 1 litre. The only exceptions are for people with medical conditions and babies. Check with your travel agent to find out the
specifications for each country and airline. Also check for travel
warnings through your travel agent, airline or Department of Foreign
Affairs and Trade (http://www.dfat.gov.au/).

If travelling on a long-haul flight, reduce the risk of developing
deep vein thrombosis (DVT) by wearing support leggings, available
from chemists or at the airport. Try to minimise foot swelling because
it puts strain on the kidneys and makes recovery from jet lag more
difficult. Do foot exercises every 30 minutes. Take a blow-up neck
cushion and use a foot cushion to remove pressure from the back of
your knees. They're easy to use and store.

Some airlines supply food and drink free of charge. On others,
you pay on board, so have enough money on you.

If travelling with small children, be aware that changes in air
pressure can make take-off and landing painful for them. For small
babies, breastfeeding or bottle feeding can clear their ears. For older
children, have a yawning competition or give them a piece of barley
sugar to suck on. If this doesn't work and they're in pain, put your
mouth over their nose and mouth and give one short puff of air. It
will make them yawn.

BUSES

You're more likely to have to carry your luggage over a greater distance when travelling by bus, so keep it to the barest minimum and don't take luggage that you can't lift yourself. Noise can be irritating on a bus so pack earplugs or headphones. Take a neck pillow and a small torch or light on a key chain for reading. You're more likely to become sick on a bus or ship than on any other mode of transport. If you're prone to motion sickness, keep your eyes on the horizon and have medication with you.

TRAINS

The experience varies according to which class you're travelling in. Some trains have a carriage to store luggage, while in others, luggage is stored at the end of the carriage or in racks above the seats. It's a good idea to take some food with you even though your train may have a dining car or staff that brings food through the carriages. You may want to book a sleeping carriage if travelling overnight. Shannon likes to sleep like a log in a private room on an overnight train.

SHIPS

Cruises have become more popular and accessible. The idea of lying on a sun bed with a changing landscape or seascape rolling by is appealing. Many people become seasick and there are two reasons for it: one is low viscosity in the inner ear; and the other is brain confusion. Have some medication with you. Another trick is to find the stillest part of the ship with the farthest view, even if it's only to see the uninterrupted horizon. If you see something stable, your brain can find some equilibrium.

HIKING AND CAMPING

You'll need a sleeping bag, backpack, hiking shoes, map, compass, GPS, water, first-aid kit, string, pocket knife, noisemaker (such as a whistle), dehydrated rations and a mobile phone. Shannon suggests also taking a 1.8 x 1.8-metre plastic sheet with you. It can become an instant tent, water catcher or umbrella. A felt hat is another versatile item when hiking and camping. It can protect you from the sun, insulate you in the cold and can even become a billy if needed. Another comfy option is to take a mattress—buy a self-inflating one or you may prefer to make your own.

COMFY CRAFT

HOW TO MAKE YOUR OWN TRAVEL MATTRESS

When Shannon travelled around Australia, she constructed a mattress using empty wine cask bladders. You'll need 12 empty bladders and 2 thin layers of foam (90 x 180 x 1cm). Place one layer of foam on the floor, position 6 bladders on either side of the foam, with the dispenser nozzle facing outwards, and glue them in place with foam and plastic glue. Make a crosshatch line of glue over the top of the bladders and put the second layer of foam over it. Blow up the bladders before sleeping to make a very lightweight, compact and comfy bed. And of course, don't drink all the cask wine at once!

CARS

Cars are usually pretty comfy to begin with, but there are several additions that will make going on long trips in the car even comfier. For starters, always keep a blanket and a blow-up pillow in the car— you never know when you might need them! Shannon likes to keep a *Slurpex*, a chamois or paper towels in the glove box to pick up spills or defog windows. Keep a small, lightweight tarpaulin in the boot in case you need to change a tyre in the rain. Windscreens can be broken on long journeys, so it's a good idea to store a temporary windscreen made of plastic and double-sided tape (available from your local car mart) to get you to the next service station.

If there's a strange smell, check the air conditioning. The vents are generally located near the door. If there's a stale odour, hang a damp tea bag with lavender oil in front of the vent.

Always have your car serviced before a big trip. Check the oil, tyre pressure and water level. And always check that the spare tyre is in good condition. Have your mobile phone charged and road service membership up-to-date. Remember maps, street directories and keep contact numbers for accommodation in the car in case you get lost or are running late.

Have a damp washer in a zip-lock bag to wipe hands and faces and a box of tissues. Keep a supply of healthy low-sugar and low-fat nibbles to stave off hunger pangs and help settle tummies. If travelling with carsick people, have a 5-minute walk break every 30 minutes and encourage them to focus on the horizon, which settles the stomach, rather than on other cars on the road. Have garbage bags and zip-lock bags handy for passengers with unstable tummies.

GAMES FOR KIDS ON LONG CAR JOURNEYS

I spy—is a classic. In case you're not familiar with it, the game starts with the person who is 'in' choosing something they can see outside the car window. They then say, 'I spy with my little eye, something beginning with…' and select the letter of the alphabet that their chosen secret object begins with. Then everyone else in the car has to find the identity of the secret object by suggesting things that begin with that letter until they guess correctly. Whoever gets the right answer is 'in' next.

Travelling piquet/car bingo/spotto—make a list on paper of objects that kids have to identify and tick off on the journey. Some examples include a pink car, yellow truck, letterbox, horse and so on.

Numberplate game—find numberplates that begin with each letter of the alphabet.

Have a sing-a-long—either with a CD or unplugged.

HOW TO WASH A CAR

In these times of water restrictions, it's important to wash the car with the least amount of water. This technique uses 2 buckets of water. Add $\frac{1}{2}$ tablespoon of dishwashing liquid to a bucket of warm water. With a soft sponge, begin cleaning the car, starting with the roof. Clean one side of the car then the other side. Clean the hubcaps, numberplate and wheels and throw the dirty water over the car. Then pour 1 bucket of fresh water over the car and wipe dry with a chamois or *Slurpex*.

Don't clean the car on a hot day because the soap will stick to the duco.

FISH SAUCE CRISIS: Steve's question

Q: I don't know how, but one of the kids managed to spill fish sauce in the back of the car. The smell is awful.

A: Fish sauce is high in oil and protein. To prevent the protein setting, break it down by applying soap and cold water with an old toothbrush then apply paper towel and firm pressure. Repeat many times. It's important not to get any heat on the stain.

TOOLKIT FOR ROAD EMERGENCIES

Jennifer's car got wedged on a steep driveway. When she rang her dad for advice on what to do, he suggested putting some hessian bags under the tyres for traction, as though this was a handy item in the back of her car! Fortunately, the tow-truck guy came to the rescue. It is a good idea to have a basic toolkit for your car. First, see what comes with the car. Shannon suggests the car should have disposable gloves, a torch, a small first-aid kit, screwdrivers—both Phillips head and flathead—a pair of pliers, a jack, a shifting spanner, a hammer, a piece of wire, some foil and a pair of pantyhose! She reckons a pair of pantyhose works a treat if your exhaust pipe drops, you need a temporary fan belt in a hurry or a tow rope!

FLAT BATTERY

If you get a flat battery, it may be caused by incorrect pH balance from low water levels in your battery. To dilute the acid, top it up with water. Undo the vent caps of the battery and fill them with water to the top of the separators and plates. Then tap a spanner on the side of the battery so the electrolytes mix in. If the car still won't start, get a new battery.

CAT CURSE: Clyde's question

 A cat always curls on the bonnet of my car and leaves paw marks all over it. Is there a solution?

 Cats hate camphor, so rub *Vicks VapoRub* along the edge of the bonnet and replace frequently.

HINT

HOW TO JUMP-START A CAR

Before you do anything, read your car manual. Some modern cars are computerised and cannot be jump-started. If there are cracks in the battery or it's frozen, don't try to jump-start it. To jump-start, the first thing to do is find jumper leads and another car with a battery voltage the same as yours. There are two terminals on a battery—positive (+) coloured red and negative (-) coloured black. Attach one end of the lead to the dead battery's positive terminal. Attach the other end of the same lead to the positive terminal of the working battery. Attach the other lead to the negative terminal on the working battery and the other end to the engine block of the car with the dead battery. The engine block is generally any unpainted metal under the bonnet. Do not attach the negative lead to the dead battery. Stand back from the bonnet of the car. Start the car with the working battery. Wait for a few minutes then try to start the car with the dead battery. If it doesn't start, wait for a few minutes and try again. If it doesn't work, you'll need to get a new battery. Remove the jumper leads in the reverse order you put them on.

Food

BUYING AND STORING FOOD

If we bailed you up at the fruit market and asked you how to select the best fruit and vegetables, would you be to tell us? Perhaps the growth of cities and life away from the land goes some way to explaining why we know less and less about fresh produce. Fortunately, all you need is a good sense of sight and smell and some general know-how, which we'll outline below. Try to buy fruit and vegetables in season because they will be at their best. The easiest way to tell when fresh produce is in season is by watching the price and quality. The length of time fresh fruit and vegetables can be kept varies according to how far they've been transported, how long they've been at the shop, the temperature at the shop, how well they're stacked, what they were stored next to and how often they were handled. These factors determine how long fruit and vegetables will last at your home. That's why you need to learn how to use your sense of sight and smell. We also suggest that you learn to cook by sight, smell and taste rather than by recipe. And never stop experimenting with cooking because you'll never know what wonderful creation you might discover.

How we used to keep comfy from *Pears' Cyclopaedia 33rd edition* (1928)

Vinegar is in small quantities good. It supplies a salutary and grateful stimulus to the stomach. Correcting the flatulancy of vegetable food and the putrenacy of animal aliment. But any excess of it is pernicious.

FRUIT AND VEGETABLES

APPLES

HOW TO SELECT

The best way to determine the ripeness of an apple is by looking at the base of the stem. It should be slightly green, if it's brown, it means the apple is old. Likewise, if the core is dried out, the apple is old. When you tap your knuckle on the side of an apple it should sound hollow. When you sniff the stem, it should have a fresh apple fragrance. If it has a musty smell, then it's old and likely to be floury.

HOW TO STORE

Apples keep better in the refrigerator crisper or in a cool dry space. Polish them with a pair of pantyhose before you put them in the fridge to get rid of wax and finger marks. Polishing buffs the skin and makes it crunch. It's a good idea to wash the apple again before eating. Don't refrigerate for longer than 2 weeks. Shannon's mum used to polish her apples for her school lunchbox.

Instant apple sauce

Peel and core 3 apples, preferably granny smiths. Slice into fine wedges and place in a microwave-safe dish. Add 1 teaspoon of brown sugar, 1 clove and ½ teaspoon of butter. Cover and microwave on the vegetable setting for around 3 minutes. Then whiz in a blender. Makes ½ –1 cup

Dried apples

When cooking, use tarter apples such as granny smiths, pink ladies, pippins or bonzas. To dry apples, core and cut into 5mm thick slices, place on an oven rack in a 70°C/150°F/gas mark ¼ oven for 2–3 hours.

You can also dry them in the microwave using microwave drying racks.
Cooking time will vary according to the kind of microwave you have.

ARTICHOKES

HOW TO SELECT	They should be green with a moist stalk, very firm to the touch with a fresh grassy smell. The leaves should be tight with a hint of purple to the head.

HOW TO STORE	Artichokes last for about 1 week in the fridge crisper, but this will vary. They're off when the stem or leaves become spongy.

Basic artichoke recipe

Peel the outer leaves of each artichoke and trim the stem. Cut in half
vertically from the base to the top and remove the choke or fluffy bit
in the middle. Place the outer leaves in the bottom of a microwave-
safe dish and add enough water to just cover the leaves. Lay the
artichokes face down on the leaves. Add juice of ½ a lemon,
1 teaspoon of olive oil and a pinch of salt. Cover and microwave on
the leaf vegetable setting or until tender. Test tenderness with a
skewer. You can stuff the centre of the artichoke with smoked salmon
and sour cream, prosciutto, tomato and chopped basil or garlic butter.
You can also eat the cooked outer leaves, which are great for dips.

ASPARAGUS

HOW TO SELECT	Fresh asparagus has juicy, stiff stems and no wrinkles. If the ends have shrunk, they've been out for too long.

To keep asparagus moist, store upright in a glass of water in the fridge. Asparagus will remain fresh for around 4 days. If the bottom is woody, hold an asparagus spear in both hands and snap off the end. It will break at the point where the asparagus has turned woody. Don't discard the woody bits: they may be too chewy to eat, but they still have flavour and are perfect for making stocks. Store them in a labelled plastic bag in the freezer.

Basic asparagus recipe

Steam whole asparagus for no longer than 3 minutes (asparagus goes soggy if cooked for too long). Season with lemon juice and cracked black pepper, or whatever spices you prefer, and add some shaved parmesan cheese for a kick. If you cook asparagus in the microwave, half cover in orange juice and add 1 teaspoon of butter. Cover and cook for 2 minutes or until just tender. Orange juice stops the strong smell and brings out the flavour of the asparagus.

AVOCADOS

There are different avocados for every month of the year and each one has its own way of ripening. The best way to tell if an avocado is ripe is to lightly tap on it with your knuckle. Don't squeeze them because they bruise easily. A ripe one sounds solid. If there's a hollow sound, it's not ripe. The stem should be just brown and not puckered. Check the skin for gall marks, which appear as little brown dots. These are actually an insect which burrows into the avocado. Avoid selecting these avocados if you can or chop the area away if you find them. The best way to cut an avocado is to use a sharp knife and cut lengthways around the entire avocado from top to bottom. Then twist one side against the other to release. To remove the seed, tap a large knife into the seed so it sticks, then twist the knife and the seed should pop away from the flesh.

Avocados are best kept out of the fridge except if cut—the cold stops the ripening process. If you use only half an avocado and you want to store the rest for later, leave the seed in, run it under cold water and while it's damp, put a small piece of plastic wrap over the cut surface, then put it in the fridge. Sprinkling lemon juice on avocado prevents browning but it also changes the taste, so the water and plastic wrap option is preferable. To ripen an avocado, put it in a paper bag with a banana, which gives off the ripening chemical, ethylene, and leave for about 24 hours.

Avocado sauce for veal scaloppine

Cut 1 avocado into 4cm thick slices. Mix lemon juice, salt, 1 crushed garlic clove and 1 tablespoon of cream or sour cream and sprinkle over the avocado. Warm through, without stirring, in a small frying pan or chafing dish. Place avocado sauce on just cooked veal and serve. **Serves 4**

BANANAS

Everyone has a different preference for eating bananas. Some people like them ripe, soft and sweet and others prefer unripe bananas with a bit of tang. The way to determine ripeness is by looking at the stem. Ripe bananas have a black or brown stem. The stem should only be brown right at the very tip.

Keep bananas out of the fridge or they'll go brown. Use overripe bananas in baking (banana bread, banana and chocolate chip muffins or banana cake) or as compost on the garden— ferns and rainforest plants love them.

Pilli

Pilli is a Tahitian and Norfolk Island recipe that uses green or unripe bananas. Two-thirds fill a casserole dish or cake tin with 10 sliced green bananas. Sprinkle over some brown sugar and the juice of 1 lemon or the juice of 2 oranges. Add 2 teaspoons of self-raising flour, gently toss until the bananas are well coated and pour over 1 beaten egg. Bake in a 100°C/200°F/gas mark ½ oven for 45 minutes or until tender and golden brown. The pilli may take up to 1 ½ hours to cook—the cooking time varies according to how green the bananas are. The finished dish has a light, crispy top and is fudgy inside. **Serves 8**

BEETROOT

HOW TO SELECT

Choose beetroot bulbs that are unwrinkled, hard to the touch and rich in colour. The leaves should look crisp.

HOW TO STORE

Remove the leaves—and use them in salads or as a cooked vegetable—so moisture isn't extracted from the beetroot. Store in the fridge crisper for up to 1 week. After this, they start to shrink and go rubbery. Cooked beetroot can be stored for 2–3 days in the fridge or placed in the freezer and stored for months. Pickled beetroot will last for up to 6 months.

Basic beetroot recipe

The easiest way to cook beetroot is to place the bulbs, with the skin still on, in a microwave-safe dish. For 1–2 large beetroot, add 1cm of water and 1–2 tablespoons of white vinegar. Cover the container and microwave, using the root vegetable setting, for 5 minutes for each

beetroot or until tender. When cooked, place in a bowl of cold water,
put on some disposable gloves and rub off the skins with your hands.
If roasting beetroot, wrap them in foil so they retain their moisture
and flavour and roast at 200°C/400°F/gas mark 6 for 55 minutes or
until tender. To pickle, slice the cooked, peeled beetroot, sprinkle with
salt, place in a container and cover with any type of vinegar. Each
type of vinegar will create a different taste. As a rule of thumb, the
darker the vinegar, the sweeter it is. Leave it in the fridge until ready
for use. It will last for 6 months.

HOW TO SELECT

Look for the blue bloom, make sure the bottom of the punnet is dry—old blueberries tend to sweat—and check carefully for mould. If the blue bloom is slightly pistachio green, it's mould.

HOW TO STORE

Remove the blueberries from the punnet, wash and dry them on paper towel before returning them to the punnet. This removes any mould spores or fruit fly.

BLUEBERRIES
Toffee blueberries

Mix 250g of blueberries with ½ a beaten egg white. Melt 3 tablespoons of caster sugar on a low heat, making sure it doesn't brown.
If it does brown, add water, 1 teaspoon at a time, until sugar syrup is
clear. Stab each blueberry with a toothpick and place, one by one, in
the sugar syrup for about 10 seconds. Transfer to a sheet of foil on
the benchtop, lining up the berries. Place the blueberries in the fridge
until the light crispy toffee that appears to be frosted is set. Serve in a
bowl and pass with toothpicks and mascarpone mixed with the seeds
scraped from 1 vanilla bean. **Serves 10**

BOK CHOY

HOW TO SELECT

Bok choy leaves should be dark green, firm with a strong grassy smell. The base should be moist when cut.

HOW TO STORE

Wash bok choy and store in the fridge crisper for a couple of days.

Steamed bok choy

Wash and chop the bok choy leaves. Steam until wilted but still crisp. Drizzle over soy sauce and a little sesame oil.

BROCCOLI/BROCCOLINI

HOW TO SELECT

Broccoli heads should be green, tight, firm and compact with a blue haze: the bluer, the better. There shouldn't be any brown or dark marks or bruising. The cut end should be pale green and very crisp. The flowers should not be opened. If they open, the broccoli goes yellow. Broccolini stems should be stiff and the head green with a blue haze. Avoid broccolini with flowering buds.

HOW TO STORE

Trim the broccoli stem with a cross, stand in water and place in the coldest part of the fridge crisper for 7–10 days. Broccolini should be stored in the fridge for 3–4 days.

Steamed broccoli/broccolini

Chop the broccoli into florets and steam until the stem is just tender. Serve plain or with lemon and garlic. Steam whole broccolini in the same manner.

BRUSSELS SPROUTS

HOW TO SELECT

Brussels sprouts should be pale green and hard with tight leaves and no pin holes. The holes indicate worms.

HOW TO STORE

Don't wash brussels sprouts before storing or they go limp. Store in the coldest section of the fridge crisper for up to 4 weeks and wash just before cooking.

Brussels sprout coleslaw

Shred 1kg of brussels sprouts using the fine blade on a mandoline. Add 100g of grated carrots and 125g of finely sliced dried apricots. Sprinkle over lemon juice and olive oil and toss. **Serves 6**

TIP

Cook brussels sprouts in orange juice rather than water to prevent the strong smell and to give a lovely flavour. Pour enough orange juice into a microwave-safe container to come 1cm up the sides, add brussels sprouts, cover, and microwave until tender.

CABBAGES

Cabbage should have tightly packed leaves, be hard and have a fresh clean smell. When you tap your knuckle against it, it should sound solid.

Cut off the core of the cabbage and make a cross in the base. Put the cabbage in a large plastic bag with a small amount of water and sit the base over the water.

Shannon's family recipe for cooking cabbage

Put a small handful (about the size of an egg) of breadcrumbs in a small piece of muslin, tie with a piece of kitchen twine and place in with cabbage when cooking. Cabbage cooked in this manner can be used in many ways, as the bread absorbs all the bitter juices making the cabbage easy to digest. Another advantage to this style of cooking is that the breadcrumbs absorb almost all of the pungent smell that usually accompanies cabbage cooking.

To prevent the strong smell of cabbage, add a piece of apple to the cabbage when cooking.

CAPSICUMS

No matter what the colour, capsicum should be firm, shiny and sound hollow when tapped. The stem should be bright green and firmly attached. There shouldn't be any dark or soft spots.

Store capsicum in the crisper until they soften, which could be any time from 3 days to 3 weeks. You can make a green capsicum go red by placing it in a brown paper bag with a banana.

Roast capsicum

The easy way to roast a capsicum is to place it under a very hot grill and roast it, turning often, until the skin is evenly blackened. Transfer to a plastic bag, seal and leave for 3 minutes. Remove the capsicum from the bag and peel off the skin.

Stuffed capsicum

Slice 2 red capsicums in half lengthways and remove pith and seeds. Finely slice some cabbage in a mandoline. To each cup of cabbage, add 1 cup of cooked rice and ¼ cup of finely chopped red onion. Stuff the mixture into the red capsicum halves, sprinkle over grated parmesan cheese and roast in a fan-forced 180°C/350°F/gas mark 4 oven for 10 minutes or until the capsicum starts to blacken on the sides and the parmesan cheese is golden brown.

TIP

You can stuff capsicums with many ingredients, such as minced beef or shredded roast chicken, chopped bacon and chopped pineapple or mushrooms and hazelnuts. Be as creative as you like!

CARROTS

Carrots should be hard with a strong orange colour. They do come in other colours, but orange is the most common. The carrot top should be green with a sweet smell.

HOW TO STORE Store carrots in the fridge crisper for up to 1 month. They begin to go black and limp when going off.

Sweet carrots

Roughly grate 500g of carrots and finely chop 2 large onions. Put 1 dessertspoon of olive oil in a frying pan, add the carrot and onion mixture and stir constantly for 10 minutes or until tender. Just before serving, add 1 teaspoon of lemon juice and ½ teaspoon of white sugar. Kids love it! **Serves 4**

CAULIFLOWER

HOW TO SELECT Cauliflower should be waxy, white and tightly packed without any dark marks or bruising. Bits should not come off in your hand. If bits do come off, it means the flowers have opened.

HOW TO STORE Cut off the core of the cauliflower and make a cross in the base. Put it in a large plastic bag with a small amount of water and position the base over the water. Place in the crisper for up to 1 week. You can blanch cauliflower and store it in the freezer for 3 months.

Basic cauliflower recipe

Pour in enough water to come about 3cm up the sides of a large saucepan and add ½ cup of milk. Place 2 layers of cauliflower florets in the saucepan, cover, and bring to the boil. Reduce heat to low and simmer for 4 minutes or until tender. The milk keeps the cauliflower white.

CELERY

Celery should be crisp and firm and have thick stems. The ridges should be fairly flat; if they stand upright it means they've lost moisture.

Wrap the base of celery in damp paper towel and cover in plastic wrap. Store celery lying down in the crisper for up to 1 week.

Celery fingers

Cut hand-length pieces of celery, wash and dry well. Pipe a mixture of sour cream and caviar down the centre cavity.

CHERRIES

No matter the colour, cherries should be firm and glossy with green stems. Those with stems last longer. They're in season at Christmas time. Cherries are high in melatonin, the hormone that helps with sleep.

Wash first and store in a plastic bag in the fridge for up to 2 weeks (if they're not eaten before then).

Stewed cherries

Wash 1kg of cherries and place in a saucepan with 1 heaped table-spoon of white sugar. Boil for 2 minutes, allow to cool and store in sterilised jars. To sterilise jars, wash well and dry in a 100°C/200°F/gas

mark ½ oven. Fill the jars all the way to the top while still hot.
Stewed cherries keep for years. **Makes 3 large jars**

CHILLIES

Chillies should be shiny and plump with green stems.

Store chillies in a paper bag in the crisper for 3–4 weeks.
Alternatively, thread them onto a cotton thread and hang them
near the kitchen window to dry.

Quick chilli sauce

Add 1 finely chopped small red chilli to 2 teaspoons of butter,
½ teaspoon of salt and the juice of ½ a lemon. Microwave on High
for 2 minutes. To make a milder sauce, don't include the chilli seeds.
To make a sweeter sauce, add ½ teaspoon of caster sugar.

CHOKOS

Chokos should be full, bright and apple green with fairly smooth
skins and the occasional prickle.

Store chokos in a cool, dark place for up to 5 days and then
store in the crisper in the fridge.

Basic choko recipe

Peel and cut 1 choko into wedges. Peel, core and slice 1 green apple.
Steam the choko and apple until tender. Place the choko in a
microwave-safe dish, drizzle with olive oil, sprinkle over grated
parmesan cheese and grill until cheese is golden brown. You can also
microwave, cover with baking paper to brown the top. **Serves 4**

CORN

HOW TO SELECT

If the husk is on, corn should be a fresh pale green. The leaves
should be tight and the silk should be yellow, not brown. If the
husk has been removed, kernels should be shiny, plump and
cream in colour. The paler the colour of the corn, the fresher it is.

HOW TO STORE

Store corn in the husk or wrap it in plastic and store in the fridge
crisper. It can last for several weeks, especially if the husk is intact.

Corn on the cob

Strip the husk and remove the silk from 1 corn cob. Wrap the cob in
microwave-safe plastic wrap and cook in the microwave on the
vegetable setting for 4 minutes or until tender. Add a dob of butter
and eat using cob holders. **Serves 1**

CUCUMBERS

HOW TO SELECT

There are several varieties of cucumber. Crystal or gasless cucumbers should be white and firm without any soft spots and the stems should be green and fresh. If you tap your knuckles against them, they should sound heavy. Lebanese, telegraph and English cucumbers should be dark green and smooth-skinned. If the skin is rough, it's old. Australian cucumbers should be dark green and glossy. The fatter they are, the better the taste.

HOW TO STORE

Keep cucumbers in the fridge crisper for 1 week or until the skin goes limp.

Instant cucumber pickle

Peel and slice cucumber and place in a bowl with half vinegar, half water and a pinch of salt for each cucumber. Serve immediately or place in a container, cover and store in the fridge until needed. It's perfect with salads.

EGGPLANT

HOW TO SELECT

Make sure the stem is green and the skin is smooth, shiny and full-coloured. Smaller eggplants are likely to be sweeter.

HOW TO STORE

Store eggplant in the fridge crisper for 1 week. Don't leave them in plastic because they sweat and rot.

Roast eggplant

Thinly slice 1 eggplant lengthways on a mandoline. Paint each slice
with a little chilli oil and grill, turning only once after 3 minutes. The
total cooking time should be around 6 minutes. Serve hot or cold.
Serves 4

FENNEL

HOW TO SELECT
> Fennel should be full, fat and as white as possible. It should have
> a waxy feel.

HOW TO STORE
> Wrap fennel bulbs in damp paper towel, place in a plastic bag
> and store in the fridge crisper for about 3 weeks.

Warm fennel salad

Wash the fennel, trim the tops and finely slice across the bulb using a
mandoline. Melt 1 teaspoon of butter in a saucepan, add fennel and
1 finely sliced onion and cook for 5 minutes or until the fennel is
translucent. Add ½ a sliced granny smith apple and the juice of ½ an
orange, season with salt and pepper and serve.

FIGS

HOW TO SELECT
> Regardless of the colour, fig stems should be fat and milky. The
> skin should be firm but soft without any splits.

HOW TO STORE

Store figs in a paper bag in the fridge for 2–3 days.

For the cheeseboard

Wash the figs and slice them in half lengthways. Sprinkle the cut side of each fig with a little brown sugar and add a tiny knob of butter. Place on a baking tray and grill until sugar caramelises and is crisp on top.

GARLIC

HOW TO SELECT

Garlic should be full, fat, tight and hard. The skin shouldn't be flaking off.

HOW TO STORE

Garlic keeps best if air can circulate around it. Store garlic hanging in a net. If you keep it in a bowl, have a paper towel underneath. It's off when the bulbs become dried out. It lasts for up to 3 months.

Roast garlic

Trim the top off a head of garlic (not a clove, but the whole head of garlic). Do not peel. Drizzle with olive oil and add a sprinkle of thyme leaves. Place in a baking dish lined with foil and roast at 180°C/350°F/gas mark 4 for 40 minutes. Place a tea towel over the base of the garlic and squeeze garlic cloves from skin. Garlic has enzymes in its skin that are an antibiotic.

GINGER

 HOW TO SELECT — Ginger should be fat, round, hard and shiny with a silvery glow.

HOW TO STORE — Store ginger in a paper bag in the fridge crisper for up to 1 week.

Crystallised ginger

Peel and slice ginger root into 1cm thick slices. To each cup of ginger, add ½ cup of white sugar, ½ cup of water and the juice of ½ an orange. Slowly simmer in a saucepan for 1 hour. Allow to cool and spread the mixture over a sheet of foil and place in the fridge. When cool, dust with caster sugar.

GRAPES

HOW TO SELECT — Grapes should be plump and round with green stems. When you shake a bunch, they should stick to the vine. If lots fall off, they're old.

HOW TO STORE — Wash and store grapes in plastic in the fridge for about 1 week.

Sultana grape crêpes

Remove sultana grapes from the stem and chill. To make crêpes: combine 2 eggs, 1 cup of plain flour, ½ cup of milk, ½ cup of water, ½ teaspoon of salt and 2 tablespoons of melted butter in a blender and process for 45 seconds. Cover and set aside for 1 hour. Melt a little butter in a hot pan and make a batch of crêpes. Pipe a line of vanilla custard down the centre of each crêpe and top with the grapes. Roll into finger-shaped parcels and serve with a glass of champagne. Makes about 15 crêpes. **Allow 2 for each person**

GRAPEFRUIT

HOW TO SELECT

Grapefruit should be shiny and smooth skinned. There should be green under the stem.

HOW TO STORE

Store grapefruit in or out of the fridge: they will remain fresh out of the fridge for up to 2 weeks. To store for longer periods, melt some beeswax or paraffin wax and pour over grapefruit to coat the skin. They will keep like this for 1 month, sometimes longer.

Fresh grapefruit
Grapefruit is best eaten fresh. Add a little brown sugar if the flavour is too tart.

HERBS

HOW TO SELECT

The stems should be green at the tips and the leaves fresh and crisp. Choose herbs by their smell.

HOW TO STORE

Keep the herbs wrapped and wash under cold water just before use. Place herbs in a glass of water, cover with a plastic bag and store in the fridge.

TIP

To dry herbs from the garden, place them on a paper towel and heat them in the microwave. Heat them uncovered in 1-minute bursts until crisp. Except for sage and bay leaves, fresh herbs are always best.

Shannon's salsa verde

Combine coarsely chopped leaves of 1 bunch of flat-leaf parsley, 1 large sprig of mint, 1 sprig of basil, 1 sprig of coriander and 1 teaspoon of rock salt and pound using a mortar and pestle. Add the juice of 1 lemon or 1 lime and 1 tablespoon of extra virgin olive oil. Blend until smooth. **Makes about 1 cup**

Jennifer's salsa verde

Combine 3 tablespoons of coarsely chopped flat-leaf parsley, 1 tablespoon of mint, 5 anchovies, 1 tablespoon of capers, 1 tablespoon of dijon mustard, juice from ½ a lemon, 1 garlic clove, olive oil to taste and blitz to a paste using a hand-held blender. **Makes about ½ cup**

GREEN BEANS

HOW TO SELECT

Green beans come in all shapes and sizes. When you hold the ends, they should snap rather than be limp.

HOW TO STORE

Store green beans in the fridge for up to 1 week. If the beans have any mould, don't eat them because it contains bacteria. You can blanch and freeze beans for up to 3 months.

Bean and mushroom salad

Top and tail whole green beans then blanch them. (Blanching means dropping them into boiling water for 30 seconds and then dropping them into ice water until they lose their heat.) Drain and place the beans in a large salad bowl. Fry an equal quantity of mushrooms for 1 minute in a hot frying pan with a little garlic and butter. Add the mushrooms to the salad bowl, drizzle with olive oil, lemon juice and salt.

HONEYDEW MELONS

HOW TO SELECT

When tapped with your knuckle, honeydew melon should sound hollow, but heavy. The stem should be green and grassy and smell sweet. The skin should be smooth with a faint powdery blue.

HOW TO STORE

Store in the fridge for 3–4 weeks.

Sliced honeydew melon

Peel, seed and vertically slice honeydew melon. Serve on a platter with prosciutto and wasabi.

KIWIFRUIT

Kiwifruit should be hard and fuzzy with a slightly green top. If gold-coloured, it should have a slightly pointy base.

Store kiwifruit in the fridge for about 2 weeks.

Kiwifruit sorbet
Peel, chop and crush 6 ripe kiwifruit, add 2 dessertspoons of caster sugar and stir. Add 2 dessertspoons of water and continue to stir. Place in the freezer for 10 minutes, remove from freezer and stir for 30 seconds. Repeat every 10 minutes for 2 hours. **Serves 4**

LEEKS

Leeks should be very firm and white towards the base. Leaves should be tight and have a fresh smell.

Store leeks in plastic in a crisper in the fridge for up to 2 weeks. Blanch leeks in boiling water and freeze for up to 6 months.

Caramelised leek tart
Cover a flan pan with puff pastry. Place a sheet of foil over the pastry and blind bake at 180°C/350°F/gas mark 4 for 6 minutes. Wash leeks and cut into 1cm thick slices and place in upright rounds on the pastry in one layer. Brush the tops with olive oil, sprinkle with brown

sugar and powdered ginger and bake at 150°C/300°F/gas mark 2 for
40 minutes or until the leek is caramelised and the pastry golden.
Serves 6

LEMONS

HOW TO SELECT

Lemon skins should be as smooth as possible. They should feel
waxy and firm but not hard. The stem should be green. Heavier
lemons have more juice, so select by weight.

HOW TO STORE

Lemons are best kept at room temperature. If you buy lemons,
or any citrus fruit, in bulk and want to preserve them, wash in
cold water and wipe with a cloth dipped in olive oil. Then place
in the fruit bowl. Make sure you get good air flow in the fruit bowl.
If you want to store lemons for a few months, cover them in
paraffin wax. Heat the wax on the stove until it's warm enough to
be molten then pour it onto the lemons. Store wrapped in
greaseproof paper.

Preserved lemons
Wash whole lemons and place them in a microwave-safe dish with
salt and water. For each kilogram of lemons add 2 cups of salt and
enough water to cover. Cover and microwave on high for 4 minutes.
Transfer to a container and add salt until all the moisture is absorbed.
Seal, refrigerate and leave for 3–4 weeks.

TIP
You'll get more juice from a lemon if you heat it in the microwave for 30 seconds before squeezing. When grating a lemon, dip the grater in water and the rind will slip off more easily. If you want to use only a small amount of lemon juice, pierce the lemon with a knitting needle and squeeze the juice through the hole you've made. Then place the lemon in the fridge ready to use another time.

LETTUCES

HOW TO SELECT

There are many varieties of lettuce. Leaves should be full and crisp. Select the heaviest lettuce because the leaves are more tightly packed and the lettuce is juicier. Check that gourmet lettuce leaves don't have a greasy feel.

HOW TO STORE

To store lettuce, cut the bottom of the core off, cut a small cross in the stem and stand it in water for about 30 minutes before wrapping it in plastic and putting it in the fridge in the crisper. Hydroponic lettuce roots should be covered in water and plastic and stored in the fridge.

Braised lettuce

Don't throw the outer leaves of a lettuce away. They may be tough when raw but soften nicely when braised. Wash and dry the leaves and place them in a frying pan. Sprinkle with a little lemon juice, add a couple of knobs of butter and 1 teaspoon of fish sauce. Braise until tender.

LIMES

Lime skins should be as smooth as possible and feel waxy and firm but not hard. The stem should be green. Heavier limes have more juice so select by weight.

Store in or out of the fridge. They last for months. You can also wax limes as described for grapefruit. Preserve limes in the same way as lemons.

Lime and ginger cordial

Put 2 litres of water, 2 cups of sugar and a large sliced ginger root into a saucepan. Add 2 cups of lime juice and boil for 3 minutes on a high heat. Remove immediately from the heat, strain into a large glass jug and refrigerate. Dilute to taste for drinking (generally 1 litre of the mixture with 4 litres of water). Serve with ice and mint leaves or drizzle over ice-cream. **Makes 7.5 litres or 30 serves**

LYCHEES

Choose firm, red lychees with stems attached.

Store lychees in the fridge for up to 3 days.

Fresh lychees

Lychees are best peeled and eaten immediately.

MANDARINS

HOW TO SELECT

Mandarins should be firm and sweet smelling with a slightly green stem. The skin should not be loose. Test by weight. Heavier mandarins are juicier.

HOW TO STORE

Mandarins can be stored in or out of the fridge. Don't leave them out of the fridge for more than 2 days.

Ambrosia

Peel and divide 3 medium-sized mandarins into segments. Then slice across each segment and squeeze out any pips. Place in a bowl with ½ a finely chopped pineapple. Add 2 dessertspoons of toasted coconut and 1 large packet of marshmallows and stir. Add 250g of low-fat sour cream and stir again. Sprinkle over toasted coconut and refrigerate for 2 hours. Ambrosia goes well with ham and turkey.
Serves 6

MANGOES

HOW TO SELECT

Mangoes can appear to be nice on the outside and taste awful on the inside. Ripe ones are firm with a good sweet smell. If it smells of sulphur, it's off. The skin should be smooth.

HOW TO STORE

If ripe, store in the fridge for 1–2 weeks. If unripe, store out of the fridge until it ripens and then store in the fridge.

Fresh mangoes

The best way to cut mangoes is to slice down both sides of the seed.
You'll be left with 2 spheres. Criss cross over the flesh with a knife,
push the mango up from the skin and fork out the pieces. Don't
waste the flesh around the seed: cut around it and eat.

MUSHROOMS

HOW TO SELECT

Button mushrooms should be firm and quite white. The spore
casing should be closed, which means you shouldn't be able
to see the brown veins inside the mushroom. Field mushrooms
will have the brown veins showing. Choose dry field
mushrooms with an earthy smell. Avoid slimy skinned ones.

HOW TO STORE

Don't wash mushrooms under water because they'll rot and go
soggy. Instead, wipe them clean with a damp paper towel, then
store them in a paper bag in the fridge crisper for up to 2 weeks.

Garlic mushrooms

Thinly slice 500g of mushrooms on a mandoline. Melt 1 dessertspoon
of butter in a frying pan, add 4 crushed garlic cloves and cook until
opaque. Add mushrooms and cook for 4 minutes stirring constantly.
Add a pinch of dried thyme and ginger powder and cook for
30 seconds. **Serves 2**

NECTARINES

HOW TO SELECT

Nectarines should be firm, with a smooth skin, slightly green stem
and fresh smell.

> **HOW TO STORE**
>
> Nectarines attract fruit fly so it's best to store them in the fridge for up to 2 weeks.

Frosted nectarines

Drop whole nectarines into boiling water and allow them to spin for 2 minutes. Peel and dip in caster sugar. Add to a cheese platter.

ORANGES

> **HOW TO SELECT**
>
> Choose oranges according to the season. If you are unsure, ask the fruiterer for advice. Choose oranges with a smooth skin and a slightly green stem, avoid those with little brown spots.

> **HOW TO STORE**
>
> Store oranges in or out of the fridge for 4–6 weeks, or longer if waxed as described for grapefruit (see page 191).

Ham, orange and fennel (HOF) salad

Peel an orange and slice across it. Layer each slice with some ham and some finely shredded fennel. Drizzle with olive oil, add a sprinkle of sesame seeds and chill in the fridge for 30 minutes before serving.

OLIVES

> **HOW TO SELECT**
>
> Olives can be bought fresh or in a jar. Determine freshness by taste. Some bottled olives can have a bitter taste that can be improved by adding 1 teaspoon of citric acid, screwing the lid back on and shaking vigorously.

Store fresh olives in the fridge and bottled olives in the pantry until they're opened then store them in the fridge. Fresh olives last for 1–2 weeks, bottled olives last for a long time.

Hunter's chicken

Place 4 skinless chicken thigh fillets in a crock-pot and sprinkle over 1 teaspoon of ground cinnamon. Add 4 sliced potatoes, 1 x 400g can of chopped tomatoes, a sprinkle of thyme and 2 handfuls of black olives and simmer for 1 ½ hours. **Serves 4**

You can prepare your own olives! In a large saucepan, add 2 tablespoons of salt to 3 litres of water. Then add 1 teaspoon of citric acid and 1 crushed garlic clove, add 2kg of olives and cook until the olives are tender. You can flavour the olives with chilli seeds, lemon rind or garlic. Allow to sit for 2 hours then spoon into sterilised jars. To sterilise jars, wash and rinse and place in a 100 C/200 F/gas mark ½ oven until dry.

ONIONS

Red onions are very sweet. Select ones with a tight, smooth, glossy surface. Don't choose ones with flaky skins because they're drying out. Brown onions are sweet with an earthy aftertaste. Select ones that are glossy and shiny. White onions have a sharper taste with a hint of pepper. Select glossy and shiny ones. Spring onions should be fresh and green all the way to the tip with a pale bottom. Sweet gasless and green onions should be fresh and green all the way to the tip with a white pearly bulb. Chives should be pert and a deep emerald colour. Ramsons are a tiny purple spring onion with a fine top like a chive and a sweet lemon and pepper flavour. Eschalots are purple pink or golden bulbs with a more delicate flavour than onions.

HOW TO STORE

Store in a dry, dark, cool place for months. Those with green tops should be stored in the crisper in the fridge.

Red onion salad

Peel and finely slice 1kg of red onions using a mandoline. Finely chop 1kg of ripe tomatoes and 1 cup of fresh mint leaves. Make a dressing using the juice of 1 lemon, 2 tablespoons of olive oil and salt and pepper to taste. Serve with crusty bread. **Serves 10**

Brown onion and lentil dip

Boil ½ cup of red lentils until soft. Drain well. Peel and roughly chop 1kg of brown onions. Heat 1 dessertspoon of olive oil in a saucepan, add onions and cook, stirring occasionally, over high heat for 20 minutes or until onion caramelises. Add the lentils and stir for 5 minutes. Serve with Lebanese bread and hummus. **Serves 4**

White onion with parsley sauce

To make parsley sauce, combine 1 dessertspoon of butter and 1 dessertspoon of self-raising flour in a saucepan and stir until foaming. Stir in 2 dessertspoons of finely chopped parsley, ½ teaspoon of salt and 1 dessertspoon of lemon juice. Gradually add 1 cup of milk, and stir constantly until you have a thick, smooth sauce. Peel 12 large white onions and wrap them in microwave-safe plastic wrap. Cook in the microwave until soft. Top with the parsley sauce and serve. **Serves 6**

TIP

If you're running late with dinner, try the old wives' trick of cooking some onions. The smell will temporarily placate the hungry hoards.

PEELING BACK THE LAYERS: Alex's question

 This is something that has perplexed me for some time: can you still use an onion if there's mould under one of the layers?

 If it's black mould then no. Black mould makes the onion look water-soaked. If the mould is blue in colour then it's okay to eat once you've removed and washed the mouldy bits. If in doubt, throw it out.

TIP

There are various strategies to prevent tears when chopping onions. You can wash onions under the tap, but then you lose half of the juice and they don't taste the same. You can partially freeze onions, but this breaks down the cell-wall bonds and you lose part of the sugars so they won't taste the same. You can wear nose and eye goggles. You can hold a stick between your clenched teeth so you breathe through your mouth rather than through your nose. The best way is to get someone else to chop them!

TIP

Rubbing your hands with bicarb and vinegar removes smells, especially after chopping onion or chilli. Another option is to wear disposable gloves while chopping.

HOW WE USED TO KEEP COMFY FROM *PEARS' CYCLOPAEDIA 33RD EDITION* (1928)

To remove the smell of onions, rub the hands after peeling with a stick of celery and the odour will be entirely removed.

PASSIONFRUIT

> **HOW TO SELECT**
>
> Passionfruit skin varies and isn't an indicator of ripeness. The best way to determine ripeness is by the weight of the passionfruit. If it feels as light as a ping pong ball, then it's dried out inside.

> **HOW TO STORE**
>
> Store passionfruit in a fruit bowl. The length of time will vary according to the temperature and freshness of the passionfruit. It's off when it becomes light, rattles and is very wrinkly. Don't store in the fridge.

Preserved passionfruit pulp

To preserve passionfruit pulp, combine ½ cup of passionfruit pulp, ½ an aspirin and ½ teaspoon of sugar. It lasts for up to 3 weeks in the fridge. Store in an airtight container.

PAPAYA

> **HOW TO SELECT**
>
> The papaya (or pawpaw as it is often incorrectly called) skin should be smooth and lightly oiled. The stalk should be slightly green and smell sweet and musky. Unripe papaya smells sour and lemony. If it smells like vomit, it's well and truly off.

> **HOW TO STORE**
>
> Store papaya in the fridge until it begins to smell off. Remove from the fridge and allow to come to room temperature before eating.

Fresh papaya

Papaya is best eaten fresh with a squeeze of lemon juice. Don't throw away the seeds, they make a great alternative to peppercorns when making sauces or in marinades to tenderize meat.

PINEAPPLES

HOW TO SELECT

To work out when a pineapple is ready to eat, stand the pineapple upright, hold one of the centre leaves and pull at it. If the leaf comes away easily, it's ripe. If you have to yank at it, it's not ripe. The smell should be sweet and sugary. If it has a musty smell, it's old. Colour is not an indicator. If it's not ripe, place it in a paper bag with a banana to help the ripening process.

HOW TO STORE

Store pineapples upright in the fridge. If you lay them on one side all the sugar falls to that side. They can be stored for a very long time. The way to tell when they're off is when the end becomes brown and smells mouldy.

HOW TO PEEL

Top and tail the pineapple to the flesh and slice off all the skin. Place the pineapple on its side—you'll see the burrs running in a spiral around the pineapple—and using a sharp carving knife, cut at a 45-degree angle along one side of the burr spiral starting at the bottom and working your way around to the top. Then cut along the other side of the burr spiral at an angle so you create a wedge. The wedge will come away. When you're finished, you'll have a frilly looking but burr-free pineapple.

Pineapple with sweet mint sauce

Mix 2 teaspoons of dried mint, 2 teaspoons of sugar, 2 teaspoons of brown vinegar and 4 teaspoons of hot water. When cool, drizzle over cut pineapple. It's a great side dish for hot curries or anything with a lot of chilli because the acidic pineapple cuts through the heat!

PLUMS

HOW TO SELECT

No matter the variety, plums should be firm, but not hard, with a shiny skin. The stem should be slightly green. The smell should be of fresh sugar. If a plum smells like an apple, it's going off. If a dark coloured plum smells like petrol, it's going off. Never serve overripe black plums to children—the children may become a bit intoxicated!

HOW TO STORE

To ripen, store in the fruit bowl until it smells like fresh sugar. If ripe, store in the fridge for up to 5 days. Don't store in the crisper.

Plum chutney

Wash 500g of plums and place them in a crock-pot. Add 2 large pork hocks, a small handful of peppercorns, a sprinkle of salt and 1 dessertspoon of balsamic vinegar. Leave in the crock-pot on high for 2 hours or until tender. Serve in summer or winter. **Serves 4**

PARSNIPS

HOW TO SELECT

Parsnips should be hard and not wobbly. Colour is not an indicator. The top should be a fresh green.

HOW TO STORE

Store parsnips in a paper bag in the crisper.

Roasted parsnip and carrot

Peel and slice 500g parsnips and 500g of carrots. Toss in a bowl with 1 teaspoon of sugar, ½ teaspoon of salt, juice from ½ an orange and 1 tablespoon of olive oil. Place in a microwave-safe dish, cover, and cook in 3-minute bursts until soft.

PEACHES

HOW TO SELECT

Peach skins should have a soft, even bloom without too many speckles. They should be firm but not hard.

HOW TO STORE

Store peaches in the fridge for 4–7 days.

Caramelised peaches

Cut peaches in half and remove the seeds. Mix 1 teaspoon of brown sugar, 1 teaspoon of butter and a little ground cinnamon.Spread over cut side of the peach and place under the grill on a low heat for around 20 minutes or until top is caramelised.

PEARS

Pears should have a smooth skin and be just firm. Green or Packham pears should have a glossy finish with even speckles. Corella pears should have a bright red flash to the skin. Winter Coles or Beurre Boscs should be an even, rusty brown colour. If the flesh near the stem gives a little, it's ripe. Check with your fruiterer if they have been refrigerated and ask for a suggested ripening period.

When ripe, store pears in the fridge. If not ripe, keep in a fruit bowl.

Poached pears
Peel 4 firm pears leaving the stems intact and place in a small baking dish with 3 cups of good red wine, 1 tablespoon of brown sugar, a pinch of salt and 1 teaspoon of butter. Place in 180°C/350°F/gas mark 4 oven and bake, occasionally spooning the sauce over the pears, for 30 minutes. Serve with mascarpone. **Serves 4**

Pear and rocket salad
Pear is great in a salad of rocket and parmesan cheese with a balsamic-vinegar dressing. Thinly slice 1 pear and toss with 3 cups of rocket. Scatter over shaved parmesan cheese, ½ tablespoon of balsamic vinegar, 1 ½ tablespoons of extra virgin olive oil and season with salt and pepper. **Serves 2**

PEAS

Fresh peas should have juicy shells and snap when you pinch them with your fingers. They should be bright green with green tops. Frozen peas are also acceptable to use.

Store fresh peas in a paper bag in the crisper for up to 3 weeks. Store frozen peas in the freezer for up to 6 months.

Pod dippers
Once you've removed the peas from their pods, wash the pods and use them as dippers in Spicy Pea Dip or your other favourite dips.

Spicy pea dip
Mix 500g of fresh green peas, ½ cup of water, 1 tablespoon of lemon juice, ½ teaspoon of sugar and 1 small bunch of chopped coriander. Microwave until tender. Gently mash with 250g of sour cream and stand in the fridge until chilled. **Makes about 2 cups**

It's a great idea to keep sour cream in the fridge so you can make a dip whenever you need to.

POTATOES

There are many varieties of potato. Make sure they are firm with as few eyes as possible to make peeling easier. There shouldn't be any green in the potatoes. Ideally, potatoes should be sold in sacks or black plastic.

Potatoes should be kept in a cool, dark place where air can circulate. Rub the eyes off before storing them. If you store them with no light, no moisture and plenty of air, they can last for up to 1 year. Only keep them in the fridge if you have a cockroach problem.

Milk-sautéed potatoes

Wash and slice 4 large potatoes on a mandoline. Peel and slice 1 onion on a mandoline. Drizzle a little olive oil into a ceramic dish and layer the potato and onion alternately in the dish. Pour over a small quantity of skim milk, sprinkle with grated parmesan cheese and ground paprika, place a sheet of baking paper on top and cook in the microwave for 20 minutes or until the top is golden brown. Cut into squares. **Serves 6**

PUMPKIN

When you tap your knuckle against the pumpkin, it should sound like knocking on a solid, wooden door. The stem should be slightly green but dried at the tip. When you push the core with your thumb it should be hard.

Store uncut pumpkin, with the stem facing upwards, in a cool, dark place for up to 1 year. Check the stem each month and trim the excess dry parts: don't trim too much away. If you remove the stem, the pumpkin will rot. When cut, store in the fridge for 2–4 days.

Chicken and pumpkin pasta sauce

Cut 1 chicken breast into cubes and brown in a little olive oil for
3–4 minutes. Add 1 ½ cups of cooked pumpkin cubes, ½ teaspoon of
basil and 150g of blue cheese and cook on low heat until the mixture
forms a paste. Spoon over cooked and drained pasta. **Serves 3**

RADISHES

HOW TO SELECT

There are several varieties of radish: red, white and green. Red
radishes and small white radishes should be firm with a velvety
coat. Large white radishes, also known as daikon, look like big
white carrots and should have smooth shiny skins. If there's any
movement when you squeeze them, they'll be chalky in the
middle. No matter what their colour is, the tops should be a fresh
green.

HOW TO STORE

Trim the tops and any excess root and wash thoroughly. Place
radishes in a resealable container, cover with water and a pinch
of salt. Seal and store in the fridge for about 1 week.

Radish mice

Remove the green tops from fresh radishes making sure you don't cut
into the radish. Don't remove the root—this is the mouse's tail. Take
a small slice from either side of the green tip—this is the mouse's
face. Push a black peppercorn on either side to create the eyes. With
a sharp knife, make another cut to form ears. Place in iced water and
the ears will stand up. These are a great decoration for a cheese
board and are edible as well!

RASPBERRIES

HOW TO SELECT

Raspberries should be plump and not damp. They should have a dry, slightly bluish bloom and no stems.

HOW TO STORE

Remove raspberries from the punnet and rinse the punnet in water. Place a piece of paper towel inside the punnet, replace the raspberries and place in the fridge for 3–4 days. Don't wash raspberries until you're ready to eat them.

Lamb with raspberry and thyme coulis

Pan-fry 6 lamb cutlets and set aside to rest. Retain the cutlet juices in the frying pan and add 1 punnet of raspberries, 6 sprigs of fresh thyme, ½ teaspoon of butter, 1 teaspoon of balsamic vinegar, 1 pinch of dried sage and 1 pinch of salt. Gently stir over medium heat for 2 minutes or until the raspberries soften. Spoon the sauce over the cutlets and serve. **Serves 3**

ROCKMELONS

HOW TO SELECT

When selecting rockmelon, look at its core. If the stem is slightly green, curling in and sweet smelling, it's ripe. If the stem is dark green and grassy smelling, it's not ripe. Check the pale side of the rockmelon as this rots first. There shouldn't be any soft spots on the melon. Then go by weight. Heavier ones will have fewer seeds and be the freshest.

HOW TO STORE Store green or unripe rockmelons in a fruit bowl. If ripe, store in the fridge for up to 3 weeks.

Sweetened rockmelon

Peel, seed and chop 1 rockmelon into 2cm cubes. Place in a bowl, add 1 tablespoon of icing sugar and the juice of ½ an orange, stir and refrigerate for 30 minutes. **Serves 4**

SILVERBEET

HOW TO SELECT Stems should be crisp, white, juicy and pert. Leaves should be shiny, curly and a deep emerald green.

HOW TO STORE Cut off the bottoms and stand silverbeet stems in a big jug of water. Store outside the fridge and eat as soon as possible.

Steamed silverbeet

Starting at the base of each silverbeet leaf, run a knife along the stem to the tip of the leaf, hold the stem and allow the leaf part to fall into a bowl. Run the knife along the other side of the stem and allow the leaf to fall into the bowl. You will be left with the stem, which you can give to the kids to play with as swords! Wash the leaves thoroughly and drain. Put a small amount of water in a large pan, add silverbeet leaves and a finely shredded green apple. (The apple takes away any bitter aftertaste.) Steam until soft and serve with a knob of butter and a squeeze of lemon juice.

SNOW PEAS

<table>
<tr><td>HOW TO SELECT</td><td>Snow peas should have a fresh green top and snap when broken in half. The skin should be smooth.</td></tr>
</table>

<table>
<tr><td>HOW TO STORE</td><td>Wash, dry and store snow peas in a paper bag in the fridge crisper for up to 3 weeks. Don't store in plastic or they will sweat.</td></tr>
</table>

Snow pea finger

Pipe sour cream and red caviar onto a snow pea and arrange a ribbon of smoked salmon on top. Instant, elegant finger food!

SPINACH

<table>
<tr><td>HOW TO SELECT</td><td>Stems should be crisp, green, juicy and pert. Leaves should be shiny and a fresh green colour. English spinach yellows as it ages.</td></tr>
</table>

<table>
<tr><td>HOW TO STORE</td><td>Cut off the bottoms and stand spinach stems in a big jug of water. Store outside the fridge and eat as soon as possible.</td></tr>
</table>

Lebanese spinach triangles

Gradually add Greek-style or Lebanese natural yoghurt to 2 cups of self-raising flour and mix with a fork until it forms a light fluffy ball that isn't sticky. Then knead it. Pull off sections of dough and form into flat circles as big as your hand. Place a small handful of finely shredded spinach in the centre, add a sprinkle of chilli and lemon juice. Fold over the edges 3 times to form a triangle. Paint the outside with olive oil and a sprinkle of salt and bake in a 200°C/400°F/gas mark 6 oven for 15–20 minutes or until golden. **Serves 6**

SQUASH

HOW TO SELECT

Make sure squash skins are bright yellow and smooth without any brown spots. The top should be a fresh green.

HOW TO STORE

Store squash in a paper bag in the fridge crisper for about 1 week.

Steamed squash with parmesan cheese
Top and tail the squash and steam lightly. Sprinkle with olive oil and lemon juice and serve with grated parmesan cheese.

STRAWBERRIES

HOW TO SELECT

Check the bottom of the punnet and make sure there's no moisture. The strawberries should be a deep, red colour and have a shiny skin. The tops should be a fresh green and not wilted. Strawberries grow better in the southern parts of Australia.

HOW TO STORE Remove the strawberries from the punnet and wash. Place a paper towel at the base of the punnet. Dry the strawberries, return them to the punnet and store in the fridge. How long they last will depend on where they come from: Queensland strawberries last for 4–5 days; Victorian strawberries last for 7–10 days.

Mozzarella strawberries

Remove the stems and vertically slice into each strawberry until you almost cut through. Dip a thin slice of mozzarella cheese in balsamic vinegar and slide it into the slot in the strawberry. Serve with crusty bread and mint leaves for a romantic breakfast.

SWEET POTATOES

HOW TO SELECT Sweet potato or kumera can be orange, purple or white in colour. Select ones with an even width because they're easier to peel. They should be hard with dry ends. There shouldn't be any soft spots or mould. Peel white sweet potato under water so it doesn't go green.

HOW TO STORE Sweet potato should be kept in a cool, dark place where air can circulate for up to 1 month. Only keep them in the fridge if you have a cockroach problem.

Baked sweet potato and coconut

Peel 500g of sweet potato and cut it lengthways into 2cm thick slices. Toss in olive oil and slightly overlap the slices in a roasting dish. Add 2 knobs of butter, sprinkle with 2 tablespoons of desiccated coconut and 2 tablespoons of brown sugar. Roast in 180°C/350°F/gas mark 4 oven for 20–30 minutes or until tender. **Serves 2**

TOMATOES

Tomatoes should be firm but not hard. No matter what the variety, the colour should be vibrant with smooth, slick shiny skins.

For bought tomatoes, wash and dry and place in a plastic bag in the fridge crisper for about 1 week. If growing your own, eat as soon as they are ripe without refrigeration.

Sweetened tomatoes

Using 1 medium-sized tomato per person, blanch the tomatoes by dropping them into boiling water for 10 seconds. Remove them, drop into chilled water and peel. Slice each tomato into eights and place them in a bowl with a pinch of salt, a pinch of caster sugar and ½ teaspoon of balsamic vinegar. Stir and serve. Kids love them because there's a hint of sweetness and the skin doesn't get caught in their teeth.

Don't you hate it when you can't get the tomato sauce to flow from the bottle? You bash your hand against the end of the bottle and get a major rush of sauce. An easier way to release the sauce is to put a table knife or straw down the centre then remove it; the air releases the vacuum.

WATERMELONS

HOW TO SELECT

Watermelon should sound hollow when knocked on with your knuckle. Neither the stem nor the core should feel soft. The skin should be glossy.

HOW TO STORE

Keep watermelon in a cool, dark place until ready to cut. Once cut, cover watermelon in plastic wrap and store in the fridge. Uncut watermelons last for up to 2 months. Cut watermelons last for about 1 week. If you're not sure whether an uncut watermelon is ripe, cut a small triangle into the melon with a clean sharp knife. If it's not red, it's not ripe. Replace the triangle and store. It will keep ripening.

Lebanese watermelon salad
Slice and deseed watermelon and cut into 1cm cubes. Place in a bowl with a good handful of fresh mint leaves and 2 handfuls of 1cm cubed feta cheese. Give the mixture a light tumble and serve as a summer dessert.

ZUCCHINI

HOW TO SELECT

Zucchini should have firm, glossy skin and green tops.

HOW TO STORE

Store unwashed zucchini in a plastic bag in the fridge crisper for up to 1 week. Wash before preparing.

Stuffed zucchini
Use 1 zucchini per person. Slice zucchini lengthways, scoop out

seeds with a spoon and chop finely. Place zucchini shells in a microwave-safe dish. Combine zucchini seeds, ¼ finely chopped red onion, 2 dessertspoons of ricotta and stir. Place the mixture into the zucchini shells, cover with a sheet of baking paper and cook in the microwave in 2-minute bursts until tender.

MEAT, POULTRY AND SEAFOOD

BEEF

HOW TO SELECT

Beef can come in a range of colours from a light, bright red through to dark burgundy. It should never have a hint of brown or green. If it does, it's off. The cut surface should be glossy and slick with a fresh, clean, salty smell. Fat on the meat should not be wrinkled or coming away. If it smells or if the skin is greasy, don't use it. The reason why you should only eat fresh meat is because it carries bacteria. The smaller the amount of meat in a piece, the more likely it will go off. If in doubt, throw it out.

Choose mince by its bright colouring and minimal juices in the tray.

TIP

Meat that sits in blood rots more quickly, so avoid buying meat in trays if you can. Use a good-quality butcher with a high turnover.

HOW TO STORE

If you intend to use the beef in the next 2 days, store it in the fridge on a bottom shelf to avoid blood dripping onto other food. There is some dispute about whether storing meat in plastic makes it sweat. Shannon thinks it's fine to use plastic. Foil is another option as is storing the meat on a plate with a glass lid. To eat later, store in the freezer—in or out of the tray—for up to 3 months.

HOW TO STORE AFTER COOKING

If cooked all the way through you can keep meat for up to 1 week in a sealed container. You can also freeze meat after cooking but you must bring it to boiling point before eating. You can only freeze cooked meat once. You can't defrost and then refreeze because of bacteria. If there's any odour to the meat, throw it away.

HINT

HOW TO TELL IF STEAK IS WELL DONE

The easiest way to work out how well a steak is cooked is the folded fist test. Make your hand into a fist and press the skin below your thumb and forefinger. That's how the steak should feel when it's well done. Relax your hand so thumb and forefinger are softly touching then press the same area of skin. This is medium. Open your hand to a relaxed position and press the skin below your thumb. This is rare.

Only turn steak once. The more you turn it, the tougher it gets. It's time to turn the steak when blood starts rising to the surface. For rare steaks, once turned, blood should still sit on top of the steak. A medium steak will have a little blood. And well done won't have any blood at all. Meat will shrink less if it's cooked longer at a lower temperature.

LAMB

HOW TO SELECT

Lamb should be a similar colour to beef but a touch darker. The fat should be fairly white. The meat should be firm but not hard without any dry bits on the edges. Dry bits indicate it's going off.

HOW TO STORE

If the lamb is to be used within 2 days, remove it from the plastic wrapping, store on a plate, cover with a glass lid and place in the fridge. To eat later, store in the freezer for up to 3 months. Defrost meat in the fridge or in the microwave using the defrost setting. Defrost it at 10 per cent less than the weight of the lamb. For example, if the lamb weighs 1kg, set the defrost setting at 900g. Meat defrosted all the way to the end of the cycle cooks some bits and toughens it.

TIP

If you're out of powdered gravy, combine $1/2$ teaspoon of instant coffee, a pinch of mustard powder, 1 tablespoon of plain flour and $1/2$ tablespoon of butter, oil or pan juices and stir well.

PORK

HOW TO SELECT

Pork should be pale pink with a fresh slick feel. It shouldn't feel greasy. The fat should be rigid and opaque. If the fat is transparent, it's going off.

HOW TO STORE

If cooking in the next 2 days, remove from plastic wrapping, put it on a plate, cover with a glass lid and store in the fridge. If minced, it can only be stored for 24 hours. Both can be stored in the freezer for up to 3 months.

KANGAROO

HOW TO SELECT
Kangaroo should be deep burgundy in colour and even in tone. If there's colour variation and it's lighter in one part, it's old. If the meat is dark or blackish in colour or has a pungent odour, it's off. There shouldn't be much blood in the tray.

HOW TO STORE
Kangaroo is very lean and goes off more quickly, so it's best to keep it in the freezer unless eating right away.

HOW TO COOK
Never cook kangaroo on high heat. Cook kangaroo on medium-high heat for 3–4 minutes on each side. For well done, turn the stove off and cover the meat after cooking for another 3–4 minutes so that it doesn't toughen. You can store cooked kangaroo in the fridge for up to 1 week. If the meat is cooked medium or rare, it can be kept in the fridge for only 2 days. Cooked kangaroo can be frozen for up to 3 months.

TIP
To tenderise meat, use 1 teaspoon of vinegar, 2 tablespoons of oil and $1/2$ teaspoon of bicarb soda in a bowl. Add your favourite herbs as well. This can also be used as a marinade.

HAM AND BACON

HOW TO SELECT
A cooked leg of ham should have dry skin with no wet or greasy spots. Select bacon in the same way and avoid rind with bristle in it.

HOW TO STORE

Store ham in a calico bag in the coldest part of the fridge for up to 3 weeks. It must be completely enclosed to prevent it from sweating, drying out and rotting. Change the bag once a week. The meat will keep better if you don't cut the skin away. Instead, pull it back like a flap. Alternatively, slice up all the ham and store it in plastic containers with freezer paper between slices and freeze for up to 3 months. Store bacon in the fridge for up to 2 weeks. You can freeze bacon but place paper towel between each layer for easy access.

TIP

If bacon is slimy, smelly and going hard around the edges, throw it out. It's off if the fat becomes transparent.

Bacon crispies

Remove bacon rind keeping part of the fat with it and cut into 3cm long slices. Place in a pan over high heat and cook, turning constantly, until golden brown. It will spit, crackle and pop, so be careful.

CHICKEN AND TURKEY

HOW TO SELECT

Chicken and turkey skin should be full, light in colour and opaque. If it's transparent and you can see the musculature, it's old. The smell should be fresh: if there's even a hint of sulphur, throw it out. Make sure it's not greasy. Free-range and organic chickens are available: select based on your preference.

HOW TO STORE

Poultry can be stored in the fridge for 24 hours. Make sure it's not sitting in blood. Remove from plastic wrapping, store on a plate and cover with a glass lid. Chicken can be frozen after cooking but don't leave it for more than 1 month in the freezer. Thaw either in the fridge or microwave.

HOW TO COOK

To test if chicken is cooked, pierce the thigh joint with a skewer. If the juice runs out pink, it's not cooked. If the juice runs out clear, it's cooked. To make chicken crispier, pat dry with paper towel before cooking. Place it on a rack in a baking dish to allow the heat to circulate.

FISH

HOW TO SELECT

If buying a whole fish, the eye should be glassy like a marble and not milky. The scales should be flat and smooth. The fins and tail should open easily when flexed. Fillets should feel soft and jelly-like, not greasy. They should have a fresh, briny smell. If it smells of ammonia, it's off. Always check if the fish has been pre-frozen because once it's thawed, you must cook it. You can't refreeze.

TIP

To stop fish going off in the car on the way home from the fishmonger, store it in an *Esky* or insulation bag.

HOW TO STORE

When it comes to storing fish, the colder the better. Keep it on ice even in the fridge. Fish can only be kept in the fridge for 24 hours. It's best stored in the freezer until ready to use. It can be thawed quickly or cooked frozen.

TIP

One hassle with fish can be the bones. There's an easy way to remove them. Lay the fish fillet on a board and rub the flesh backwards from tail to head with clean wet hands. You'll feel the bones. Remove them with tweezers. Keep a pair of tweezers in the kitchen for this purpose.

HOW TO PREPARE

If you don't have a fish scaler, put the fish into a large tub with plenty of water. Hold the fish by the tail and using a soup spoon with a large edge run it from the tail to the head in a swift, flicking motion. Continue until there are no scales left. If the fish hasn't been gutted, place the tip of the knife just behind the fins on the bottom of the fish and slice forward along the fish until you reach the jaw. Use your fingers to gut the fish and rinse thoroughly. If removing the head, cut just behind the gills. Feel with your fingers from the back to the front of the fish for any scales. Pay particular attention to the area around the fins. There's nothing worse that a rogue scale getting stuck in your teeth!

HOW TO COOK

Fish cooks very quickly. As a general rule, cook fish according to its thickness. A 25mm thick fish takes less than 10 minutes to cook. The fish is cooked as soon as the flesh has whitened.

Smoked salmon

Always make sure the plastic wrapping is tight and without any bubbles. Once opened, make sure the covering is secure and that there are no air bubbles. If it's not covered, it can go off. Consult the use-by date.

SEAFOOD

Prawns—whether green or cooked, the colour should be even and the shell hard and shiny. If the shell is soft, it's old. The whiskers should be intact. If none are left, it's not fresh. These days, prawns are cryovac sealed as soon as they are caught. The flavour, apparently, isn't affected, but it does mean you can't refreeze already thawed frozen prawns.

Bugs and lobster—raw bugs and lobster should have bright, shiny shells without any slime. You should be able to move the tail. If it's rigid, it's not fresh. Cooked bugs and lobster should have a fresh sea smell. If they smell rancid, they're off.

Oysters—if the shell is shucked and open, the flesh should be plump and moist. It should be pale in colour, except for the ruffle. If it's starting to go green or yellow, it's not fresh. Unshucked or closed oysters should be completely closed. If they're slightly open, it suggests gases have built up and they're off. Store on ice or on an ice slurry.

Mussels—should always be tightly closed when you buy them. If you're buying just the meat, it will be frozen. Don't eat any mussels that do no open after cooking. Likewise with cockles and scallops.

Scallops—scallops can come with or without the coral (orange part). Find out where the scallops are sourced because the disc from stingray is often substituted for scallop.

Raw squid—can vary in colour. The skin should always be slick and slightly squeaky when you rub your finger over it. Raw **calamari** should be fresh, white and slightly transparent. If it's opaque, it's old. The same rule applies to **octopus**.

If garbage night is a few days away and you don't want to leave seafood rotting in the bin, wrap prawn shells and other seafood in newspaper, put in a plastic bag and store in the freezer until garbage night. That way you won't stink the place out. Alternatively, freeze and save for stock.

DAIRY, EGGS AND BREAD

DAIRY

Always check use-by dates. If buying milk from a small shop with low turnover, take 2 days off the use-by date. Always choose milk with the longest use-by date. The same applies to yoghurt and cream. Store at 4 degrees or less. Ice-cream should be stored in the freezer.

If you can't buy sour cream, use pouring cream and to each 300ml carton, add 1 teaspoon of white vinegar and shake well.

If you don't want to spend hours with a fork or beater whipping cream, put the cream in a sealed container and shake vigorously. It's quicker and ready to store in the fridge when you're finished.

HOW TO
STORE
Cheese and butter should be kept in the dairy compartment of the fridge. It's a great chill spot and the temperature doesn't vary too much. Because cheese absorbs odours it should be kept covered; plastic wrap is fine. Cheese can be susceptible to mould. To stop it going mouldy, add a couple of drops of white vinegar to paper towel and rest it on the bottom of the container. This won't affect the flavour of the cheese. Camembert and brie are best served at room temperature so remove them from the fridge 30 minutes before serving. Mersey Valley cheese is best served cold. Wrap blue cheese in foil or it will sweat.

You can freeze milk but be aware that it expands when frozen so the container can't be full or it will explode. Remove 1 glass before freezing. When you're ready to use the milk, thaw it in the fridge. Cream freezes well. Cheeses don't freeze well. If you do need to freeze cheese, first dust it with cornflour to stop it going greasy and powdery.

EGGS

HOW TO
STORE
Even though most fridges have egg storage areas, it's best to keep them in their box, which helps maintain a constant temperature and guard against the eggs absorbing odours. Eggshells are semi-permeable and very absorbent. In winter, it's all right to leave eggs out of the fridge.

HINT
Fill a glass with water and place the egg in it. If the egg floats, it's rotten. If the egg sinks, it's fresh. Eggshell is a semi-permeable membrane and over time, gas is absorbed. That's why a rotten egg floats and why it smells so bad when off. Shannon's daughter loves doing the test.

TIP

Write on boiled eggs with a non-toxic marker so you don't confuse them with the others. Shannon puts little faces on them!

TIP

If your eggs are overboiled or cool too slowly, the yolk becomes grey. Turn them into devilled eggs! Just slice the egg in half, remove the yolk and mash it with a little butter, mayonnaise and curry power. The curry powder adds yellow and covers the grey. Replace the yolks and sprinkle with paprika.

TIP

To cook scrambled eggs in the microwave, combine 2 eggs with the juice of 1 orange and $1/2$ teaspoon of dried parsley flakes. Microwave for 1 minute, stir, then microwave for 30 seconds. It may need more cooking depending on the microwave.

TIP

If you don't have egg rings, use the outside ring of a large onion which you can also eat.

BREAD

It's easy to tell when bread goes off because it goes mouldy. Throw away the whole loaf because mould spores will be right through the bread. Depending on how much bread you eat, store in the fridge or freezer. Some people like using bread bins but it's not a good idea with Australian weather, particularly humidity.

TIP

To freshen bread, dampen a paper towel with water and put it inside a small paper sandwich bag. Place in the microwave for 10 seconds, remove, wrap it around the bread and leave for 2–3 minutes before using for sandwiches.

FREEZING FOOD

Always label and write the date on food wrapping when it's put in the freezer so you know long it's been there. Don't store bread in the freezer for more than 4 weeks. Don't keep meat for longer than 3 months. Fruit and vegetables can be stored a little longer. Anything water-based shouldn't be stored for more than 3 months. When freezing chicken, give it a dusting of cornflour or plain flour—you can also add a pinch of ginger—to stop it from sweating. Plastic takeaway containers are a perfect size for freezing meal-sized portions of meat. Put a piece of plastic freezer bag between the layers and always thaw in the fridge.

HINT

HOW TO DEFROST SAFELY

Many people are under the false belief that food can be defrosted at room temperature. They think that you can pull a piece of meat out of the freezer and leave it on the bench while they're at work. This isn't the most hygienic habit. It's better to place the frozen item on a plate and leave it in the fridge to defrost. It takes longer but there's less risk of bacteria growing. Using the microwave defrost setting is also acceptable, but always remove the items from any plastic wrapping. Place on a paper-towel lined plate and cover with baking paper. To stop the edges cooking, cook at 10 per cent less than the weight of the meat. So for 1 kg of lamb, set the microwave at point 9 on the defrost setting. Another practice to avoid is placing the frozen item in a sinkful of boiling water. Again, bacteria can thrive. You can soften food with cold water but you must do it by hand. Never soak meat because it changes the temperature and produces bacteria.

FOOD PREPARATION

Before preparing any food, wash your hands thoroughly. Also wash any fruit and vegetables because you never know who's touched them. If wavering about whether you need to wash, keep this in mind: the two worst places for germs are supermarket trolleys and the shelf in front of bank tellers!

The basic food-handling procedures to observe include:

Be careful using chopping boards. Uncooked meat and unwashed vegetables can carry bacteria. Have a chopping board for meat and another for vegetables.

Prepare and chop washed salad vegetables first. Then wash and cut root vegetables and store them in a bowl. Then wash your board immediately.

Don't leave food sitting on the benchtop because bacteria thrive when the temperature rises.

Put food back into the fridge as soon as you can. Hot items should be covered and allowed to cool to room temperature before being placed in the fridge. Cover any food out of the fridge.

To prevent tomato paste from going mouldy, always use a clean spoon and leave the covered jar upside down in the fridge. You can also spoon tomato paste into ice-cube trays, cover each square with plastic wrap and store in the freezer for months.

COMFORT FOOD

We use food to make us feel better. Comfort food is a sure-fire way to warm the heart and soothe the soul. Take care: it can also expand the waistline! Here are some comfort classics.

CHEESE ON TOAST

Toast one side of a slice of bread under the grill until golden. On the untoasted side, layer your favourite thinly sliced vegetables with fine layers of grated cheese (the cheese bonds the vegetables together), finishing with a layer of cheese . Place it under the grill until the edges of the toast are dark brown but not black. The harder the cheese you use, the more it will brown and crisp.

HOT CHOCOLATE

For each cup of milk, use 2 tablespoons of chopped chocolate or chocolate buttons. Heat milk in a saucepan, gradually add choc bits and stir. If you like the flavour, add cinnamon or nutmeg. Pour the hot chocolate into a cup and place a marshmallow on top. It will melt and form a delicious foam on top. Yum!

HOMEMADE VEGETABLE SOUP

This is a quick way to make vegetable soup but you need to have a juice extractor. The best part is there's no chopping. Put your favourite vegetables through the juicer and transfer the extracted juices to a pot. Remove the pulp from the juice catcher and add it to the liquid in the pot. Bring the mixture to the boil then allow it to simmer for 10 minutes. Make sure it boils, especially if the soup contains potato, sweet potato, onion or any starchy vegetables, otherwise it will have an odd taste. This soup makes a great base for stews if you want to add meat.

CUCUMBER AND PRAWN SOUP
Peel 6 large cucumbers, add a bunch of chopped coriander and process in a blender. Add salt, pepper, lime juice and 1 table-spoon of sour cream. Float 3 prawns per dish on top and garnish with sprigs of coriander. **Serves 6**

WICKED DOUBLE CREAM AND CHOCOLATE DIP
Crush a Flake-style chocolate bar into filings and stir it through a bowl of double cream. Use it as a dip for strawberries or other fruit.

QUICK LIQUEUR CHOCOLATES
Melt 1 packet of dark chocolate drops in a double boiler. Combine 5 tablespoons of Grand Marnier, 1 packet of orange jelly and $^1/_2$ cup hot water and stir until the jelly dissolves. Pour the mixture into a large 5mm thick tray and place in the freezer for 10 minutes. Remove and cut into bite-sized pieces. While cold, dip the squares in the warm melted chocolate. Place them on waxed paper and transfer to the fridge to set. You can vary the kind of chocolate coating you use. Be warned that it's very alcoholic!

COCONUT ORANGE
Peel the outside of an orange and remove all the pith. Slide a small sharp knife between the skin and each segment and remove segments. Sprinkle the segments with desiccated coconut or (for over 18-year-olds) kirsch. Serve as a dessert or as a treat.

FOOD DISASTERS

What to do if you've added too much salt

If you've added too much salt, add 1 teaspoon of lemon juice. You could also add a couple of slices of apple, which will give the meal a sweet taste.

What to do if you've burnt something

If the burn is really bad, throw it out and start again: no one likes to eat charcoal. For a mild burn, put 2 slices of bread at the bottom of a cooking bowl and pour the burnt contents on top. This will draw off the moisture and reduce the ashy taste. Ash contains salt so adding something acidic, such as lemon juice or orange juice, will also lessen the ashen flavour.

What to do if you burn the milk

Remove the scorched taste from burnt milk with a pinch of salt.

What to do if you've added too much chilli

Chilli is a strong alkali so you can reduce its intensity with strong acids such as lemon, yoghurt, pineapple and vinegar.

What to do if you've added too much sugar

Reduce the intensity of sugar with a spritz of lemon juice.

What to do if you accidentally use salt instead of sugar

If you've added salt instead of sugar to a cake mix, there's nothing you can do but start again. To prevent it happening again, make sure you label containers well.

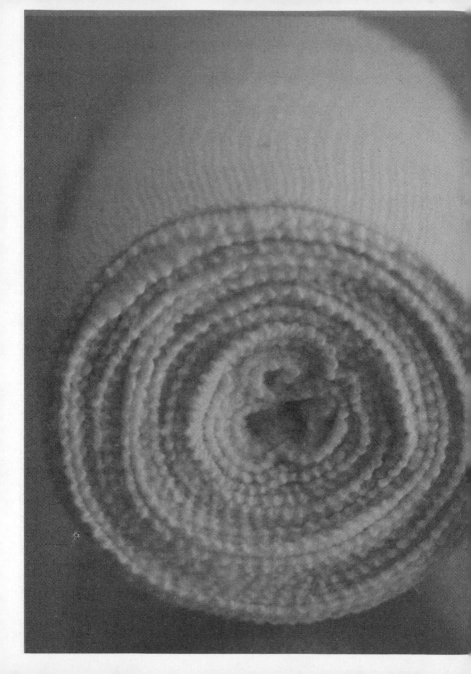

First Aid

Having some knowledge of first aid is really important. The information listed below is general. **Do not pick this book up in a crisis**. In the case of an emergency, ring 000. We also suggest you do a first-aid course through an accredited organisation, such as St John Ambulance Australia.

HOW WE USED TO KEEP COMFY FROM *FORTUNES IN FORMULAS FOR HOME, FARM AND WORKSHOP* BY HISCOX AND SLOANE (1944)

To kill nits and lice, use 1 dracham of oil of pennyroyal, 8 ounces of turpentine and sufficient kerosene to make to 1 gallon. This will kill lice, bedbugs and their eggs.

FIRST-AID KIT

A basic first-aid kit should contain: *Band-Aids*, sterile eye pads, triangular bandages, safety pins, wound dressings in various sizes, *Micropore* tape, crepe bandages, elastic bandages, small scissors, splinter probe, disposable gloves, tweezers, eye-wash solution, alcohol swabs and hand towels. It should also contain painkillers, such as paracetamol and aspirin, papaw ointment, antiseptic cream, tea tree oil.

SERIOUS INCIDENTS

Always seek immediate medical attention. Call emergency on 000.

Snake bites—a recent study on snake bites, which included brown snakes, tiger snakes, black snakes and sea snakes, at Perth's Princess

Margaret Hospital revealed that most people were bitten on the foot or leg and 70 per cent of children with snake bites received the wrong first aid. **Call 000 for an ambulance** and apply pressure over the bite as soon as possible. Wrap a broad bandage along the limb starting just above the bite area. Wrap down to the lowest portion of the limb—to push the poison away from the heart—then continue wrapping upwards, covering the entire limb if possible. If you don't have a bandage, clothes—such as a T-shirt torn into strips or pantyhose—can be used. The bandage needs to be tight, but not so tight that it stops circulation. Do not remove the bandage. Next. immobilise the limb by placing splints down either side of the limb, or create a sling so movement is minimal. This technique is known as the pressure immobilisation bandage and was developed by Australian Dr Struan Sutherland in the 1970s. Don't worry about identifying the snake. A sample of its venom can be taken at the hospital.

Spider bites—if possible, put the spider in a jar to take with you to the hospital or clinic. Find someone to help you because some spiders inject a neurotoxin and mouth-to-mouth resuscitation may be needed. Don't take any risks, if you are unsure, **Call 000 for an ambulance**. All bites from large black spiders should be treated as a funnel web bite and a pressure immobilisation bandage should be applied (see Snake Bites above). You can go into cardiac arrest minutes after being bitten by a funnel web spider so call an ambulance immediately. Red back spider bites require application of an ice pack. Once again, **seek medical help immediately.** Children will react differently to each toxin so seek medical help.

Choking—if the person isn't breathing, **call 000 for an ambulance** operator can give advice. It's likely you'll be asked to perform CPR so that oxygen can still get to the brain until help arrives. To prevent choking in small children, make sure food is mashed well and placed at the front of the mouth when eating. This makes children use their tongue and jaws to chew and even though you increase the risk of dribble and spit, it's much better than a choking child! If food is placed at the back of the mouth, they may not chew it properly.

Poisons—call the Poisons Information Centre on 13 11 26 anywhere in Australia and a health professional will give advice on first aid and contact for hospitals. Keep any remaining poison, any box or container and any vomited matter to help identify the poison.

Heatstroke—this can take the form of headache, dizziness, nausea, vomiting, abdominal cramp, collapse and unconsciousness. The face is pale, cold, clammy and sweaty and the pulse is weak. If the person is conscious, put them in a cool place and give them lots of cool water. If unconscious, bend their knees so their feet are on the ground which forces blood to the torso and head. If their breathing is distressed, place them in the recovery position. Bathe the pulse points in cool water.

Fainting—is generally caused by a fall in blood pressure and can be caused by shocking news or standing in a hot stuffy environment. After fainting, lie them prone and bend their knees so their feet are on the ground; this forces blood to the torso and head. Loosen clothing, get some fresh air and give sips of water. If unconscious, make sure there's fresh air, remove false teeth, loosen clothing and place in the recovery position (see following page). If breathing is impaired, use artificial respiration. If they are breathing but it's not noisy, turn the head to one side. If breathing is noisy, turn them into a three-quarter prone position. Do not give food or fluids while unconscious. Allow sips of water if consciousness returns.

THE RECOVERY POSITION

Lie the patient on their side with the lower arm at right angles in front of them and the upper arm across the chest with the hand resting flat under the cheek. Straighten the bottom leg along the ground and bend the upper leg towards the waist.

RESUSCITATION

The procedure for resuscitation is currently being reviewed but this is the general process. First, remove the person from danger. Call 000 for an ambulance. Check the ABC—Airway, Breathing, Circulation. Position the patient on their back. being careful of the spine. If the person isn't breathing or doesn't have a pulse, begin cardio-pulmonary resuscitation (CPR). These are the guidelines for performing CPR from St John Ambulance Australia (http://www.stjohn.org.au/emergency.htm):

1. Giving compressions—kneel beside the patient, one knee level with the head and the other with the patient's chest. Locate the lower half of the sternum (breastbone) in the centre of the chest. Place the heel of the hand on the lower half of the sternum (breastbone) and place the heel of the other hand on top of the first hand. Interlock the fingers of both hands and raise the fingers. Do not apply pressure over the patient's ribs, upper abdomen or lower part of the sternum. Position yourself vertically over the patient's chest. With your arms straight, press down on the sternum (breastbone). Press down about one-third of the chest. For infants under 1-year-old, place two fingers (index and middle) over the lower half of the sternum (breastbone). Press down about one-third of the chest.

2. Release the pressure—compressions and release should take equal amounts of time.

3. Repeat compressions—give 30 compressions at the rate of approximately 100 per minute.

4. Giving breaths—tilt the patient's head gently back and lift the chin (slightly for infants). Give 2 breaths.

5. Continue CPR—return the hands (fingers for infants) to the correct position on the patient's chest. Continue compressions and breaths at a ratio of 30:2 until medical help arrives. Never leave an unconscious patient alone.

COMMON COMPLAINTS AND INJURIES

Bee sting—there are two parts of a bee sting—the needle and the sac. Both parts must be removed. To do this, brush underneath the pointy part of the sting using a paddle pop stick or fingernail. Don't pull on the protruding part of the sting because this will squeeze the venom sac and inject more poison. Marigold or calendula petals and white vinegar soothe the sting. Ice also relieves a bee sting by slowing the spread of the sting toxin and relieving swelling. Watch for allergic reactions and anaphylaxis.

Tick—wipe kerosene along the skin next to the tick. Don't apply the kerosene directly because the tick could inject more toxins. The kerosene fumes will make the tick retract its head from the skin. Then use fine point tweezers at the very base of the tick to pull it out. You must get the head out. Keep the tick in a glass jar in case you get an infection and have to go to hospital. Check the rest of the body as well. The spray variety of *Aerogard* contains a kerosene-like substance which can help to remove ticks.

Dog bite—if the skin is broken, seek medical advice, a tetanus injection may be needed. Wash the bite in 2 cups of water and ½ teaspoon of tea tree oil and apply a bandage.

Burn—for minor burns, run under cold water for 10 minutes or apply a silver sulphadiazine cream, also known as *Silvadene*, which is obtained by prescription only. Don't put any greasy substance on a burn. For major burns, seek the advice of your nearest hospital.

Splinter—it depends on how deeply the splinter has penetrated. If shallow, rub sideways with a blunt probe. If deep, but there's sufficient splinter out of the skin, use tweezers in line with the splinter. For a surface splinter, use the eye of a needle, not the point. Put the splinter through the eye of the needle, twist and pull. For persistent splinters, place ¼ teaspoon of *Vegemite* over it and bandage. The yeast in *Vegemite* forms a poultice which extracts the splinter.

> **TIP**
>
> *Ichthyol*, a drawing ointment, is an old-fashioned remedy for boils, splinters and blisters. It is available from chemists, although you may have to get them to order it in. Jennifer remembers her grandmother applying the black liquid for boils. Some people even use it for bad pimples or ingrown hairs.

Foreign body in eye—for small foreign bodies, fill an eye glass with boiled and cooled salty water or just boiled and cooled water and rinse out the eye. If it's not embedded, remove with the corner of a clean handkerchief, twirled up and moistened with boiled water. If embedded, close the eyelid, make a circle of cotton wool around the eye like a donut, then cover the eye so there's no pressure. It's better to cover both eyes so the patient isn't tempted to move their eye at all. Seek medical help. Never probe an eye with anything harder than a finger or rubber probe. Be careful not to scratch the lens.

Insect in ear—fill the ear with olive oil and a few drops of surgical spirit, such as methylated spirits. The insect will float and may be removed. For anything else in the ear, seek medical advice.

Foreign body in nose—get the patient to breathe through their mouth and seek medical help.

Chilli burn—Jennifer heard about a woman who had to go to the emergency department at hospital after suffering burns from chopping too many chillies. The treatment at the emergency department was to apply bicarb soda! It's a good idea to wear disposable gloves when chopping chilli, especially when doing large amounts. You can also coat your fingers in olive oil. Washing your hands doesn't always remove the strong alkali and a casual brush of your eye will be extremely painful!

Tinea—treat with diluted tea tree oil.

Pimples—treat with diluted tea tree oil or *Ichthyol* (see page 343).

Blisters—use silicone gel *Band-Aids*. To soften new shoes, roll the rear of the heel forward towards the toe and allow it to bounce back. Soften the edges by running an emery board around the inside edges of the straps and along the upper. It's an obvious point, but never buy ill-fitting shoes. Always buy shoes at the end of the day when your feet are most swollen.

Nits/head lice—everyone hates nits! Just mention them and you feel like scratching. It's become such a problem in Australia that researchers estimate that 10–40 per cent of school children currently have lice. Proprietary products are available but they're often very harsh (especially on sensitive scalps) and Shannon has found that head lice become immune to most of them, one by one. This means you can end up using one product after another trying to find the one that your local lice are not immune to. She recommends applying unsweetened orange juice to the hair and using a nit comb to comb out the eggs. Add a couple of drops of tea tree oil to shampoos and conditioners and in the bath to prevent them.

The most important thing to remember, no matter which solution you use, is that you must comb out all of the nits. Schools now organise nit-busting days where cheap hair conditioner is rubbed into students' hair and nit combs are taken through the hair. The conditioner stuns lice for 20 minutes.

A researcher at James Cook University offers this advice:

Apply conditioner to dry hair aiming to cover each strand of hair from root to tip with a layer of conditioner. Detangle the hair with an ordinary comb. Immediately comb the hair with a fine tooth comb or plastic nit comb. Wipe the conditioner from the fine tooth comb onto a tissue and look for lice and eggs. Repeat the combing for every part of the head at least five times.

Head lice live in the hair and come down to the scalp to feed by sucking blood. So head lice formulations must be applied to all parts of the hair. A complete regime consists of two treatments seven days apart. The first kills the climbers and the second kills the juvenile lice hatched from the eggs over the intervening six days. No product currently available kills all eggs.

One bit of good news. Head lice die once they leave the head so you don't have to wash all the pillowcases, sheets and towels in the house!

Bluebottle sting—the most recent research recommends applying hot water at 46°C/115°F for 20 minutes, however, this can be difficult to access at the beach. Vinegar and lemon also alleviate the pain.

Nosebleed—with normal childhood nosebleeds, place a chilled cloth on the back of the child's neck and pinch the bridge of the nose with your fingers. If the bleeding doesn't stop in 5 minutes or is very fast, seek medical aid. Never put a child's head back while their nose is bleeding because they can drown in their own blood. Encourage the child to breathe through their mouth.

Hiccups—to cure hiccups, drink a teaspoon of white vinegar and force yourself to shudder. This causes the vinegar to bubble in your throat and confuses the nervous system. Once you confuse the nervous system, you'll stop hiccupping.

Sandflies—to soothe the itching, mix cold tea and methylated spirits in equal parts or dab a little lavender oil or white vinegar on the bites. Bicarb soda and water made into a paste also works, but don't use this on children under the age of two because their skin could react to the bicarb.

Sunburn—have a cool but not hot shower and apply the prescription cream, *Silvadene*. Aloe vera gel is also soothing for burns, although some people are allergic to it. Rub a cut tomato over the burn for temporary relief.

Warts—apply white sap from a dandelion plant but only to the wart itself or you will burn the surrounding skin. There are many old wives' tales about removing warts and they're all fanciful. One supposed remedy was to rub a piece of meat over the wart and then bury the meat in the garden. As the meat rotted, so the wart was supposed to magically fall off! It doesn't work.

Toothache—flush your mouth with ½ teaspoon of salt and warm water and gargle. Salt is a great antiseptic. Floss in case there's food caught in your teeth. For temporary relief, mix ¼ teaspoon of oil of cloves with 1 tablespoon of boiled cooled water and apply with a cotton bud to the area. Consult your dentist.

TIP

If you feel bloated and uncomfortable after a big meal, run your hand anti-clockwise over your stomach.

TIP
Relieve the itching of chickenpox by applying mint tea to the skin. A cool bath with several mint tea bags added works very well at providing relief to itchy children.

HINT
HOW TO REMOVE A BAND-AID ON A CHILD
Children love putting *Band-Aids* on but hate having them removed. One way to loosen the glue is to rub tea tree oil over the *Band-Aid*. Another way is to play this game. Get them to count '1, 2, 3' and then shout 'yah'. As they let out the 'yah', rip the *Band-Aid* off. Adrenalin goes up when you shout so they won't feel as much pain.

TIP
Bandages should be washed in very hot water to sterilise them and rolled up to preserve the elastic. To roll, use a butter knife as the core of the fold. Lay the knife over one end of the bandage, roll bandage along the blade and remove the knife. When applying a bandage, always have the edge of the roll on the outside.

TIP
To fix a broken fingernail, cut a small patch from a tea bag and glue it on with superglue. Smooth with a nail file, then paint on your favourite nail polish.

TIP
To make a quick antiseptic for minor cuts, dissolve salt in boiled water or apply apple cider vinegar.

HOW WE USED TO KEEP COMFY FROM *PEARS' CYCLOPAEDIA 33RD EDITION* (1928)

Creosote resembles carbolic acid in odour and has antiseptic properties. It is procured by the fractional distillation of cold tar. It has a sedative as well as antiseptic action on the skin and so forms an invaluable ingredient of healing ointments. It will often allay toothache on application to decaying teeth and makes a good pill for the staying of stomachic nausea.

HINT

HOW TO MAKE YOUR OWN SOOTHING LINIMENT
Empty a jar of *Vaseline* into a microwave-safe bowl, add a couple of drops of oil of wintergreen, a pinch of chilli powder, a couple of drops of lavender oil and a drop of peppermint oil. Cook it in the microwave for 1 minute or until the mixture has softened to a thick liquid. Stir well and return to the *Vaseline* container. You can add a few drops of food colouring so you don't confuse it with *Vaseline*. Relabel the jar and it's ready to use on sore muscles.

OLD-FASHIONED REMEDIES FOR COMMON AILMENTS

To lessen the incidence of **migraine**, mix 1 teaspoon of red clover tea with 1 teaspoon of powdered kelp, cover with 1 cup of boiling water and steep for 5 minutes. Have 1 cup a day over 2 weeks and the recurring migraine will dissipate. Continue to drink at least 1 cup a week.

To lessen **morning sickness**, drink ginger tea and eat green pineapple before getting out of bed or have some dry crackers beside the bed to eat before you stand up.

Drinking raspberry leaf tea will help **PMT** and **cramping**.

To cure a **tension headache**, put the juice of a lemon in a cup of coffee.

Deal with **intestinal threadworms** by eating lots of grated carrot and drinking carrot juice. This works particularly well with children. If you think a child has threadworm, make sure they have a warm bath before bed and once asleep, take a torch and look at their backside. The worms come out at night. Prevent worms by getting children to wash their hands, especially after playing with animals. For **tapeworms** and **flatworms**, consult a doctor.

To cure a **hangover**, eat steamed endives with a few drops of lemon juice and a sprinkle of salt. Endives assist liver and kidney function and help process the alcohol. It works if you eat it before or after your overindulgence.

For a **child's cough or cold**, wrap sage and thyme in a tissue secured with an elastic band. Put this inside their pillow and they'll sleep better.

For a **child's bronchial cough or wheeze**, take 2 whole nutmegs and pierce them end to end with a bodkin. Thread a piece of ribbon through both nutmegs and hang it around the child's neck. Encourage the child to spin the beads along the string. Nutmeg is a bronchial dilator and raises adrenalin.

To get rid of **puffy red eyes**, lie down for 10 minutes, place a tea bag dampened with a little witch-hazel on each eye, then remove and rinse eyes.

Make your own heat bag for **aches and pains**. Mix rough-ground buckwheat, a couple of sprigs of lavender, ½ teaspoon of thyme, ½ teaspoon of sage, place in a cotton bag and stitch it up. Put it in the microwave for 1–2 minutes and apply to the sore spot. When Shannon was caring for a chronically ill relative, she made a vest, which means the patient can sit up and move around, from calico, and added several pockets to it so that heat bags could be located where the pain was. Calico washes easily.

HINT

HOME REMEDY FOR A COLD

Mix the juice of 2 lemons, 1 teaspoon ginger powder, 1 teaspoon chamomile tea leaves, 1 teaspoon dried thyme leaves, 1 teaspoon dried sage leaves, 1 teaspoon dried mint leaves, 2 tablespoons honey and 1 teaspoon dried green or black tea leaves. Steep with 2 cups of boiling water for 5 minutes, strain thoroughly and add 3 teaspoons of the mixture to a cup of hot water and sip. If your throat is really sore, add 1 clove to the mixture. If your breathing is wheezy, add $1/4$ teaspoon of grated nutmeg or ground nutmeg. If you feel nauseous, triple the amount of chamomile. If you have stomach cramps, add 1 teaspoon raspberry leaves. Keep the mixture in a sealed container in the fridge or freezer and use it when you need it.

CARING FOR SICK PEOPLE

No one likes to be sick, but if you're caring for someone who's unwell, there are many things you can do to make life more comfortable for them. Sometimes dealing with minor problems makes the bigger ones more manageable. This includes applying heat to an ache, a cool washer to a hot forehead or even having your face washed, your hair brushed or a gentle massage.

There are two times in the day when patients tend to feel worse. One is around sunset, the other is between 2 and 3 o'clock in the morning. These downtimes are related to circadian rhythm, where the body uses energy at different rates. Ease these swings by administering medication before these times.

Sickbed checklist:

Pillows—fluffed and puffed with spare clean pillowcases.

Bowl—in case of vomiting.

Towels—for spills.

Glass of water within easy reach.

Box of tissues.

Spot for medicines.

Sterile wipes.

TV, DVD, CD, radio, books or cards for entertainment.

Hairbrush and other toiletries—add a little conditioner to a spray bottle of water for tangled hair.

Bin lined with plastic for easy disposal.

Vase of fresh flowers.

There's nothing worse than stagnant air when you're spending extended time in a room so be aware of airflow. Even in winter, allow a crack of fresh air in through the window. You can always heat the room and keep the window slightly open. Keep the room clean and fresh smelling.

To lessen the smell of vomit, put a ring of toothpaste on the inside rim of a bucket. Peppermint also settles the stomach.

Have someone accompany a sick person to the doctor. When you're feeling sick, you don't always absorb all the information.

HOW TO CHANGE A BED WITH SOMEONE IN IT

If needed, place a towel under the patient. Fold the new base sheet in half lengthways, that is, from top to bottom. Roll the patient on their side and roll the old sheet halfway up behind them. Then place the new sheet behind them and fold half the sheet over the mattress and tuck in. You've now got half of the old sheet and half of the new sheet positioned. Roll the patient to the other side of the bed over the new sheet. Remove the old sheet and unroll the new sheet and tuck in.

Talcum powder massage

When people have been lying in bed with a temperature, they get hot, sweaty and uncomfortable. One way to settle them for sleep is with a talcum powder massage. Wipe their back with powder, then apply a little to your hands and massage into the skin.

Wash your hands before and after being with a sick person to help prevent the spread of germs.

A comfy tip for sick people is to warm their bed socks in a dryer.

AMENITIES

Don't over-cover fevered patients with piles of blankets. They'll feel the cold but that's because their temperature is higher than normal. The best kind of blanket is an open weave cotton one: they're easy to wash, are inexpensive and they breathe.

Make sure you have the ability to block or increase light with curtains, blinds and/or lights. If someone has a headache, it's important to be able to darken the room.

For itching or rashes, put 2 teaspoons of dried mint into a pot of hot water, allow it to steep and strain. Chill it in the fridge and apply with a cotton ball to any itchy spots or add ½ cup of the mixture to a bath of blood-heat water.

TIP

If using calamine lotion on children, draw it on with a cotton bud forming flowers or aeroplanes—they'll think it's fun.

WHEN TO SEEK MEDICAL HELP

Normal body temperature is 37°C/98°F but this can vary by around 0.6°C/33°F throughout the day. A fever is considered at an oral temperature of 37.8°C/100°F (38°C/100°F in children). Seek medical advice for extreme fatigue, lassitude, any loss of consciousness, dizziness, unexplained rashes, shaking or chills, if vomit contains pus or blood, if vomiting continually, if there's blood in stools, if diarrhoea continues for more than 24 hours, if you cough blood, if sputum is opaque or coloured. **Always err on the side of caution and seek medical advice.**

HOW TO TAKE A TEMPERATURE

There are many kinds of thermometer available, including digital, liquid crystal, ear and disposable. Glass thermometers containing mercury are no longer recommended. For children, reusable adhesive temperature strips are available that attach to the forehead. The most common way to take a temperature is orally as long as the person is able to breathe through their nose. If they can't, use the armpit. The way to take the temperature is to place the thermometer under the tongue at the back and close the lips around it. Leave for the required time. Remove and read. For an armpit reading, which is less accurate than an oral one, place the thermometer under the arm with the bulb in the centre of the armpit. Close the arm firmly, cross it over the chest and leave for 3 minutes. In some cases, it could take longer to register. A temperature in the armpit is lower than the temperature in the mouth. Rectal thermometers should only be used by qualified medical practitioners or on doctor's instructions. Clean thermometers in cool soapy water, rinse in surgical spirit and store.

HOW TO PERFORM A SPONGE BATH

If the patient can't shower, organise a sponge bath at least once a day with a warm washer. Start at the face: wipe it with a washer and pat it dry with a soft towel. Clean the neck, shoulders, arms and hands. Then clean the torso, hips and legs. Turn the patient over and get a new washer. Start at the neck and work down the back making sure to massage as you go. People who spend extended time in bed can get bedsores or bruises. Make sure you dry them thoroughly. A little talcum powder will help keep skin soft and supple, help absorb sweat and ensures that they're dry. Never apply it directly, but sprinkle onto a soft towel and wipe the towel across the skin. Talcum powder in the air can cause problems for people with respiratory problems.

CONVALESCENT FOOD

Mashed vegetables

Mashed foods are great. Steam or microwave potato, sweet potato, broccoli, add a splash of milk and salt and pepper to taste.

Chicken soup

You might have heard that chicken soup is the perfect dish for someone who's sick. It does have the ring of an old wives' tale to it but there are some good reasons why chicken soup is a good choice. Chicken is high in protein, which aids healing, soft vegetables add good carbohydrates, which give energy, and because it's been boiled, it's easy to digest, absorbs quickly and is gentle on sore throats. Just make sure you don't use too much salt.

Rinse 1 boiler chicken (also known as a soup chook, these are an older chicken and taste better than regular chicken) and joint. Place into a large saucepan with 2 teaspoons of salt and 4 litres of water. Cover and boil for 30 minutes. Strain stock through a colander into a saucepan. Using two forks, strip the meat from the bones of the chicken and place the bones, fat and tendon to one side for disposal. Shred meat finely and return to the stock. Return to the stove and bring to the boil. Add 1 large or 2 medium grated carrots, 3 finely chopped celery stalks, 2 large finely chopped onions, 1 finely chopped tomato, 1 finely chopped potato and a generous handful of finely chopped curly leaf parsley. Add a pinch of pepper and boil for 20 minutes or until vegetables are tender. To skim fat from soup, place a clean paper towel on top and remove the paper towel (and fat) with tongs. You can add ½ handful of pearl barley or rice for a thicker soup.

Coddled eggs
Egg coddlers are available but can be expensive, instead use a glass-covered container small enough to contain the egg and not much more. For 1 egg, add any of the following fillings you like: a little chopped bread, onion, bacon, tomato, cheese, herbs and spices to taste. Add ½ teaspoon of butter, cover and put in the microwave in 30-second bursts until the white has firmed.

Bread porridge
Cut 2 slices of bread into 1.5cm squares. Place in a bowl, cover with warm skim milk and sprinkle lightly with white sugar. This is great for bedridden sick kids, especially those with sore throats.

How we used to keep comfy from *Pears' Cyclopaedia* 33rd *edition* (1928)

Invalid beef tea custard: Where eggs may be given, the following forms a nice change for the invalid from ordinary beef tea and is usually much appreciated. Beat up two yolks and one white of new laid eggs, a pinch of salt, and a small cupful of beef tea made either from fresh beef or any good essence. Put into a small basin and steam it over a saucepan much smaller than the basin so that the latter will not touch the bottom of the saucepan. The water should only simmer. The custard may be baked by putting it in a small dish and placing it the oven until set.

If the patient has diarrhoea or gastroenteritis, serve light, non-acidic food. Anything too rich or strong in flavour will upset the stomach. Serve clear soups without any onion. Add water if serving juice. If the patient has been vomiting, low-salt dry biscuits are ideal. Keep up liquids.

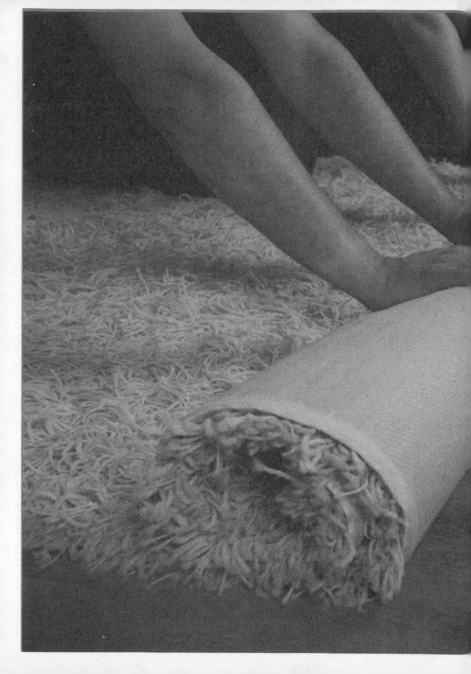

Oddments

In every home there are bits and bobs that don't really belong anywhere or go with anything. So it is with this assorted information about being comfy. Here's our miscellaneous bowl of goodies to help make your house a home.

HIS AND HERS

Moving in together can become stressful when tastes don't match. He might love modern furniture and she might love antiques. She might love pastel colours and he might like bold ones. How can these styles be melded? Because there are so many paints, wallpapers, patterns and fabrics available, there will be a style you can both agree upon. While you'll have to compromise on many items, a style that you both like can be brokered. You might choose his pattern and her colours. You might have streamlined bedding and fluffy pillows. You might have modern furniture with antique handles. It's a good idea to buy a completely new doona cover and sheets that you both like. When a hoarder and a minimalist fall in love, special patience and consideration is required. Hoarders shouldn't put every *objet d'art* on display and minimalists shouldn't forbid a few items. Allow a hoarder to have a display cabinet or area in a room that's not allowed to overflow. Or you may choose to divide the house into minimalist and hoarder zones. It's all about accommodation and being accommodating.

GOODS AND SERVICES

Make it a priority to build relationships with service providers. Probably the best way to find good tradespeople is by word of mouth. Ask neighbours and friends if they can recommend anyone. Find out if they completed the job on time and on budget. Have a look at work they've done previously. If you can't get a recommendation, look in the local newspaper. Always make sure the service provider is accredited, which can usually be checked online. Check they have public liability insurance, workers' compensation and home warranty insurance. It's usual to get three quotes for a job. Write down all your expectations, including the price, for the job and have them sign the bit of paper before they begin work. It's also good to have a clean-up clause. Build a relationship with your local hardware store, the handy salespeople are a fantastic source of knowledge.

In many instances, you must use professionals for work, particularly with electricity, gas and plumbing. If unsure, check with your local council. As a rule, you're not allowed to touch anything behind a power point. Even with jobs that you can do yourself, it's worthwhile having a professional sight and inspect the work to make sure it's up to standard. If any work affects the structural integrity of the house, you'll need a professional.

You might watch programs on TV made in other parts of the world without the same building standards. Don't use them as a guide on what you can or can't do around your home. For instance in Italy, you don't get a building permit until you've completed your building; that's certainly not the case in Australia.

DUST

Dust is the enemy of electronics and humans. Dust labours your breathing even in a small way. If a room is dusty and musty, don't reach for the fragrance spray because the petrochemical oils in the spray will penetrate the electronics. Instead, clean the room or put a negative ion generator in to lower the amount of dust. Another option is to get a bowl and half fill it with bicarb soda and put some drops of your favourite essential oil on top. Leave it in the room to help keep the air fresh and pleasantly fragranced.

INSTRUCTIONS AND WARRANTIES FILE

One of Jennifer's friends always forgets how to change the clock on
the oven when daylight-saving changes. It's a good reason to store
all instruction guides and warranties in a designated spot. Either
store them in a filing cabinet or place them in loose-leaf plastic
sheeting in a folder. Some people, such as Shannon's husband Rick,
love reading instruction manuals; others don't even flick through
them. It's worthwhile reading basic operating instructions because
you'll get more from the item. It also means you'll know which page
to go to in an emergency. If you've misplaced yours, many large
manufacturers now have these manuals available online. If they
don't, ring or write and they can send you a new one.

TURNING A RENTAL INTO A HOME

Some rentals are incredibly schmick, others can look a little worn. In
either case, you need to put your stamp on a property and make it
your home. There are many things you can do to improve the look.
The first thing to do before moving into a rental property is to clean it
thoroughly. Consider repainting the walls, but you must ask the real
estate agent or owner first. They may offer to cover the cost of the
paint and deduct some rent. If you can't repaint the walls, use wall
hangings or art. Wall hangings could be sections of chiffon or another
light fabric suspended against a wall with wiring. If you use lighter
fabrics it means you won't need heavy hooks and it gives an airy feel.
The heavier the fabric, the heavier the look, which is fine for winter
but too stuffy for summer. Soften colours with lighting. Bright lighting
against salmon or orange hues will soften them. Lights with cream or
soft yellow shades will warm a colour and make it more vivid. Cover
ugly walls with panels of fabric, large pieces of furniture or large
works of art. If the curtains are really horrible, remove the rental

ones, launder them, fold them flat and store them, then put up your
own curtains. This will make a huge difference to the look of the
place.

If you move house often, you'll feel more comfy if you keep a
similar layout. If your furniture doesn't coordinate, use slipcovers and
repaint furniture, such as wardrobes or shelving, so that it matches.
Make sure you choose a neutral colour, such as grey, because it goes
with any other colour: white gets dirty easily and black can be too
heavy and oppressive.

Line shabby kitchen cupboards and drawers with heavy plastic
sheeting which is easy to wipe clean. It's available by the metre and
in a variety of weights, colours and designs from hardware stores.
Because it lasts a long time you can take the plastic sheeting with
you when you leave the rental and move into the next house. Avoid
using contact because it's difficult to remove and wears quite quickly.
If the cupboard doors are tatty, remove them and the hinges and have
open shelving. Keep the doors and hinges to reattach before you
move again. Open shelving is a great way to inhibit cockroaches
because they don't like the light. Use huge wooden chopping boards
to cover nasty benchtops. If the kitchen is small, make it as unclut-
tered as possible. If space is at a premium, you may have to store
plates and dishes near the dining area rather than in the kitchen. You
can also add small plastic-coated wire shelves inside your cupboards.
They're lightweight, inexpensive and available from department
stores and two-dollar shops.

Most kitchens don't have carpet, which is fortunate because it's
very unhygienic. If you find yourself in a rental that does, protect it
(and your bond) by placing stiffened heavy duty plastic over the top of
it. It's much easier to clean than carpet.

If the carpet is worn or unattractive, use rugs to cover it, but make
sure the carpet is clean first. If it's not clean, you may get nasty
smells and mould and mildew. You may need to put several small

HOW TO MAKE A CHIFFON WALL HANGING

There's a bit of work in this but it will dramatically improve the look of a wall without making a permanent change. From a hardware store buy wire the thickness of a coat-hanger and slightly longer than the width of your planned wall hanging. Create a loop half-way along the wire by winding the wire over itself. The wall hanging will be hung from this loop. Sew the top of the chiffon so that the wire can be threaded through it. You could also sew the side edges and bottom of the piece of chiffon if you want to stop the fabric from fraying, but that's optional. Thread the chiffon along the wire, making a small slot in the chiffon to allow the loop to come through. Then hang the wall hanging on a screw or nail from the loop.

HOW TO MAKE A TEMPORARY LIME WASH SLURRY

If you have high-gloss enamel walls, change the colour with this temporary lime wash slurry. Buy lime wash from paint suppliers. Follow instructions to mix, then paint it on the walls with a rag. When it's time to move, wipe it off with water and a sponge. You can also soften the colour of enamelled walls with equal parts powdered milk, powdered chalk (in any colour) and water. It will look like thin paint. The room will smell for a couple of days, but it will dissipate. You can remove it whenever you need to by washing it off.

rugs together. You can create a patchwork look with the small rugs. Tie them by their tassels in the shape you need. They can be arranged and rearranged according to the shape of the room.

IF YOU MOVE REGULARLY

Moving house is a very stressful experience. If you're someone who does it often, minimise the trauma with these tactics. Rather than using cardboard boxes, keep large plastic boxes with lids and wheels. It also means you'll have fewer pests, which are attracted to cardboard. If putting items into storage, make sure you have a sealed area rather than a caged one because it's less likely vermin will get in. Also use a good-quality surface spray on packing.

When packing, use butchers' paper rather than newspaper because you won't get ink stains. Invest in large cotton matted fabric off-cuts available from removalists. It's sterile, can be washed and used again. Pack and label boxes according to the room they came from rather than the room they're going to. It's easier for you to remember. Keep a master list of what's in the boxes. Find a good removalist and stick with them. They'll become used to your moving criteria and it will ease your stress because you know they can do the job well. You may also get a special deal.

There are several ways to make a place feel like home quickly. One way is to pack an essentials box with everything you need for the first few days. Include items such as enough cups, plates and cutlery for a meal, salt and pepper, an electric jug, tea and/or coffee, clean sheets, soap, towels, toilet paper, toothpaste, hairbrush, *Band-Aids*, talcum powder and pyjamas. Have a few items you love—such as a favourite, colourful throw—that can be set up easily. For Jennifer, it's using her own sheets and doona on the bed. It makes life more comfy, offers some consistency and feels less like living in a hotel.

You can't always take plants with you when you move, but you can take the same pot and refill it with similar plants.

Meeting local service providers also helps you settle into a new area.

> **TIP**
> Be aware that one way to get a longer lease is by renting a commercial/residential property.

Make sure you keep medical files up-to-date so that you can take them to your new doctor. This also applies to school files. The post office can redirect your mail but if you move a lot, keep a post office box so that your postal address will remain constant. Have your phone messages forwarded as well. A mobile phone and an up-to-date address book are essential for constant movers.

Meet the neighbours: at the very least meet your next-door neighbours. Knock on their doors and say hello. Another way to introduce yourself is to print a 'We're here' card and leave it in your neighbours' letterboxes. If your memory is poor, write their names down.

RENOVATING AND REDECORATING HINTS

If you're living in a house while it's being renovated, minimise the amount of dust by sealing the room you're working in. You can do this with old bed sheets or heavy-duty plastic fixed over doorways and windows. Shannon prefers using plastic sheeting because it also cuts noise down. Make sure you place doormats at the outside of the door so you don't track dirt from one room to another. Make sure curtains and blinds in other parts of the house are in good condition because having tradespeople around can invade your privacy.

Keep a sample of everything you use, from carpet, paint, timber, tiles and so on. If anything needs to be patched later on, you'll be able to find a match.

Be careful of toxins when removing paint. Old paints may contain lead, arsenic or a variety of other toxic nasties. Lead is absorbed into the blood by breathing or through contact with skin. If paint is older than 15 years, test your walls and furniture with a lead-testing kit available from paint stores. They have instructions with them. If the item or area does contain lead, wear a mask and completely cover yourself with clothes and gloves so that nothing can touch your skin. Test for arsenic with a kit, particularly in older houses. Arsenic was generally in the green and blue range of paint colours. If there are traces in the paint you're removing, make sure you're fully covered and masked. Arsenic, like lead, can be absorbed through the pores of the skin as well as through the mouth, eyes, nose and ears. If in doubt, seek professional help.

TIP

When painting a room or your home, it's always a good idea to make a note of the paint name and brand you have used. Paint the colour on some white cardboard and write the name, brand and number on the back. When it's dry, keep it in your filing cabinet.

GIFT IDEAS FOR PEOPLE WHO HAVE EVERYTHING

Turn a photo into a jigsaw, placemat, calendar or mug.

Bake cakes and slices and package them decoratively.

Cook a meal and present it in a beautiful bowl.

Give some potted fresh herbs.

Write a gift certificate giving an hour of your time for babysitting or helping to organise a party.

INDEX

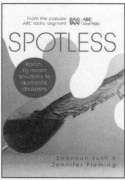